THE MACARTHUR NEW TESTAMENT COMMENTARY

2 PETER & JUDE

John MacArthur

MOODY PUBLISHERS/CHICAGO

Editor: Garry Knussman
Cover Design: BlueFrog Design

Library of Congress Cataloging-in-Publication Data

MacArthur, John, 1939-
    2 Peter and Jude / John MacArthur
        p. cm. — (The MacArthur New Testament commentary)
    Includes index.
    ISBN-13: 978-0-8024-0770-2
    1. Bible. N.T. Peter, 2nd—Commentaries. 2. Bible. N.T. Jude—Commentaries. I. Title:
Second Peter and Jude. II. Title.

BS2795.53.M24 2005
227'.93077–dc22

                                                                            2005015329

We hope you enjoy this book from Moody Publishers. Our goal is to provide high-quality,
thought-provoking books and products that connect truth to your real needs and chal-
lenges. For more information on other books and products written and produced from
a biblical perspective, go to www.moodypublishers.com or write to:

Moody Publishers
820 N. LaSalle Boulevard
Chicago, IL 60610

7 9 10 8 6

Printed in the United States of America

To Rick Holland—
my fellow pastor at Grace Community Church who always
encourages me by his loyal friendship, faithful service, zealous
leadership, and exceptional expository preaching.

Contents

Preface

It continues to be a rewarding, divine communion for me to preach expositionally through the New Testament. My goal is always to have deep fellowship with the Lord in the understanding of His Word and out of that experience to explain to His people what a passage means. In the words of Nehemiah 8:8, I strive "to give the sense" of it so they may truly hear God speak and, in so doing, may respond to Him.

Obviously, God's people need to understand Him, which demands knowing His Word of Truth (2 Tim. 2:15) and allowing that Word to dwell in them richly (Col. 3:16). The dominant thrust of my ministry, therefore, is to help make God's living Word alive to His people. It is a refreshing adventure.

This New Testament commentary series reflects this objective of explaining and applying Scripture. Some commentaries are primarily linguistic, others are mostly theological, and some are mainly homiletical. This one is basically explanatory, or expository. It is not linguistically technical but deals with linguistics when that seems helpful to proper interpretation. It is not theologically expansive but focuses on the major doctrines in each text and how they relate to the whole of Scripture. It is not primarily homiletical, although each unit of thought is generally treated as one chapter, with a clear outline and logical flow of thought.

Most truths are illustrated and applied with other Scripture. After establishing the context of a passage, I have tried to follow closely the writer's development and reasoning.

My prayer is that each reader will fully understand what the Holy Spirit is saying through this part of His Word, so that His revelation may lodge in the mind of believers and bring greater obedience and faithfulness—to the glory of our great God.

Introduction to 2 Peter

Second Peter (along with Jude) is viewed by some as the "dark corner" of the New Testament. As a result, it is not often preached, studied, discussed, or quoted. The book is even neglected in scholarly circles, where critics dismiss it as a pseudonymous (forged) letter, unworthy of serious study.

But the church of Jesus Christ ignores this epistle at its peril. After all, Peter wrote it to help believers face a world filled with subtle spiritual deception. Knowing that his death was imminent (1:14), the apostle wanted to remind his readers of the truths he had already taught them, so that those truths would continue to safeguard them after he was gone (v. 15). Peter also knew that the deadly threat of false teachers loomed large on the horizon; he wanted to expose the apostates in order to expel their demon doctrines from the church.

Never has Peter's warning been more timely than it is today. The rapid advancement of mass media, coupled with the church's lack of discernment, has allowed doctrinal error to spread like wildfire. False teachers propagate their heresies via television, radio, the Internet, books, magazines, and seminars—doing whatever they can for their own self-promotion. In the process, their deceit lures multitudes to exchange the truth for utter lies (cf. 1 Tim. 1:19; 2 Tim. 2:16–18). To make matters worse, some in today's church, motivated by cowardly fear of rejection or misguided notions of love, are reluctant to expose today's apostates. Instead of countering error, they either embrace it or ignore it in the name of tolerance.

The apostle Peter, however, had no qualms about denouncing the deceivers who threatened his beloved flock. He recognized them for what they were: wolves in sheep's clothing (Matt. 7:15; Acts 20:29), lurking to devour the ignorant with their beguiling lies. Peter understood that false teachers are the emissaries of hell and pawns of Satan, motivated by the love of money, power, prestige, and prominence. Because they are masters of deception, they successfully peddle the doctrines of demons to unsuspecting souls, marketing eternal ruin as if it were eternal life.

The only sure defense against their tactics is found in the truth of God's Word. Peter knew this, of course, which is why he penned this epistle. As a true man of God, he was deeply concerned to protect those under his spiritual care.

AUTHOR

Peter was the acknowledged leader and spokesman of the apostles; as such, his name heads all four New Testament lists of the Twelve (Matt. 10:2–4; Mark 3:16–19; Luke 6:13–16; Acts 1:13). Along with his brother Andrew (who introduced him to Jesus [John 1:40–42]), he ran a fishing business on the Sea of Galilee (Matt. 4:18; Luke 5:1–3). The two brothers were originally from the village of Bethsaida (John 1:44), but later moved to the larger nearby town of Capernaum (Mark 1:21, 29). Their business was a successful one, as evidenced by the spacious house they owned in Capernaum (Mark 1:29, 32–33; Luke 4:38). We know that Peter was married, because Jesus healed his mother-in-law (Luke 4:38), and his wife accompanied him on his missionary travels (1 Cor. 9:5).

Peter's full name was Simon Barjona (Matt. 16:17), literally "Simon son of Jonas" (or John; cf. John 1:42). Simon was a common name in first-century Palestine. (There are eight other Simons mentioned in the New Testament: Simon the Zealot [Matt. 10:4]; Simon the half-brother of the Lord [Matt. 13:55]; Simon the leper [Matt. 26:6]; Simon of Cyrene, who was drafted to carry Jesus' cross [Matt. 27:32]; Simon the Pharisee, at whose home Jesus ate a meal [Luke 7:36–50]; Simon the father of Judas Iscariot [John 6:71]; Simon the magician [Acts 8:9–24]; and Simon the tanner, with whom Peter stayed in Joppa [Acts 9:43].) At their first meeting, Jesus named him Cephas (John 1:42; cf. 1 Cor. 1:12; 3:22; 9:5; 15:5; Gal. 1:18; 2:9, 11, 14), which is Aramaic for "rock"; "Peter" is its Greek equivalent (John 1:42).

On occasion, Peter is called "Simon" in secular or neutral settings (e.g., in reference to his house [Mark 1:29; Luke 4:38], his mother-in-law [Mark 1:30; Luke 4:38], or his business [Luke 5:3, 10]). At such times the use of the name has no spiritual implications. More often, however, he is referred to as "Simon" to mark the key failures in his life—those times when he was acting like his old, unregenerate self.

For example, in Matthew 17:24–25 Peter brashly assured the tax collectors that Jesus would pay the two-drachma tax levied for the upkeep of the temple. Reminding him that as God's Son, He was exempt from paying the tax, Jesus addressed Peter as "Simon" (v. 25). On another occasion, while out on the Sea of Galilee, Jesus said to Peter, "Put out into the deep water and let down your nets for a catch" (Luke 5:4). Peter was skeptical and hesitant to follow the Lord's advice; after all, Jesus had been a carpenter and was a rabbi, not a fisherman. No doubt somewhat exasperated, "Simon answered and said, 'Master, we worked hard all night and caught nothing, but I will do as You say and let down the nets'" (v. 5). The staggering haul of fish that resulted from his obedience (vv. 6–7) opened Simon's eyes to the reality of who Jesus is, so Luke, by the Spirit's inspiration, called him by his new name: "Simon Peter . . . fell down at Jesus' feet, saying, 'Go away from me Lord, for I am a sinful man, O Lord!'" (v. 8).

Following one of the Twelve's recurring debates as to which of them was the greatest, Jesus warned proud, overconfident Peter of his impending betrayal: "Simon, Simon, behold, Satan has demanded permission to sift you like wheat" (Luke 22:31). In fact, it was on the night of that betrayal that Peter was again called Simon, this time because he could not stay awake in the Garden of Gethsemane (Mark 14:37).

After the resurrection, Jesus called Peter "Simon" for the last time. Tired of waiting for the Lord to appear (Matt. 28:7), Peter impulsively announced, "I am going fishing" (John 21:3). Dutifully following their leader, the rest of the disciples said to him, "We will also come with you." But those whom Jesus called to be fishers of men (Matt. 4:19) He did not allow to again become mere catchers of fish: "and that night they caught nothing." The next morning Jesus met the unsuccessful crew on the shore, where He prepared breakfast for them. Afterward, He asked Peter three times, "Simon, son of John, do you love Me?" (John 21:15–17), and three times Peter affirmed his love for the Lord.

A few weeks later, the Holy Spirit descended on Peter and the rest of the apostles, and from then on the "Rock" lived up to his name. He took the lead in finding a replacement for Judas Iscariot (Acts 1:15–26), fearlessly preached the gospel (Acts 2:14–40; 3:12–26), boldly confronted the Jewish authorities (Acts 4:8–20), unhesitatingly disciplined sinning church members (Acts 5:1–11), and zealously denounced false teachers

(Acts 8:20). Moreover, it was through Peter's ministry that the doors of the church were thrown open to the Gentiles (Acts 10:1–11:18).

After his appearance at the Jerusalem Council (Acts 15:7–12), Peter all but disappeared from the historical record of the New Testament until he wrote his epistles. Paul alluded to Peter's missionary travels in 1 Corinthians 9:5, but the extent of those travels is not known. Nonetheless, the Scriptures indicate that he visited Antioch (cf. Gal. 2:11–21) and probably traveled to Corinth (cf. 1 Cor. 1:12) and throughout Asia Minor (cf. 1 Peter 1:1). According to tradition, Peter perished in Rome, as did Paul, during Nero's persecution (see further comments under "Date, Place of Writing, and Destination" below).

PETRINE AUTHORSHIP DISPUTED

While not normally wanting to dignify unbelieving skeptics, in this case it is helpful to see how this epistle rises to inspired integrity in the face of assaults on its legitimacy.

The authorship of 2 Peter has been disputed more sharply and to a greater extent than the authorship of any other New Testament book. Yet the letter itself plainly claims to have been written by "Simon Peter, a bond-servant and apostle of Jesus Christ" (1:1). The Greek text actually reads, "Simeon Peter," using the Hebrew form of Peter's name used elsewhere of him only in Acts 15:14. Such only strengthens the author's claim to be Peter, since a forger would not likely have used an obscure form of Peter's name. In 1:14 the author referred to Christ's prediction of his death (cf. John 21:18); in 1:16–18 he claimed to have been an eyewitness (of which there were only three; Matt. 17:1) of the Transfiguration; in 3:1 he referred to an earlier letter (1 Peter) that he wrote to his readers; and in 3:15 he referred to Paul as his "beloved brother," thus making himself the great apostle's spiritual peer. Those personal allusions further strengthen the letter's claim to have been written by Peter—a claim that should be allowed to stand unless there is compelling evidence to the contrary. As will be seen shortly, no such evidence exists.

Perversely, many critics view the personal allusions as the work of a forger attempting to pass himself off as Peter. Ironically, many of those same critics argue that 1 Peter was not written by Peter either—precisely because 1 Peter *lacks* sufficient personal allusions to him. As Daniel B. Wallace remarks, "In reading the literature, one cannot help but see an element of caprice and double standard, where scholars have already made up their minds despite the evidence" ("Second Peter: Introduction, Argument, and Outline" [Biblical Studies Press: www.bible.org, 2000]).

In addition to the epistle's personal allusions to events in Peter's life, there are similarities between the language of 2 Peter and Peter's speeches in Acts. The verb translated "received" (1:1) appears only three other times in the New Testament, one of which is in Acts 1:17; "godliness" is used four times in 2 Peter (1:3, 6, 7, 3:11), but elsewhere (outside of the Pastoral Epistles) only by Peter in Acts 3:12 (NKJV); the "day of the Lord" (3:10) appears in Acts 2:20, and only in 1 Thessalonians 5:2 and 2 Thessalonians 2:2 in the rest of the New Testament. The use of those uncommon words further suggests that the apostle Peter penned this epistle.

Many scholars, however, are not content to accept the epistle's claims at face value. Instead, they insist that it was written decades after the apostle's death by someone claiming to be Peter. To support their rejection of the letter's authenticity, critics advance several arguments.

First, they note that the early church was slow to accept 2 Peter as part of the canon of Scripture. The first person to explicitly state that Peter wrote it was Origen, early in the third century. Critics claim there is no trace of the epistle's existence until that time. Further, although Origen accepted it as a genuine writing of Peter, he noted that others had doubts about its authenticity. Writing in the fourth century, the church historian Eusebius of Caesarea also expressed doubts about 2 Peter. He did not reject it, but included it among the New Testament books whose authenticity was disputed. The silence of the church fathers before the time of Origen is taken to be a tacit denial of 2 Peter's authenticity.

Critics also point out several alleged historical problems that, they claim, indicate the epistle could not have been written in Peter's lifetime. First, they maintain that the reference to Paul's letters (3:15–16) reflects a time when those letters had been collected and recognized as Scripture. That, they argue, did not happen until long after Peter's death. Second, they believe the false teachers in view were second-century Gnostics. Third, the writer refers to "your apostles" (3:2) and says that the "fathers" (who are assumed to be the first generation of Christians) had already died (3:4). From a critical perspective, that suggests 2 Peter was written by someone who was neither an apostle nor one of the first generation of believers. Finally, critics argue that the reference to Christ's prediction of Peter's death (1:14) derives from John 21:18. John's gospel, however, was not written during Peter's lifetime.

A convincing argument in the minds of many critics is 2 Peter's alleged literary dependency on Jude. Since they date Jude later than Peter's lifetime, it follows that Peter could not have written 2 Peter. Further, they insist that an apostle would not borrow so extensively from a non-apostolic source.

Relentless critics also point to supposed differences in style, vocabulary, and doctrine between 1 and 2 Peter. The Greek of the first epistle, they suggest, is polished and sophisticated, while that of the second is coarse and stilted, replete with grandiose language and difficult constructions. The critics claim that the vocabulary of the two epistles is also very different, and 2 Peter shows a knowledge of Greek culture and philosophy far beyond the grasp of a simple Galilean fisherman. Finally, in their reckoning, many doctrinal themes found in 1 Peter are absent from 2 Peter. All of those factors lead many skeptics to insist that the same author could not have written both epistles.

Upon closer examination, however, each of the above arguments utterly fails to disqualify Peter as the author of this epistle.

It is true that the external attestation to 2 Peter in the writings of the church fathers is less extensive than that for most of the other New Testament books. It is, however, far more complete than the attestation given to any of the books excluded from the canon. In fact, 2 Peter was never rejected as spurious (even by Fathers who had questions about its authenticity—such as Eusebius), nor was it ever attributed to anyone other than Peter.

While Origen was the first to attribute 2 Peter to Peter, others before him were familiar with the epistle. Origen was an astute literary critic, and he would not likely have been taken in by a recent forgery. Moreover, he repeatedly quoted the epistle as Scripture, strongly implying that 2 Peter was known and accepted as canonical long before his time. The epistle's inclusion in the third-century Bodmer papyrus P[72] also indicates that it was considered part of the canon by that time. (The monumental fourth-century manuscripts Codex Sinaiticus and Codex Vaticanus and the fifth-century manuscript Codex Alexandrinus also include 2 Peter.)

Origen's teacher, Clement of Alexandria, wrote a commentary on the catholic (general) epistles, including 2 Peter (Eusebius *Ecclesiastical History*, 6.14.1). By writing a commentary on the book, Clement indicates that he considered 2 Peter to be Scripture (and therefore authentic). Furthermore, Clement's testimony provides strong evidence that the epistle's canonicity was generally accepted by the church in the first half of the second century.

Further evidence of the epistle's existence and acceptance at that time comes from Justin Martyr (c. A.D. 100–165). In his *Dialogue with Trypho*, Justin wrote, "And just as there were false prophets contemporaneous with your [the Jews] holy prophets, so are there now many false teachers amongst us, of whom our Lord forewarned us to beware" (82.1). That passage bears a striking resemblance to 2 Peter 2:1, "But false prophets also arose among the people, just as there will also be false teachers among you, who will secretly introduce destructive heresies, even denying the Master who bought them, bringing swift destruction upon themselves." That the Greek word translated "false teachers" (*pseudodidaskaloi*) appears before Justin's time only in 2 Peter 2:1 further suggests that Justin was borrowing from 2 Peter.

The apocryphal *Apocalypse of Peter,* dating from the first half of the second century, shows clear evidence of literary dependence on 2 Peter. In the early part of the second century, the *Epistle of Barnabas* (5.4) declares "that a man shall justly perish, who having the knowledge of the way of righteousness forceth himself into the way of darkness," a passage reminiscent of 2 Peter 2:21: "For it would be better for them not to have known the way of righteousness, than having known it, to turn away from the holy commandment handed on to them." Similarly, *Barnabas* 15.4, "In six thousand years the Lord shall bring all things to an end; for the day with Him signifyeth a thousand years; and this He himself beareth me witness, saying; Behold, the day of the Lord shall be as a thousand years," appears to have been drawn from 2 Peter 3:8: "But do not let this one fact escape your notice, beloved, that with the Lord one day is like a thousand years, and a thousand years like one day."

The *Shepherd of Hermas,* also dating from the early years of the second century, says, "Go, and tell all men to repent, and they shall live unto God; for the Lord in His compassion sent me to give repentance to all, though some of them do not deserve it for their deeds; but being long-suffering the Lord willeth them that were called through His Son to be saved" (*Similitude* 8.11.1). The similarity to 2 Peter 3:9, "The Lord is not slow about His promise, as some count slowness, but is patient toward you, not wishing for any to perish but for all to come to repentance," is remarkable.

That 2 Peter was known in the second century is further suggested by two Gnostic works, *The Gospel of Truth* and *The Apocryphon of John,* which contain probable allusions to it.

At about the same time that the apostle John penned the book of Revelation (the midnineties of the first century), Clement of Rome wrote, "Let this scripture be far from us where He saith, 'Wretched are the double-minded, which doubt in their soul and say, "These things we did hear in the days of our fathers also, and behold we have grown old, and none of these things hath befallen us" ' " (*1 Clement* 23.3). Clement seems to be echoing 2 Peter 3:4, which reads, "Where is the promise of His coming? For ever since the fathers fell asleep, all continues just as it was from the beginning of creation." Both passages relate the skepticism of false teachers, and both go on to warn that judgment is coming (*1 Clement* 23.5; 2 Peter 3:10).

Two other passages in *1 Clement* use Greek phrases found in the New Testament only in 2 Peter and in no other extrabiblical writing of that era. Both use the phrase translated "excellent (the NASB renders the same Greek word "Majestic") glory" in reference to God (*1 Clement* 9.2; 2 Peter 1:17); both also describe the Christian faith as "the way of truth" (*1 Clement* 35.5; 2 Peter 2:2).

Finally, if 2 Peter was written before Jude, then Jude is the earliest document to cite it (see the discussion of the relationship between Jude and 2 Peter in the "Introduction to Jude" later in this volume). The critics' argument that 2 Peter's supposed literary dependence on Jude proves it was written after Peter's lifetime depends on two assumptions. First, the author of 2 Peter had to have borrowed from Jude. Second, Jude had to have been written after Peter's lifetime. Neither assumption, however, can be proved.

The internal evidence indicates that 2 Peter came first, since Peter employed future tenses to describe the false-teaching apostates (2:1–3; 3:3). Jude, on the other hand, in paralleling 2 Peter, used tenses that say those who were prophesied had arrived (Jude 4). He used no future tenses with reference to the apostates.

The above-mentioned extrabiblical citations make a strong case that 2 Peter was known in the church from the first century onward. It is true that none of the Fathers who alluded to 2 Peter before the time of Origen cited 2 Peter as a source. Yet that is not unusual; the Apostolic Fathers cite 1 Peter twenty-nine times without naming Peter, and Romans thirty-one times without naming Paul (see Robert E. Picirilli, "Allusions to 2 Peter in the Apostolic Fathers," *Journal for the Study of the New Testament* 33 [1988], 74). (For a summary of the allusions to 2 Peter in the writings of the church fathers prior to the time of Origen, see also Michael J. Kruger, "The Authenticity of 2 Peter," *Journal of the Evangelical Theological Society* 42/4 [1999], 649–56; B. B. Warfield, "The Canonicity of Second Peter," in John E. Meeter, ed., *Selected Shorter Writings of Benjamin B. Warfield*, vol. 2 [Phillipsburg, N.J.: Presbyterian and Reformed, 1973], 49–68.)

The allusions to 2 Peter in the church fathers do not prove Peter wrote his second letter. But they do remove the objection that the alleged lack of external attestation rules out a date in Peter's lifetime. It also explains why the epistle was eventually accepted by the church as canonical; it was not a second-century forgery as many modern critics allege, but had a pedigree reaching back into apostolic times. Kruger notes the significance of 2 Peter's ultimate acceptance by the church as part of the canon of Scripture:

> In our quest to determine the authenticity of 2 Peter we cannot over-
> look the fact that 2 Peter, despite the reservations of some, was finally
> and fully accepted by the church as canonical in every respect. The
> fact that 2 Peter faced such resistance—resistance coupled with the
> incessant competition of pseudo-Petrine literature—and *still* prevailed

proves to be worthy of serious consideration. Is it so easy to dismiss the conclusions of Origen, Cyril of Jerusalem, Gregory Nazianzen, Ephiphanius [sic], Athanasius, Augustine, Rufinus, Jerome, and the church councils of Laodicea, Hippo, and Carthage? Thus, if the epistle of 2 Peter held such a firm position in the fourth-century canon, then perhaps the burden of proof should fall on those who suggest it does not belong there. ("Authenticity," 651, emphasis in original.)

It is unwarranted for modern critics to assume that those ancient scholars were credulous and unsophisticated. On the contrary, the very councils that accepted 2 Peter as canonical also rejected other works that claimed Peter as their author (such as *The Gospel of Peter, The Preaching of Peter, The Teaching of Peter, The Apocalypse of Peter, The Acts of Peter and the Twelve Apostles, The Epistle of Peter to Philip,* and *The Letter of Peter to James*). They recognized that 2 Peter clearly stood out from those forgeries as divinely inspired Scripture.

The alleged historical difficulties raised by the critics do not prove that 2 Peter could not have been written during Peter's lifetime. The reference to Paul's letters (3:15–16) need not be forced to mean *everything* Paul wrote; it merely speaks of those epistles Peter was aware of when he wrote 2 Peter. Nothing in the text speaks of a collection of Paul's inspired letters or implies that either Peter or his readers were familiar with all of them. That Paul's letters were already circulating among the churches during his own lifetime is clear from Colossians 4:16.

Nor is it an anachronism, as some charge, for Peter to refer to Paul's inspired letters as Scripture (3:16). The apostles knew that what they wrote under the inspiration of the Holy Spirit (John 14:26) was Scripture on a par with the Old Testament. Paul repeatedly claimed to be writing the very words of God. In 1 Corinthians 2:13 he declared, "which things we also speak, not in words taught by human wisdom, but in those taught by the Spirit, combining spiritual thoughts with spiritual words," while in 14:37 he added, "If anyone thinks he is a prophet or spiritual, let him recognize that the things which I write to you are the Lord's commandment." He commended the Thessalonians because "when [they] received the word of God which [they] heard from [him], [they] accepted it not as the word of men, but for what it really is, the word of God" (1 Thess. 2:13; cf. 2 Cor. 13:3; 1 Peter 4:11–12).

Neither does the evidence support the claim that the false teachers in view in 2 Peter were second-century Gnostics. The elements of their heretical teaching were common to the first century, while the characteristic teachings of second-century Gnosticism (e.g., cosmological dualism, an evil demiurge who created the evil physical world, salvation through secret knowledge) are absent from 2 Peter. Charles Bigg writes,

> Every feature in the description of the false teachers and mockers is to be found in the apostolic age. If they had "eyes full of adultery," there were those at Corinth who defended incest. If they "blasphemed dignities," there were those who spoke evil of St. Paul. They profaned the Agape [the love feast or communion service], so did the Corinthians. They mocked at the Parousia [the return of Christ], and some of the Corinthians denied that there was any resurrection. (*A Critical and Exegetical Commentary on the Epistles of St. Peter and St. Jude*, The International Critical Commentary [Edinburgh, T. & T. Clark, 1902], 239)

Nor does 2 Peter discuss the key issues of the second century (e.g., the role of bishops in church government, fully-developed Gnosticism, and Montanism). The failure to mention specific second-century issues is especially noticeable in 3:8, "But do not let this one fact escape your notice, beloved, that with the Lord one day is like a thousand years, and a thousand years like one day." One of the major beliefs of the second century was chiliasm, an early form of premillennialism. If 2 Peter was written in the second century, it is unlikely that its author would have failed to mention chiliasm in connection with 3:8.

The author had already called himself an apostle (1:1), so the reference to "your apostles" (3:2) could not mean he was excluding himself from their number. Since the apostles were given by God to the church (cf. 1 Cor. 12:28; Eph. 2:20; 4:11–12), it was fitting for Peter to describe them (himself included) as "your apostles." The "fathers" in view in 2 Peter 3:4 were not the first generation of Christians, but the Old Testament patriarchs. Both the context (the flood; vv. 5–6) and the usage of the phrase "the fathers" support that interpretation. In the New Testament (John 6:58; 7:22; Acts 13:32; Rom. 9:5; 11:28; 15:8; Heb. 1:1) and in the writings of the apostolic fathers, that phrase refers not to the first generation of Christians, but to the Old Testament patriarchs.

Nor is it necessary that the mention of Peter's impending death (1:14) derives from John 21:18. Obviously, Peter was there when Jesus made that prediction, and he heard it with his own ears.

Much has been made of the differences in style between Peter's two epistles. But the differences are not as significant as many confidently assert. The commentator Joseph Mayor, who denied that Peter wrote 2 Peter, nevertheless admitted, "There is not that chasm between [1 and 2 Peter] which some would try to make out" (cited in D. Edmond Hiebert, *Second Peter and Jude: An Expositional Commentary* [Greenville, S.C.: Unusual Publications, 1989], 12). Nor do the two brief epistles that Peter wrote provide enough material to definitively establish his style.

Some argue that the vocabulary of the two epistles is so different that the same author could not have written both books. However, the percentage of words common to 1 and 2 Peter is roughly the same as the percentage common to 1 Timothy and Titus, both written by Paul and similar in content. It is also similar to the amount of common vocabulary found in 1 and 2 Corinthians (Kruger, "Authenticity," 656–57).

The difference in vocabulary and style between 1 and 2 Peter can be accounted for in part by their different themes: 1 Peter was written to comfort those undergoing persecution, 2 Peter to warn of the danger of false teachers. Though it adds nothing to the argument, the differences in style may reflect that Silvanus (Silas) acted as Peter's amanuensis for 1 Peter (1 Peter 5:12), a common practice in Peter's day. Under the apostle's direction, Silvanus may have smoothed out his grammar and syntax. But since Peter was most likely in prison when he wrote 2 Peter (see "Date, Place of Writing, and Destination" on page 14), he might not have had access to an amanuensis and thus may have written the epistle in his own hand.

The charge that 2 Peter reflects a grasp of Hellenistic philosophy beyond what Peter could be expected to know not only foolishly presumes to know what Peter actually knew, but also overlooks the influence of Peter's environment on him. He was born and reared in Galilee, which even in Isaiah's day was known as "Galilee of the Gentiles" (Isa. 9:1). Nearby was the Gentile region known as the Decapolis (Matt. 4:25; Mark 5:20; 7:31). Further, it is now known that many of the Hellenistic terms Peter used were in common usage in his day. The apostle used terms his readers were familiar with, without investing them with the shades of meaning that the Greek philosophers gave them.

Despite the supposed differences in style of 1 and 2 Peter, there are remarkable similarities between the books. The wording of the salutations of both epistles, "May grace and peace be yours in the fullest measure" (1 Peter 1:2) and "Grace and peace be multiplied to you" (2 Peter 1:2), is identical in the Greek, and the phrase is found nowhere else in the New Testament. Other words common to both books but rare in the rest of the New Testament include *aretē* ("excellence"; 1 Peter 2:9; 2 Peter 1:3, 5), *apothesis* ("removal," "laying aside"; 1 Peter 3:21; 2 Peter 1:14), *philadelphia* ("love of the brethren," "brotherly kindness"; 1 Peter 1:22; 2 Peter 1:7), *anastrophē* ("behavior," "way of life," "conduct"; 1 Peter 1:15, 18; 2:12; 3:1, 2, 16; 2 Peter 2:7; 3:11), and *aselgeia* ("sensuality"; 1 Peter 4:3; 2 Peter 2:2, 7, 18). Further, 2 Peter, like 1 Peter, contains Semitic expressions consistent with Peter's Jewish background.

Although the different themes of each epistle required Peter to address different doctrinal issues, there is nonetheless a commonality in their teaching. Both letters speak of God's prophetic word revealed in the Old Testament (1 Peter 1:10–12; 2 Peter 1:19–21), the new birth (1 Peter 1:23; 2 Peter 1:4), God's sovereign choice of believers (1 Peter 1:2; 2 Peter 1:10), the need for personal holiness (1 Peter 2:11–12; 2 Peter 1:5–7),

God's judgment on immorality (1 Peter 4:2–5; 2 Peter 2:10–22), the second coming of Christ (1 Peter 4:7, 13; 2 Peter 3:4), the judgment of the wicked (1 Peter 4:5, 17; 2 Peter 3:7), and Christ's lordship (1 Peter 1:3; 3:15; 2 Peter 1:8, 11, 14, 16; 2:20; 3:18).

There are only two possibilities regarding the authorship of 2 Peter. Either it was written by Peter as it claims, or it is pseudonymous and the work of a forger who pretended to be Peter. If the latter is true, the author would have been a hypocrite as well as a liar—a deceiver condemning false teachers for being what he himself was and giving severe warning about divine judgment.

Furthermore, if the book was written by a forger, it is difficult to see what the forger's motive was. The authors of pseudonymous works usually attached the name of a prominent person to their writings to give credence to their false teaching. But 2 Peter contains no teaching that contradicts the rest of the New Testament. Since it is entirely orthodox, the epistle could have easily gone out under the author's own name. The author even notes that the false teachers (whom he is condemning) rejected the apostolic authority of Paul (3:16). In fact, they were unimpressed with authority of any kind (2:1, 10). Thus, a forged appeal to apostolic authority would not have added much to the author's argument (especially since, in so doing, he would have been guilty of the very hypocrisy he was denouncing).

Pseudonymous works were also sometimes written because people were fascinated to know more about the significant figures of the early church. But 2 Peter contains no new information about Peter.

There are numerous other difficulties with the view that 2 Peter is pseudonymous. For example, the difference in style between the two epistles is hard to account for, since most pseudonymous authors attempted to copy the style of the person they were pretending to be. Also, a forger would not have had Peter confess his inability to understand Paul's writings (3:15–16); pseudonymous authors tended to glorify their heroes (the stated "authors") and exaggerate their abilities. Nor would a pseudonymous author have referred to Paul as "our beloved brother" (3:15). The writings of the early church do not speak of the apostle in such familiar terms. For instance, Polycarp referred to him as "the blessed and glorious Paul" (*Epistle to the Philippians*, 3.1), Clement called him "the blessed Paul" (*1 Clement*, 47:1), and Ignatius described him as "Paul, who was sanctified, who obtained a good report, who is worthy of all felicitation; in whose footsteps I would fain be found treading" (*Epistle to the Ephesians*, 12.2).

Some argue that the writing of pseudonymous books (so-called pious forgeries) was an accepted practice. Since everyone knew that someone else wrote the book in the purported author's name, no deception was involved. But the obvious question is, What purpose would there be in writing a pseudonymous document if everyone knew it was pseudonymous? In the case of 2 Peter, why would a pseudonymous author have included all the personal allusions to Peter if his readers knew Peter did not write the epistle?

Despite the claims of some scholars, there is no evidence that the early church accepted the practice of pseudonymity. On the contrary, "No one ever seems to have accepted a document as religiously and philosophically prescriptive which was known to be forged. I do not know a single example. . . . We are forced to admit that in Christian circles pseudonymity was considered a dishonorable device and, if discovered, the document was rejected and the author, if known, was excoriated" (L. R. Donelson, *Pseudepigraphy and Ethical Argument in the Pastoral Epistles* [cited in Thomas R. Schreiner, *1, 2 Peter, Jude,* The New American Commentary (Nashville: Broadman & Holman, 2003), 272]).

From the beginning, the church rejected forged documents. In 2 Thessalonians 2:2, Paul warned the Thessalonians "not [to] be quickly shaken from your composure or be disturbed either by a spirit or a message or a letter as if from us, to the effect that the day of the Lord has come." Even at that early stage in the church's history, forgers were circulating letters purporting to be from Paul so they could more easily spread false doctrine. Hence the apostle warned his readers not to be fooled, and he took steps to authenticate his letters that were genuine (2 Thess. 3:17; cf. 1 Cor. 16:21; Gal. 6:11; Col. 4:18). The bishop who wrote the pseudonymous work *The Acts of Paul and Thecla* was removed from office, even though he protested that he had written it out of love for Paul and a desire to honor him (Tertullian *On Baptism, XVII; The Ante-Nicene Fathers* vol. 3 [reprint; Grand Rapids: Eerdmans, 1973], 677). The Muratorian Canon, a second-century list of New Testament books, rejected two forged letters purporting to have been written by Paul "since it is not fitting that poison should be mixed with honey" (cited in F. F. Bruce, *The Canon of Scripture* [Downers Grove, Ill.: InterVarsity, 1988], 160). At about that same time Serapion, the bishop of Antioch, offered the following explanation for rejecting the spurious *Gospel of Peter:* "We, brethren, receive Peter and the other apostles as Christ himself. But those writings which falsely go under their name, as we are well acquainted with them, we reject, and know also, that we have not received such handed down to us" (cited in Eusebius *Ecclesiastical History,* 6.12).

The New Testament placed a premium on truthfulness (cf. John 19:35; Rom. 3:7; 1 Cor. 13:6; 2 Cor. 4:2; 7:14; 13:8; Eph. 4:15, 25; 5:9; Col. 3:9; 1 Tim. 2:7; 3:15). The Holy Spirit, the "Spirit of truth" (John 14:17; 15:26; 16:13; 1 John 5:6), could never inspire a forgery. Therefore, the early church rightly rejected all such works. Had 2 Peter been a forgery, they would have rejected it too.

Thus, despite the skepticism and doubts of modern critics, the best answer to the question of who wrote 2 Peter is "Simon Peter, a bond-servant and apostle of Jesus Christ" (1:1).

DATE, PLACE OF WRITING, AND DESTINATION

According to tradition, Peter suffered martyrdom near the end of Nero's persecution. Because Nero died in A.D. 68, Peter's death must have taken place before that time. Second Peter appears to have been written shortly before the apostle's death (1:14), perhaps in A.D. 67 or 68. Peter does not say where he was when he wrote this epistle. But since his death was imminent, and he was martyred in Rome, he probably wrote it while in prison there. Unlike the first epistle, 2 Peter does not name its recipients. However, since this was the second letter he had written them (3:1), they were likely the same people (or at least some of the same people) to whom 1 Peter was addressed, believers who lived in "Pontus, Galatia, Cappadocia, Asia, and Bithynia" (1 Peter 1:1), provinces located in Asia Minor (modern Turkey).

OCCASION

Peter wrote his first epistle to comfort and instruct believers who were facing the external threat of persecution. Peter in this letter addresses the even more deadly threat of false teachers who would arise within the church. The apostle warned believers to be on the alert against their deceiving lies. Its vivid and incisive depiction of heretics and apostates is comparable only to Jude's.

Peter did not identify specific heresy. As noted above under "Author," it lacked the hallmarks of second-century Gnosticism. Whoever these heretics were, they were like many others who have denied Christ (2:1); twisted the Scriptures, including Paul's writings (3:15–16); followed instead the "cleverly devised tales" (1:16) of "destructive heresies" (2:1); mocked the second coming of Christ (3:4) and the coming judgment (3:5–7); practiced immorality (2:2, 13–14, 19); despised authority (2:10); were arrogant and vain (2:18); and sought material gain (2:3, 14). Second Peter serves not only as a much-needed rebuke of the false teachers of Peter's day, but it also gives characteristics common to the false teachers of every age. Because wickedness of life flows from heretical doctrine,

Peter focused more on their godless behavior than on the specific teachings they propagated. In the words of the Lord Jesus Christ,

> You will know them by their fruits. Grapes are not gathered from thorn bushes nor figs from thistles, are they? So every good tree bears good fruit, but the bad tree bears bad fruit. A good tree cannot produce bad fruit, nor can a bad tree produce good fruit. Every tree that does not bear good fruit is cut down and thrown into the fire. So then, you will know them by their fruits. (Matt. 7:16–20)

OUTLINE

Salutation (1:1–2)

I. Avoiding False Teaching by Understanding Salvation (1:3–11)
   A. It Is Sustained by God's Power (1:3–4)
   B. It Is Confirmed by Christian Graces (1:5–7)
   C. It Results in Abundant Reward (1:8–11)

II. Avoiding False Teaching by Understanding the Scriptures (1:12–21)
   A. They Are Confirmed by Apostolic Witness (1:12–18)
   B. They Are Inspired by the Holy Spirit (1:19–21)

III. Avoiding False Teaching by Understanding False Teachers (2:1–22)
   A. Their Infiltration (2:1–3)
   B. Their Judgment (2:4–10a)
   C. Their Impudence (2:10b–13a)
   D. Their Impurity (2:13b–17)
   E. Their Impact (2:18–22)

IV. Avoiding False Teaching by Understanding the Future (3:1–18)
   A. The Certainty of the Day of the Lord (3:1–10)
   B. The Practical Implications of the Day of the Lord (3:11–18)

The Believer's Precious Faith—Part 1: Its Source, Substance, and Sufficiency (2 Peter 1:1–4)

1

Simon Peter, a bond-servant and apostle of Jesus Christ, To those who have received a faith of the same kind as ours, by the righteousness of our God and Savior, Jesus Christ: Grace and peace be multiplied to you in the knowledge of God and of Jesus our Lord; seeing that His divine power has granted to us everything pertaining to life and godliness, through the true knowledge of Him who called us by His own glory and excellence. For by these He has granted to us His precious and magnificent promises, so that by them you may become partakers of the divine nature, having escaped the corruption that is in the world by lust. (1:1–4)

John Murray, one of the foremost Reformed theologians of the twentieth century, wrote the following about the profound and superlative significance of the atonement:

> The Father did not spare his own Son. He spared nothing that the dictates of unrelenting rectitude demanded. And it is the undercurrent of the Son's acquiescence that we hear when he says, "Nevertheless not my will, but thine, be done" (Luke 22:42). But why? It was in order that eternal and invincible love might find the full realization of its urge and purpose in redemption by price and by power. Of Calvary the spirit is

> eternal love and the basis eternal justice. It is the same love manifested
> in the mystery of Gethsemane's agony and of Calvary's accursed tree
> that wraps eternal security around the people of God. "He that spared
> not his own Son, but delivered him up for us all, how shall he not with
> him also freely give us all things?" (Rom. 8:32). "Who shall separate us
> from the love of Christ? shall tribulation, or distress, or persecution, or
> famine, or nakedness, or peril, or sword?" (Rom. 8:35). "For I am per-
> suaded that neither death nor life nor angels nor principalities nor
> things present nor things to come nor powers nor height nor depth nor
> any other creature will be able to separate us from the love of God
> which is in Christ Jesus our Lord" (Rom. 8:38, 39). That is the security
> which a perfect atonement secures and it is the perfection of the atone-
> ment that secures it. (*Redemption—Accomplished and Applied* [Grand
> Rapids: Eerdmans, 1955], 78)

Without question, God's redemption of sinners unto eternal life through
the atoning work of His Son Jesus Christ is, for all those who believe,
God's most precious gift. With salvation's certainty in view, Peter opens
his second letter by enriching his readers concerning three great truths
about it: its source, its substance, and its sufficiency.

SALVATION'S SOURCE

**Simon Peter, a bond-servant and apostle of Jesus Christ, To those
who have received a faith of the same kind as ours, by the righteousness of our God and Savior, Jesus Christ:** (1:1)

According to the custom of his day, the apostle opened his epistle
with a standard salutation, appropriately identifying himself as the author.
Simon, the Greek form of the Hebrew "Simeon," the father of one of the
twelve tribes of Israel, was a common Jewish name (cf. Matt. 13:55; 26:6;
27:32; Acts 1:13; 8:9; 9:43). **Peter** is from a Greek word that means "rock"
(Cephas is its Aramaic equivalent; see John 1:42; 1 Cor. 1:12; 3:22; 9:5;
15:5; Gal. 1:18; 2:9, 11, 14). The apostle used both names to ensure that the
letter's recipients knew exactly whom it was from.
Identifying himself as **a bond-servant,** Peter humbly and grate-
fully placed himself in the position of submission, duty, and obedience.
Some of the greatest leaders in the history of redemption bore the title
servant (e.g., *Moses,* Deut. 34:5; Ps. 105:26; Mal. 4:4; *Joshua,* Josh. 24:29;
David, 2 Sam. 3:18; Ps. 78:70; *all the prophets,* Jer. 44:4; Amos 3:7; *Paul,*
Rom. 1:1; Phil. 1:1; Titus 1:1; *James,* James 1:1; *Jude,* Jude 1), and it eventually became a designation suitable for every believer (cf. 1 Cor. 7:22; Eph.
6:6; Col. 4:12; 2 Tim. 2:24). In Peter's day, to willingly call oneself **a bond-**

servant (*doulos,* "slave") was to severely lower oneself in a culture where slaves were considered no better than animals. Whereas that practice may have been demeaning socially, it was honorable spiritually. It was to acknowledge that one was duty bound to obey his master, no matter what the cost. Of the sense in which this is true of Christians, William Barclay explains:

> (i) To call the Christian the *doulos* of God means that he is inalienably possessed by God. In the ancient world a master possessed his slaves in the same sense as he possessed his tools. A servant can change his master; but a slave cannot. The Christian inalienably belongs to God.
> (ii) To call the Christian the *doulos* of God means that he is unqualifiedly at the disposal of God. In the ancient world the master could do what he liked with his slave. He had the same power over his slave as he had over his inanimate possessions. He had the power of life and death over his slave. The Christian belongs to God, for God to send him where He will, and to do with him what He will. The Christian is the man who has no rights of his own, for all his rights are surrendered to God.
> (iii) To call the Christian the *doulos* of God means that the Christian owes an unquestioning obedience to God. Ancient law was such that a master's command was a slave's only law. Even if a slave was told to do something which actually broke the law, he could not protest, for, as far as he was concerned, his master's command was the law. In any situation the Christian has but one question to ask: "Lord, what wilt *Thou* have me to do?" The command of God is his only law.
> (iv) To call the Christian the *doulos* of God means that he must be constantly in the service of God. In the ancient world the slave had literally no time of his own, no holidays, no time off, no working-hours settled by agreement, no leisure. All his time belonged to the master. (*The Letters of James and Peter,* rev. ed. [Philadelphia: Westminster, 1976], 345–46; emphasis in the original)

Although Peter viewed himself humbly as a bond-servant, he also represented himself nobly as an **apostle of Jesus Christ,** one officially sent forth by Christ Himself as a divinely commissioned witness of the resurrected Lord, with authority to proclaim His truth (Matt. 10:1; Mark 3:13; 16:20; Luke 6:13; Acts 1:2–9, 22; 1 Cor. 9:1; 1 John 1:1; cf. Matt. 28:19–20; John 14:26; 16:13). Peter, in presenting himself in these terms, sets a pattern for all in spiritual leadership: the submissive, sacrificial anonymity of a slave, combined with the dignity, significance, and authority of an apostle.

The apostle sent this letter **to those** same believers who received his first one. They were part of God's elect scattered in the Gentile regions of "Pontus, Galatia, Cappadocia, Asia, and Bithynia" (1 Peter 1:1). Those believers were predominantly Gentiles, but certainly Jewish Christians were also among the recipients of the letter, which Peter most likely wrote in A.D. 67 or 68, about one year after writing his first epistle (for details, see the Introduction to this volume).

The manner in which Peter described his readers is theologically rich, albeit brief, and points to the divine source of salvation. **Have received** implies believers' salvation is a gift. The verb (*lagchanō*) means "to gain by divine will" or "given by an allotment" (as in the biblical practice of casting lots to learn God's will; cf. Lev. 16:8–10; Josh. 7:14; 1 Sam. 14:38–43; 1 Chron. 25:8–31; Prov. 16:33; 18:18; Jonah 1:7; Acts 1:16–26). Clearly it refers to something not obtained by human effort or based on personal worthiness but issued from God's sovereign purpose. Peter's readers received **faith** because God graciously willed to give it to them (cf. Acts 11:15–17; Gal. 3:14; Eph. 1:13; Phil. 1:29).

A faith here could mean *the* objective faith, as in the doctrines of the Christian faith, or it could denote subjective belief. But it is best to understand it in this context without the definite article (in contrast to Jude 3) as subjective faith, the Christian's power to believe the gospel for salvation. Even though belief in the gospel is commanded of all, so that all are responsible for their obedience or disobedience—and in that sense it is the human side of salvation—God still must supernaturally grant sinners the ability and power to believe unto salvation (Eph. 2:8–9; cf. 6:23; Rom. 12:3; 1 Cor. 2:5). Peter began his first epistle writing about divine choice and election in salvation, whereas here he refers to the human response of faith. God's sovereignty and man's responsibility form the essential elements of salvation. Only when the Holy Spirit awakens someone's dead soul in response to hearing or reading the gospel is saving faith initiated so the sinner can embrace redemption (cf. Acts 11:21; 16:14).

Further evidence that faith here is subjective comes from Peter's description of his readers' faith as **of the same kind as ours.** The word rendered **same kind** (*isotimon*) means "equally valuable," or "of equal privilege." It designated that which was equal in rank, position, honor, standing, price, or value. This would make no sense if referring to the body of gospel truth, since that truth has no equal. Each believer has received faith as a personal gift, a faith that is the same in nature, the precious gift of God, which brings equal spiritual privileges in salvation to all who receive it (cf. John 17:20; Acts 11:15–17; 13:39). Among the faithful, God sees no distinctions among Christians; as Paul wrote, "There is neither Jew nor Greek, there is neither slave nor free man, there is neither male nor female; for you are all one in Christ Jesus" (Gal. 3:28; cf. v. 26; Rom. 10:12–13).

All the elect have received, as a gift, the faith that saves. Ephesians

2:8–9 says, "For by grace you have been saved through faith; and that not of yourselves, it is the gift of God; not as a result of works, so that no one may boast." These verses have profound meaning and far-reaching application.

> Our response in salvation is **faith,** but even that is **not of ourselves** [but is] **the gift of God. Faith** is nothing that we do in our own power or by our own resources. In the first place we do not have adequate power or resources. More than that, God would not want us to rely on them even if we had them. Otherwise salvation would be in part by our own **works,** and we would have some ground to **boast** in ourselves. Paul intends to emphasize that even faith is not from us apart from God's giving it.
>
> Some have objected to this interpretation, saying that **faith** (*pistis*) is feminine, while **that** (*touto*) is neuter. That poses no problem, however, as long as it is understood that **that** does not refer precisely to the noun **faith** but to the act of believing. Further, this interpretation makes the best sense of the text, since if **that** refers to **by grace you have been saved through faith** (that is, to the whole statement), the adding of **and that not of yourselves, it is the gift of God** would be redundant, because grace is defined as an unearned act of God. If salvation is of grace, it has to be an undeserved gift of God. Faith is presented as a gift from God in 2 Peter 1:1, Philippians 1:29, and Acts 3:16. . . .
>
> When we accept the finished work of Christ on our behalf, we act by the **faith** supplied by God's **grace.** That is the supreme act of human faith, the act which, though it is ours, is primarily God's—His **gift** to us out of His **grace.** When a person chokes or drowns and stops breathing, there is nothing he can do. If he ever breathes again it will be because someone else starts him breathing. A person who is spiritually dead cannot even make a decision of faith unless God first breathes into him the breath of spiritual life. **Faith** is simply breathing the breath that God's **grace** supplies. Yet, the paradox is that we must exercise it and bear the responsibility if we do not (cf. John 5:40). (John MacArthur, *Ephesians,* MacArthur New Testament Commentary [Chicago: Moody, 1986], 60–61)

Peter's use of the pronoun **ours** most likely had in view the conflict between Jews and Gentiles in the church. The book of Acts records that he was heavily involved in that issue in the early days of the church. Peter explained to separatist Jewish brethren his encounter with the Gentile Cornelius' household:

> But Peter began speaking and proceeded to explain to them in orderly sequence, saying, "I was in the city of Joppa praying; and in a trance I saw a vision, an object coming down like a great sheet lowered by four

corners from the sky; and it came right down to me, and when I had fixed my gaze on it and was observing it I saw the four-footed animals of the earth and the wild beasts and the crawling creatures and the birds of the air. I also heard a voice saying to me, 'Get up, Peter; kill and eat.' But I said, 'By no means, Lord, for nothing unholy or unclean has ever entered my mouth.' But a voice from heaven answered a second time, 'What God has cleansed, no longer consider unholy.' This happened three times, and everything was drawn back up into the sky. And behold, at that moment three men appeared at the house in which we were staying, having been sent to me from Caesarea. The Spirit told me to go with them without misgivings. These six brethren also went with me and we entered the man's house. And he reported to us how he had seen the angel standing in his house, and saying, 'Send to Joppa and have Simon, who is also called Peter, brought here; and he will speak words to you by which you will be saved, you and all your household.' And as I began to speak, the Holy Spirit fell upon them just as He did upon us at the beginning. And I remembered the word of the Lord, how He used to say, 'John baptized with water, but you will be baptized with the Holy Spirit.' Therefore if God gave to them the same gift as He gave to us also after believing in the Lord Jesus Christ, who was I that I could stand in God's way?" (Acts 11:4–17; cf. 10:1–48)

At the Jerusalem Council Peter reiterated the truth that God plays no favorites concerning the salvation and spiritual privileges of Jews and Gentiles:

But some of the sect of the Pharisees who had believed stood up, saying, "It is necessary to circumcise them [the Gentiles] and to direct them to observe the Law of Moses." The apostles and the elders came together to look into this matter. After there had been much debate, Peter stood up and said to them, "Brethren, you know that in the early days God made a choice among you, that by my mouth the Gentiles would hear the word of the gospel and believe. And God, who knows the heart, testified to them giving them the Holy Spirit, just as He also did to us; and He made no distinction between us and them, cleansing their hearts by faith. Now therefore why do you put God to the test by placing upon the neck of the disciples a yoke which neither our fathers nor we have been able to bear? But we believe that we are saved through the grace of the Lord Jesus, in the same way as they also are." (Acts 15:5–11)

Therefore it should not be surprising that Peter referred to that same truth here. Among His elect, God makes no favored distinctions based on ethnicity—He gives all Christians the same saving faith with all its privileges (cf. Eph. 2:11–18; 4:5).

Believers' saving faith is available because of **the righteousness**

of . . . Jesus Christ. Sinners are given eternal life because the Savior imputes His perfect **righteousness** to them (2 Cor. 5:21; Phil. 3:8–9; 1 Peter 2:24), covering their sins and rendering them acceptable to Him. Romans 4:4–8 says,

> Now to the one who works, his wage is not credited as a favor, but as what is due. But to the one who does not work, but believes in Him who justifies the ungodly, his faith is credited as righteousness, just as David also speaks of the blessing on the man to whom God credits righteousness apart from works: "Blessed are those whose lawless deeds have been forgiven, and whose sins have been covered. Blessed is the man whose sin the Lord will not take into account." (cf. Acts 13:38–39)

This immensely important doctrine of imputed righteousness is at the very heart of the Christian gospel. Salvation is a gift from God at all points. Both the faith to believe and the righteousness to satisfy God's holiness come from Him. On the cross Christ bore the full wrath of God against all the sins of those who would believe (2 Cor. 5:18–19). Those sins were imputed to Christ so that God could impute to believers all the righteousness that was His. His righteousness fully covers the redeemed, as the prophet Isaiah beautifully expresses it, "I will rejoice greatly in the Lord, my soul will exult in my God; for He has clothed me with garments of salvation, He has wrapped me with a robe of righteousness, as a bridegroom decks himself with a garland, and as a bride adorns herself with her jewels" (Isa. 61:10).

It is noteworthy that Peter does not refer to God **our** Father here but to **our God and Savior, Jesus Christ.** Righteousness here does proceed from the Father, but it reaches every believer through the Son, Jesus Christ (cf. Gal. 3:8–11; Phil. 3:8–9). The Greek construction places just one article before the phrase **God and Savior,** which makes both terms refer to the same person. Thus Peter identifies Jesus, not just as Savior, but as God (cf. 1:11; 2:20; 3:2, 18; Isa. 43:3, 11; 45:15, 21; 60:16; Rom. 9:5; Col. 2:9; Titus 2:13; Heb. 1:8), the author and agent of salvation. The apostle made the same relation clear in his Pentecost sermon, in which he took the Old Testament truth of God and applied it to Jesus (Acts 2:21–36; cf. Matt. 1:21; Acts 4:12; 5:31).

SALVATION'S SUBSTANCE

Grace and peace be multiplied to you in the knowledge of God and of Jesus our Lord; (1:2)

In Peter's version of this familiar salutation, he reminds readers that true saints live in the realm of **grace and peace,** as the apostle Paul taught the Roman Christians: "Therefore, having been justified by faith, we have peace with God through our Lord Jesus Christ, through whom also we have obtained our introduction by faith into this grace in which we stand; and we exult in hope of the glory of God" (Rom. 5:1–2). God wants the substance of salvation **grace and peace** to **be multiplied,** to come in unending, abundant streams to His children. Similar statements fill the epistles (e.g., 1 Cor. 1:3; 2 Cor. 1:2; Gal. 1:3; Eph. 1:2). **Grace** (*charis*) is God's free, unmerited favor toward sinners, which grants those who believe the gospel complete forgiveness forever through the Lord Jesus Christ (Rom. 3:24; Eph. 1:7; Titus 3:7). **Peace** (*eirēnē*) with God and from Him in all life's circumstances is the effect of grace (Eph. 2:14–15; Col. 1:20), flowing out of the forgiveness God has given to all the elect (cf. Ps. 85:8; Isa. 26:12; 2 Thess. 3:16). "Grace upon grace" (John 1:16) is an expression that defines the boundless flow of divine favor, while peace comes with such fullness that it is divine and beyond human understanding (John 14:27; Phil. 4:7). Believers receive surpassing **grace** for every sin (Ps. 84:11; Acts 4:33; 2 Cor. 9:8; 12:9; Heb. 4:16) and abundant **peace** for every trial (John 14:27; 16:33).

All this grace and peace comes **in** (through) **the knowledge of God and of Jesus our Lord.** It is not available to those who do not know and wholeheartedly embrace the gospel. **Knowledge** (*epignōsis;* cf. 1:8; 2:20) is a strengthened form of the basic Greek word for "knowledge" (*gnōsis;* cf. 1:5, 6; 3:18). It conveys the idea of a full, rich, thorough knowledge, involving a degree of intimate understanding of a specific subject (cf. Rom. 3:20; 10:2; Eph. 1:17). The substance of one's salvation is this kind of rational, objective knowledge of God through His Word (cf. John 8:32; 14:6; 17:17; 2 John 2). This fundamental concept of knowing was first of all an Old Testament one (cf. Ex. 5:2; Judg. 2:10; 1 Sam. 2:12; Prov. 2:5; Hos. 2:20; 5:4). Paul often used the same word in relation to divine truth (Eph. 1:17; 4:13; Phil. 1:9; Col. 1:9, 10; 2:2; 3:10; 1 Tim. 2:4; 2 Tim. 2:25; 3:7; Titus 1:1). The knowledge that brings salvation derives not from feelings, intuition, emotion, or personal experience, but only from the revealed truth, based on the gospel preached in and from the Word: "So faith comes from hearing, and hearing by the word of Christ" (Rom. 10:17; cf. v. 14).

Salvation requires a genuine knowledge of the person and work of Jesus Christ (cf. Gal. 2:20; Phil. 3:10). It involves not merely knowing the truth *about* Him, but actually *knowing* Him through the truth of His Word (cf. John 20:30–31; 21:24; 2 Tim. 3:15–17; 1 John 5:11–13). Hence Peter closed this letter by exhorting his believing readers, who already possessed that saving **knowledge,** to "grow in the grace and knowledge of our Lord and Savior Jesus Christ" (3:18). Knowing the Lord in salvation is the starting point. The rest of the believer's life is a pursuit of greater knowledge of the glory of the Lord and His grace. Paul said that was his passionate pursuit: "that I may know Him and the power of His resurrection and the fellowship of His sufferings, being conformed to His death" (Phil. 3:10). He also made it clear that being consumed with the glory of His Lord was the means by which the Holy Spirit transformed him into Christlikeness (2 Cor. 3:18).

SALVATION'S SUFFICIENCY

seeing that His divine power has granted to us everything pertaining to life and godliness, through the true knowledge of Him who called us by His own glory and excellence. For by these He has granted to us His precious and magnificent promises, so that by them you may become partakers of the divine nature, having escaped the corruption that is in the world by lust. (1:3–4)

In 2 Corinthians 9:8, the apostle Paul makes an amazing statement of the overwhelming, generous sufficiency of God's salvation: "God is able to make all grace abound to you, so that always having all sufficiency in everything, you may have an abundance for every good deed." The word rendered "sufficiency" (*autarkeia*) refers to self-sufficiency, which means having all that is necessary. It further means to be independent of external circumstances and from what outside sources may provide. Believers' spiritual resources, provided lavishly by divine grace, are sufficient to meet life's demands (Phil. 4:19; cf. 2 Chron. 31:10).

But in spite of God's revelation of His tremendous generosity (cf. 1 Chron. 29:10–14), Christians often think He was somehow miserly in dispensing His grace. He may have given them enough enabling grace for justification (Rom. 3:24), but not enough for sanctification. Or some believers have been taught that they received enough grace for justification and sanctification, but not enough for glorification, and thus fear they may lose their salvation. Even if they believe there is enough grace for final glorification, many Christians still feel there is not enough for them to handle life's problems and trials. But there is no reason for any believer to doubt the sufficiency of God's grace or to look elsewhere for spiritual resources (cf. Ex. 34:6; Pss. 42:8; 84:11; 103:11; 107:8; 121:1–8; Lam. 3:22–23; John 1:16; 10:10; Rom. 5:15, 20–21; 8:16–17, 32; 1 Cor. 2:9; 3:21–23; Eph. 1:3–8; 2:4–7; 3:17–19; 1 Peter 5:7). Paul admonished the Colossians:

See to it that no one takes you captive through philosophy and empty deception, according to the tradition of men, according to the elementary principles of the world, rather than according to Christ. For in Him all the fullness of Deity dwells in bodily form, and in Him you have been made complete, and He is the head over all rule and authority. (Col. 2:8–10)

Jesus compared salvation to a wedding feast: "The kingdom of heaven may be compared to a king who gave a wedding feast for his son. . . . 'Behold, I have prepared my dinner; my oxen and my fattened livestock are all butchered and everything is ready; come to the wedding feast'" (Matt. 22:2, 4; cf. Luke 15:17–24; Rev. 19:6–9). He used that analogy because in first-century Jewish culture the wedding feast epitomized lavish celebration. In the same way, when He redeemed His own, God lavishly dispensed through the indwelling Holy Spirit all the grace and spiritual resources (Rom. 12:5–8; 1 Cor. 12:8–10; Eph. 3:20–21) they would ever need. Four essential components reminded Peter's audience of the reality of their sufficient salvation: divine power, divine provision, divine procurement, and divine promises.

DIVINE POWER

seeing that His divine power has granted to us (1:3*a*)

Whatever spiritual sufficiency believers have is not because of any power they possess in themselves (cf. Matt. 19:26; Rom. 9:20–21; Eph. 1:19; Phil. 3:7–11; 1 Tim. 1:12–16; Titus 3:5) but derives from **His divine power.** Paul expressed it this way: "Now to Him who is able to do far more abundantly beyond all that we ask or think, according to the power that works within us" (Eph. 3:20). The **power** that operates in believers is of the same divine nature as that which resurrected Christ (cf. Rom. 1:4; 1 Cor. 6:14; 15:16–17; 2 Cor. 13:4; Col. 2:12). That power enables saints to do works that please and glorify God (cf. 1 Cor. 3:6–8; Eph. 3:7) and accomplish spiritual things they cannot even imagine (see again Eph. 3:20).

His refers back to the Lord Jesus. If the personal pronoun modified God, Peter probably would not have used the descriptive word **divine** since deity is inherent in God's name. His use of **divine** pointing to the Son underscores that Jesus is truly God (cf. John 10:30; 12:45; Phil. 2:6; Col. 1:16; 2:9; Heb. 1:3) and also refutes any lingering doubt some readers may have had concerning that reality (cf. 1 John 5:20). Peter himself had been an eyewitness to Christ's divine power (1:16; cf. Mark 5:30; Luke 4:14; 5:17).

God's supply of spiritual power for believers never fails. They may distance themselves from the divine source through sin, or fail to minister and use what is available, but from the moment they experienced faith in Jesus Christ, God **has granted** His power to them. **Has granted** (*dedōrēmenēs*) is a perfect, passive participle meaning that in the past, with continuing results in the present, God permanently bestowed His power on believers.

DIVINE PROVISION

everything pertaining to life and godliness, (1:3b)

Because of their constant sins and failures as Christians, many find it hard not to think that even after salvation something is missing in the sanctification process. This faulty idea causes believers to seek "second blessings," "spirit baptisms," tongues, mystical experiences, special psychological insights, private revelations, "self crucifixion," the "deeper life," heightened emotions, demon bindings, and combinations of various ones of all those in an attempt to attain what is supposedly missing from their spiritual resources. All manner of ignorance and Scripture twisting accompanies those foolish pursuits, which at their corrupt roots are failures to understand exactly what Peter says here. Christians have received **everything** in the form of divine power necessary to equip them for sanctification—they have no lack at all. In view of that reality, the Lord holds all believers responsible to obey all the commands of Scripture. Christians cannot claim that their sins and failures are the result of God's limited provision. There is no temptation and no assault of Satan and demons that is beyond their resources to overcome (1 Cor. 10:13; 12:13; 1 Peter 5:10). To stress the extent of the divine power given each believer, Peter makes the amazing statement that saints have received from God **everything pertaining to life and godliness.** Syntactically, the term **everything** is in the emphatic position because the Holy Spirit through Peter is stressing the extent of believers' self-sufficiency.

The great power that gave Christians spiritual life will sustain that **life** in all its fullness. Without asking for more, they already have every spiritual resource needed to persevere in holy living. **Life and godliness** define the realm of sanctification, the living of the Christian life on earth to the glory of God—between initial salvation and final glorification. With the gift of new life in Christ (John 3:15–16; 5:24; 6:47; Titus 3:7; 1 John 2:25) came everything related to sustaining that **life,** all the way to glorification. That is why believers are eternally secure (John 6:35–40; 10:28–29; 2 Cor. 5:1; 1 John 5:13; Jude 1, 24–25) and can be assured God will empower them to persevere to the end (Matt. 24:13; John 8:31; Heb.

3:6, 14; Rev. 2:10), through all temptations, sins, failures, vicissitudes, struggles, and trials of life.

The word translated **godliness** (*eusebeia*) encompasses both true reverence in worship and its companion—active obedience. Saints should never question God's sufficiency, because His grace that is so powerful to save is equally powerful to sustain them and empower them to righteous conduct (Rom. 8:29–30; Phil. 1:6).

DIVINE PROCUREMENT

through the true knowledge of Him who called us by His own glory and excellence. (1:3c)

In light of the divine power and provision available to Christians, the question then arises, "How does one experience those to the fullest?" The apostle indicates that it is **through the true knowledge of Him. Knowledge** (*epignōsis*) refers to a knowledge that is deep and genuine. The word is sometimes used interchangeably with the more basic term *gnōsis*, which means simply knowledge. But Peter is referring to more than a superficial knowledge of Jesus' life, death, and resurrection. Christ Himself warned of the peril of an inadequate knowledge of Him, even for those who minister in His name:

> Not everyone who says to Me, "Lord, Lord," will enter the kingdom of heaven, but he who does the will of My Father who is in heaven will enter. Many will say to Me on that day, "Lord, Lord, did we not prophesy in Your name, and in Your name cast out demons, and in Your name perform many miracles?" And then I will declare to them, "I never knew you; depart from Me, you who practice lawlessness." (Matt. 7:21–23; cf. Luke 6:46)

Personal saving knowledge of the Lord is the obvious beginning point for believers, and as with everything in the Christian life, it comes from **Him who called** them (John 3:27; Rom. 2:4; 1 Cor. 4:7; cf. Jonah 2:9). Theologically, God's call comprises two aspects: the general call and the effectual call. Theologian Charles M. Horne succinctly defined the two aspects as follows:

> The general call is a call which comes through the proclamation of the gospel: it is a call which urges sinners to accept salvation. "On the last day, the great day, of the feast, Jesus stood and cried aloud, 'If anyone is thirsty, let him come to me and drink'" (Jn 7:37, Williams; cf. Mt 11:28; Is 45:22; etc.).

This message *(kerygma)*, which is to be authoritatively proclaimed—not optionally debated—contains three essential elements: (1) It is a story of historical occurrences—an historical proclamation: Christ died, was buried, and rose (1 Co 15:3–4). (2) It is an authoritative interpretation of these events—a theological evaluation. Christ died for our sins. (3) It is an offer of salvation to whosoever will—an ethical summons. Repent! Believe!

The general call is to be freely and universally offered. "Jesus came up . . . and said, 'Full authority in heaven and on earth has been given to me. Go then and make disciples of all the nations'" (Mt 28:18–19, Williams).

The effectual call is efficacious; that is, it always results in salvation. This is a *creative* calling which accompanies the external proclamation of the gospel; it is invested with the power to deliver one to the divinely intended destination. "It is very striking that in the New Testament the terms for calling, when used specifically with reference to salvation, are almost uniformly applied, not to the universal call of the gospel, but to the call that ushers men into a state of salvation and is therefore effectual." [John Murray, *Redemption—Accomplished and Applied* (Grand Rapids: Eerdmans, 1955), p. 88.]

Perhaps the classic passage on the effectual call is found in Romans 8:30: "Whom he did predestinate, them he also called" (KJV). Other pertinent references include: Romans 1:6–7; 1 Corinthians 1:9, 26; 2 Peter 1:10.

The efficacious call is immutable, thereby insuring our perseverance. "For the gifts and the calling of God are irrevocable" (Ro 11:29, NASB). (*Salvation* [Chicago: Moody, 1971], 47–48; italics in original. See also these other New Testament references: John 1:12–13; 3:3–8; 6:37, 44–45, 64–65; Acts 16:14; Eph. 2:1, 5, 10; Col. 2:13; 1 Thess. 1:4–5; 2 Tim. 1:9; Titus 3:5.)

As in all appearances of this call in the epistles, Peter's use of **called** here clearly refers to the effectual and irresistible call to salvation.

God effects His saving call through the revealed majesty of His own Son. Sinners are drawn **by** the **glory and excellence** of Jesus Christ. In Scripture **glory** always belongs to God alone (cf. Ex. 15:11; Deut. 28:58; Pss. 8:1; 19:1; 57:5; 93:1; 104:1; 138:5; 145:5; Isa. 6:3; 42:8, 12; 48:11; 59:19; Heb. 1:3; Rev. 21:11, 23). Thus when sinners see the glory of Christ they are witnessing His deity (cf. Luke 9:27–36; John 1:3–5, 14). Unless through the preaching of the gospel (Rom. 10:14–17) they realize who Christ is (the glorious Son of God who is Savior; cf. John 20:30–31; 2 Peter 1:16–18), and understand their need for repentance, so as to come to Him in faith, pleading for salvation, sinners cannot escape hell and enter heaven.

So, when God draws sinners to Himself, they see not only Christ's glory as God, but also His **excellence** as man. That refers to His morally virtuous life and His perfect humanity (cf. Matt. 20:28; Luke 2:52; 22:27; 2 Cor. 8:9; Phil. 2:7; Heb. 2:17; 4:15; 7:26; 1 Peter 2:21–23; 1 John 3:3). All salvation blessings, power, and provision come only to those who see and believe the words and acts of the sinless God/Man (cf. John 14:7–10; Acts 2:22; 1 Cor. 15:47; 1 John 1:1–2; 5:20).

DIVINE PROMISES

For by these He has granted to us His precious and magnificent promises, so that by them you may become partakers of the divine nature, having escaped the corruption that is in the world by lust. (1:4)

Christ's glory as God and His excellence as the perfect Man attract people to a saving relationship with Him. **By these** attributes of glory and excellence **He has** accomplished all that is necessary for believers' salvation, so that He also **granted to** them **His precious and magnificent promises.** The term rendered **has granted** is from the same verb (*dōreomai*) that occurs in verse 3, again in the perfect tense, describing past action with continuing effects.

Peter describes all the salvation promises in Christ as **precious** (*timios*) **and magnificent** (*megistos*), meaning "valuable" and "greatest," respectively. These words include all the divine **promises** for God's own children contained in the Old and New Testaments (cf. 2 Cor. 7:1), such as: spiritual life (Rom. 8:9–13), resurrection life (John 11:25; 1 Cor. 15:21–23), the Holy Spirit (Acts 2:33; Eph. 1:13), abundant grace (John 10:10; Rom. 5:15, 20; Eph. 1:7), joy (Ps. 132:16; Gal. 5:22), strength (Ps. 18:32; Isa. 40:31), guidance (John 16:13), help (Isa. 41:10, 13–14), instruction (Ps. 32:8; John 14:26), wisdom (Prov. 2:6–8; Eph. 1:17–18; James 1:5; 3:17), heaven (John 14:1–3; 2 Peter 3:13), eternal rewards (1 Tim. 4:8; James 1:12).

The Lord bestows all these **so that** believers **may become** full **partakers of the divine nature.** First, **may become** is not intended to present merely a future possibility, but a present certainty. The verb builds on all Peter has written. He has said that in salvation saints are called effectually by God through the true knowledge of the glory and excellence of Christ, and thus they receive everything related to life and godliness, as well as priceless spiritual promises. It is because of all that that believers **may become,** here and now, possessors of God's own eternal life (cf. John 1:12; Rom. 8:9; Gal. 2:20; Col. 1:27). **Partakers** (*koinōnos*) is often translated "fellowship," and means "sharer" or "partner." Believers are in this life partners in the very life that belongs to God (Col. 3:3; 1 John 5:11; cf. John 6:48–51).

From what they do partake in, Peter turns to what believers do not partake in, **the corruption that is in the world by lust.** Those who share the eternal life of God and Christ have completely **escaped** the effects of sin (Phil. 3:20–21; 1 John 3:2–3; cf. Titus 1:2; James 1:12; 1 John 2:25; Rev. 2:10*b*–11). **Corruption** (*phthora*) denotes an organism decomposing or rotting, and its accompanying stench. The world's moral decomposition is driven by sinful **lust** (*epithumia*), "evil desire" (1 John 2:16; cf. Eph. 2:3; 4:22). **Having escaped** depicts a successful flight from danger, in this case the effects of one's fallen nature, the sinfulness of the decaying world, and its final destruction (cf. Phil. 3:20–21; 1 Thess. 5:4, 9–10; Rev. 20:6). At glorification, believers will be redeemed completely so that they possess eternal life in perfect holiness in a new heaven and new earth where no sin or corruption will ever exist (cf. Rev. 21:1–4; 22:1–5).

It is noteworthy that Peter borrows from the terminology of mystical, pantheistic religion that called for its adherents to recognize the divine nature within them and lose themselves in the essence of the gods. Ancient false teachers (the Gnostics) and more recent ones (Eastern mystics and New Age gurus of all sorts) have often emphasized the importance of personally attaining transcendent knowledge. The apostle Peter, however, stressed to his readers the need to recognize that only by being spiritually born anew (John 3:3; James 1:18; 1 Peter 1:23) can anyone attain true divine knowledge, live righteously as God's children (Rom. 8:11–15; Gal. 2:20), and thereby share in God's nature (cf. 2 Cor. 5:17). The false prophets of Peter's day believed that transcendent knowledge elevated people above any need for morality. But Peter countered that notion by asserting that genuine knowledge of God through Christ gives believers all they need to live godly lives (cf. 2 Tim. 3:16–17).

The Believer's Precious Faith— Part 2: Its Certainty (2 Peter 1:5–11)

2

Now for this very reason also, applying all diligence, in your faith supply moral excellence, and in your moral excellence, knowledge, and in your knowledge, self-control, and in your self-control, perseverance, and in your perseverance, godliness, and in your godliness, brotherly kindness, and in your brotherly kindness, love. For if these qualities are yours and are increasing, they render you neither useless nor unfruitful in the true knowledge of our Lord Jesus Christ. For he who lacks these qualities is blind or short-sighted, having forgotten his purification from his former sins. Therefore, brethren, be all the more diligent to make certain about His calling and choosing you; for as long as you practice these things, you will never stumble; for in this way the entrance into the eternal kingdom of our Lord and Savior Jesus Christ will be abundantly supplied to you. (1:5–11)

The doctrine of eternal security, or preservation, or perseverance of the saints, is the Spirit-revealed, objective fact that salvation is forever, while assurance is believers' Spirit-given, subjective confidence that they truly possess that eternal salvation. Though the Old and New Testaments speak much about assurance (e.g., Job 19:25; Isa. 32:17; Col. 2:2; 1 Thess.

1:4–5, NKJV; Heb. 6:11; 10:22), many who profess Jesus Christ struggle to experience it. That raises the obvious question of why some Christians lack assurance. There appears to be a complex of several reasons that believers doubt their salvation. While this division is, in some ways, artificial, since the reasons overlap, it is still helpful to sort through them.

First, some lack assurance because they sit under demanding, confrontive, convicting preaching of the law that upholds a high standard of righteousness, forces people to acknowledge their sinfulness, and causes them to feel the weight of sin and God's displeasure. Such preaching may greatly disturb some listeners and cause them to waver concerning their spiritual condition. The pulpit that features strong confrontation does not always balance that with preaching that conveys strong comfort to those under grace, which produces genuine assurance.

Second, some people feel they are too sinful to be saved, and thus they have difficulty accepting forgiveness. There may be two basic causes for this. First, the human conscience can be relentless in some sensitive souls, and it naturally offers little forgiveness, grace, and mercy to relieve conviction and guilt (cf. Ps. 58:3; Prov. 20:9). Second, holiness, the law of God, and divine justice do speak strongly against sin (cf. Isa. 35:8; 52:11; Rom. 6:13, 19); the law itself contains nothing of forgiveness (Deut. 27:26; Gal. 3:21; Heb. 10:28; James 2:10; cf. Jer. 9:13–16; Acts 13:39).

A third reason for lacking assurance is that some do not accurately comprehend the gospel. They have an erroneous notion (Arminian) that maintaining one's salvation requires their effort as well as God's. Salvation, they think, is secure as long as the believer keeps believing and avoids sinful patterns. But assurance of eternal salvation can be very elusive for the person who believes it depends partly on his own "free will" cooperation with God. Such people need a true understanding of the gospel, namely that salvation is an utterly sovereign, divine operation in which sinners' redemption (from justification to glorification) depends solely on God (John 6:37, 44–45, 64–65; 15:16; Rom. 8:31–39; Phil. 1:6; 1 Thess. 1:4–5; 2 Thess. 2:13–14; 2 Tim. 1:9; Jude 24–25).

Some believe God forgave only those sins committed until the moment of salvation and that transgressions committed after salvation remain unforgiven unless confessed, which means a person needs to keep self-consciously confessing all through his Christian life to continue receiving forgiveness. Contrary to such thinking, however, Scripture teaches that God sent His Son into the world to completely pay the price of all sins—past, present, and future—for all who believe (Isa. 43:25; 44:22; 53:5, 8, 11; 61:10; John 1:29; Rom. 3:25; 5:8–11; Eph. 1:7; 1 John 1:7; 2:2; 4:10; cf. Isa. 1:18). Furthermore, Christ's resurrection affirmed God's acceptance of that total payment (Rom. 4:25; 8:34; 1 Cor. 15:17). An accurate understanding of the completeness of forgiveness is foundational to believers' assurance.

Fourth, some people lack assurance because they cannot remember the exact moment of their salvation. Evangelicalism and fundamentalism have wrongly placed too much emphasis on a dramatic event—the so-called decision for Christ. They have so emphasized praying a prayer, raising a hand, walking an aisle, or signing a card, that when people cannot remember such an event they may wonder if their salvation is genuine. The only legitimate basis for assurance has nothing to do with a past event when one "made a decision," but is based on the reality of present trust in Christ's atoning work, as evidenced by one's present pattern of faith, obedience, righteousness, and love for the Lord (cf. 1 John 1:6–7; 2:6).

Fifth, some believers still feel the strong influence of their flesh or unredeemed humanness and wonder if they truly are a new creation in Christ (2 Cor. 5:17). One day all saints will experience complete deliverance from the flesh when they enter the heavenly realm (Rom. 8:23; 1 John 3:2; cf. 1 Cor. 15:52–57). But as long as they feel the power of the flesh warring against them (Rom. 7:14–25; Gal. 5:17), they may doubt if they are really Christ's.

But one must read Romans 7:14–25 in a balanced way. The passage does explain the reality and power of the flesh, but it also speaks of the believer's desire to do what is right (vv. 15, 19, 21), his hatred of sin (vv. 23–24), and delight in the Law of God (v. 22). The battle Paul refers to is indicative of the regenerated spirit contending against the flesh (cf. Rom. 8:5–6), and therefore is reason for saints to be confident they have new life in Christ. Unbelievers have no such struggle (Rom. 3:10–20) and no confidence in Christ.

Sixth, other Christians may lack assurance because they fail to see God's hand in all their trials. They thereby miss the strongest proof of assurance, which is a tested faith. Paul instructed the Romans,

> Therefore, having been justified by faith, we have peace with God through our Lord Jesus Christ, through whom also we have obtained our introduction by faith into this grace in which we stand; and we exult in hope of the glory of God. And not only this, but we also exult in our tribulations, knowing that tribulation brings about perseverance; and perseverance, proven character; and proven character, hope; and hope does not disappoint, because the love of God has been poured out within our hearts through the Holy Spirit who was given to us. (Rom. 5:1–5; cf. Heb. 6:10–12; James 1:2–4)

Peter earlier wrote,

> In this you greatly rejoice, even though now for a little while, if neces-
> sary, you have been distressed by various trials, so that the proof of your
> faith, being more precious than gold which is perishable, even though
> tested by fire, may be found to result in praise and glory and honor at
> the revelation of Jesus Christ. (1 Peter 1:6–7)

Trials test believers' faith, not for God's sake but theirs. He knows if their
faith is truly saving faith because He gave it to them (Eph. 2:8–9); however, they learn their faith is real because it triumphs in their trials. In
God's sovereign providence, He ordained that believers' trials and difficulties constitute the crucible from which assurance derives (cf. Job
23:10; Rom. 8:35–39).

Seventh, others lack assurance because they do not know and
obey the Word and, thus, fail to walk in the Spirit, whose ministry it is to
assure obedient Christians (Rom. 8:14–17). He does so first by illuminat-
ing Scripture for them (1 Cor. 2:9–10). The very process of illumination
means the Holy Spirit is confirming to believers that they are children of
God. Second, the Spirit testifies through salvation itself, as He reveals to
saints that Jesus Christ is indeed their Savior (1 John 4:13–14). The Spirit's
work in the hearts of the elect causes them to love Christ and dwell in the
love of God (Gal. 4:6). Third, the Spirit's testimony draws believers into
communion with God, as the expression "Abba! Father!" in Romans 8:15
and Galatians 4:6 indicates. That term of intimacy connotes a Spirit-
generated petition of praise and worship offered to the Father.

Finally, and perhaps mingled through all the previous issues,
some believers lack assurance because they are willfully sinful. Clearly,
one who walks in the flesh and fulfills its desires (Gal. 5:16–21) will not
know the blessing of spiritual fruit or the joy of assurance (vv. 22–23).
Purity and assurance go hand in hand, as Hebrews 10:22 points out: "Let
us draw near with a sincere heart in full assurance of faith, having our
hearts sprinkled clean from an evil conscience and our bodies washed
with pure water." When believers fall into sin, they may fall into doubt, as
happened on various occasions even to the psalmist (e.g., Pss. 31:22;
32:3–4; 77:1–4, 7). Whatever the causes for lack or loss of assurance, the
reliable cure is to walk in the Spirit and thereby obey God's commands
(Ezek. 36:27; John 14:26; 16:13; 1 Cor. 2:12–13).

Assurance of one's gracious standing before God is not a small
matter but is actually the supreme blessing of the Christian's experience
(Rom. 5:1; 8:38–39; cf. Ps. 3:8; Isa. 12:2). This is true because the doubter
forfeits the enjoyment of all other blessings of life in Christ (cf. Eph.
1:3–14). Assurance first causes the heart to live at the highest level of joy.

Regarding the purpose of his first letter, the apostle John told his readers, "These things [tests of salvation's genuineness] we write to you that your joy may be full" (1 John 1:4, NKJV).

Second, the blessing of assurance lifts the soul to seek God's purposes above anything else. The familiar opening words of the Lord's Prayer suggest this: "'Our Father who is in heaven, hallowed be Your name. Your kingdom come. Your will be done, on earth as it is in heaven'" (Matt. 6:9–10; cf. v. 33).

Assurance also fills the heart with gratitude and praise. The psalmist demonstrated this: "But as for me, I will hope continually, and will praise You yet more and more. My mouth shall tell of Your righteousness and of Your salvation all day long; for I do not know the sum of them" (Ps. 71:14–15; cf. 103:1–5).

A fourth blessing of assurance is that it strengthens the soul against temptations and trials. Paul exhorted the Ephesians,

> Therefore, take up the full armor of God, so that you will be able to resist in the evil day, and having done everything, to stand firm . . . in addition to all, taking up the shield of faith with which you will be able to extinguish all the flaming arrows of the evil one. And take the helmet of salvation. (Eph. 6:13, 16–17)

The helmet is best understood, not as salvation itself, but as Paul identifies it in 1 Thessalonians 5:8, "the hope of salvation." When trials and temptations assault believers, God protects them from losing their hope.

Fifth, assurance also compels Christians to love obedience. The psalmist said, "I hope for Your salvation, O Lord, and do Your commandments" (Ps. 119:166). On the other hand, the insecurity of not knowing if salvation is certain can cause people to slide more deeply into sins of fear and doubt, which lead to other transgressions.

Sixth, the blessedness of assurance calms the soul with perfect peace and rest in the midst of life's storms. Regardless of the circumstances that buffet believers, there is a divine anchor of security (Heb. 6:19).

Seventh, assurance enables believers to wait patiently upon God's perfect timing for needed mercy. If their hope rests firmly in the certainty of salvation, then believers can persevere in waiting for that hope's realization (Rom. 8:25; cf. Ps. 130).

Lastly, the blessedness of assurance purifies the heart. John wrote, "We know that when He appears, we will be like Him, because we will see Him just as He is. And everyone who has this hope fixed on Him purifies himself, just as He is pure" (1 John 3:2b–3). If believers know they will spend eternity with the Lord, enjoying their reward for earthly service to Him, that will change the way they live (cf. 2 Cor. 5:9–10).

The trustworthy, all-sufficient promises of God's Word provide a firm foundation for a strong assurance of salvation. The 1689 Baptist Confession (also known as the Old London Confession) summarizes well the doctrine of assurance:

> Although temporary believers and other unregenerate persons may be deceived by erroneous, self-engendered notions into thinking that they are in God's favour and in a state of salvation—false and perishable hopes indeed!—yet all who truly believe in the Lord Jesus Christ and love Him in sincerity, endeavouring to conduct themselves in all good conscience according to His will, may in this life be certainly assured that they are in a state of grace. They may rejoice in hope of the glory of God, knowing that such a hope will never put them to shame.
>
> Job 8:13, 14; Matt. 7:22, 23; Rom. 5:2, 5; 1 John 2:3; 3:14, 18, 19, 21, 24; 5:13.
>
> The certainty of salvation enjoyed by the saints of God is not mere conjecture and probability based upon fallible hope, but an infallible assurance of faith based upon the blood and righteousness of Christ revealed in the gospel. It also results from the inward evidences of the graces of the Holy Spirit, for to those graces God speaks promises. Then again, it is based upon the testimony of the Holy Spirit as the Spirit of adoption, for He bears His witness with our spirits that we are the children of God. Such witness results in the keeping of our hearts both humble and holy.
>
> Rom. 8:15, 16; Heb. 6:11, 17–19; 2 Peter 1:4, 5, 10, 11; 1 John 3:1–3.
>
> (*A Faith to Confess: The Baptist Confession of Faith of 1689* [rewritten in modern English; Sussex, England: Carey Publications, 1975], 43)

All that discussion leads up to the text for this chapter, in which Peter (1:5–11) concludes his opening discussion of soteriology with a detailed look at this matter of assurance. God's gift of eternal life carries with it the possibility and intention that its recipients will enjoy the full benefits of true assurance (John 10:10; Rom. 8:16; Col. 2:2; Heb. 6:11; 10:22; 1 John 3:19; cf. Ps. 3:8; Isa. 12:2). Believers who are doubtful or confused about their salvation, who succumb to fear and fail to experience the anticipation of God's promises or the full benefits of a vital faith, are out of God's will. A study of assurance further reveals that Christians who have it do not become easy targets for false teachers (like the heretics the apostle discusses in chapter 2 of this letter) and are prepared to resist their deceptions and errors (cf. Eph. 6:10–11; Jude 20–23). Peter analyzed the blessings of assurance by identifying four aspects: the effort prescribed, the virtues pursued, the options presented, and the benefits promised.

THE EFFORT PRESCRIBED

Now for this very reason also, applying all diligence, in your faith supply (1:5a)

Because of all the "precious and magnificent promises" (v. 4) God has given believers and because they have received "everything pertaining to life and godliness" (v. 3), **for this very reason** they must respond with maximum effort toward living for Christ. This prescription echoes Paul's exhortation to the Philippians:

> So then, my beloved, just as you have always obeyed, not as in my presence only, but now much more in my absence, work out your salvation with fear and trembling; for it is God who is at work in you, both to will and to work for His good pleasure. (Phil. 2:12–13)

God, through Christ, granted believers a perfect and complete salvation (cf. Eph. 1:7; 3:17–21; Col. 2:10; Titus 2:14; 1 Peter 2:9); yet, paradoxically, He requires that they work it out by **applying all diligence** (cf. Col. 1:28–29). **Applying** (*pareispherō*) means "to bring in," or "to supply besides" and implies making a strong effort to provide something necessary. In view of and parallel to God's endeavor in providing salvation, believers are compelled to call on all their regenerate faculties to live godly lives (3:14; cf. Rom. 6:22; Gal. 6:9; Eph. 5:7–9; Heb. 6:10–12). Believers must carry out that effort with **all diligence** (*spoudē*, "zeal and eagerness"), accompanied by a sense of urgency (cf. 2 Cor. 8:7).

Saving **faith** is the ground in which the fruit of Christian sanctification grows (cf. Rom. 15:13; Eph. 2:10; 5:9; Gal. 5:22–23; 2 Thess. 2:13–15; Heb. 6:11–12, 19–20; 1 John 5:13). But that faith battles the flesh and will not produce a firm sense of assurance unless saints pursue sanctification (cf. Phil. 3:12–16). The word rendered **supply** (*epichorēgeō*) derives from the term meaning "choirmaster." In ancient choral groups, the choirmaster was responsible for supplying everything needed for his group, and thus the term for choirmaster came to refer to a supplier. William Barclay provides this additional background:

> [That Greek verb] comes from the noun *choregōs,* which literally means *the leader of a chorus.* Perhaps the greatest gift that Greece, and especially Athens, gave to the world was the great works of men like Aeschylus, Sophocles and Euripides, which are still among its most cherished possessions. All these plays needed large choruses and were, therefore, very expensive to produce.
> In the great days of Athens there were public spirited citizens who voluntarily took on the duty, at their own expense, of collecting,

maintaining, training and equipping such choruses. It was at the great religious festivals that these plays were produced. For instance, at the city Dionysia there were produced three tragedies, five comedies and five dithyrambs. Men had to be found to provide the choruses for them all. . . . The men who undertook these duties out of their own pocket and out of love for their city were called *chorēgoi*. . . .

The word has a certain lavishness in it. It never means to equip in any cheeseparing and miserly way; it means lavishly to pour out everything that is necessary for a noble performance. *Epichorēgein* went out into a larger world and it grew to mean not only to equip a chorus but to be responsible for any kind of equipment. It can mean to equip an army with all the necessary provisions; it can mean to equip the soul with all the necessary virtues for life. (*The Letters of James and Peter*, rev. ed. [Philadelphia: Westminster, 1976], 298–99)

Believers must **supply** ("give lavishly or generously")—alongside all that Christ has provided—all virtues required to maintain the assurance of salvation (cf. Luke 10:20; Rom. 5:11; 14:17).

The Virtues Pursued

moral excellence, and in your moral excellence, knowledge, and in your knowledge, self-control, and in your self-control, perseverance, and in your perseverance, godliness, and in your godliness, brotherly kindness, and in your brotherly kindness, love. (1:5*b*–7)

The first virtue, **moral excellence** (*aretē*), uses the distinctive word in classical Greek for virtue. It was such a lofty term that it was used for moral heroism, viewed as the divinely endowed ability to excel in heroic, courageous deeds. It came to encompass the most outstanding quality in someone's life, or the proper and excellent fulfillment of a task or duty (cf. Phil. 4:8). *Aretē* never meant cloistered virtue, but that which is demonstrated in the normal course of living. The apostle Paul modeled the pursuit of such spiritual heroism: "I press on toward the goal for the prize of the upward call of God in Christ Jesus" (Phil. 3:14; cf. 2 Cor. 5:9; 1 Thess. 4:1, 10).

At the heart of moral excellence is **knowledge. Knowledge** refers to the divine truth that is the foundation of spiritual discernment and wisdom (Rom. 15:14; 2 Cor. 10:5; Col. 1:9; cf. Prov. 2:5–6; 9:10), the truth properly understood and applied (cf. Col. 1:10; Phile. 6). This virtue is related to illumination (cf. 2 Cor. 4:6), which is having one's mind accurately enlightened about the truth of Scripture (Col. 3:10; Titus 1:1; 2 Peter

1:3; 3:18) and involves diligent study and meditation on it (John 5:39; Acts 17:11; 2 Tim. 2:15; cf. Deut. 11:18; Job 23:12; Ps. 119:97, 105), so as to acquire "the mind of Christ" (1 Cor. 2:16).

Flowing from knowledge is a third virtue, **self-control** (*egkrateia*), which literally means "holding oneself in" (cf. Gal. 5:23). It was used of athletes who sought self-discipline and self-restraint, even beating their bodies into submission (cf. 1 Cor. 9:27). They would also abstain from rich foods, wine, and sexual activity in order to focus all their strength and attention on their training regimen. False theology (such as that propounded by the heretics of Peter's day and discussed in chapters 2 and 3) inevitably divorces faith from conduct because it cannot deliver the soul from sin's harmful effects and forces its followers to battle for self-control on their own and indulge their lusts (cf. 1 Tim. 6:3–5; 2 Tim. 2:14, 16–19; 1 John 4:1–6; Jude 16–19).

A fourth essential virtue to pursue is **perseverance,** which connotes patience and endurance in doing what is right (Luke 8:15; Rom. 2:7; 8:25; 15:4–5; 2 Cor. 12:12; 1 Tim. 6:11; 2 Tim. 3:10; Titus 2:2; Rev. 2:19)—resisting temptations and enduring in the midst of trials and difficulties.

Perseverance (*hupomonē*) is a difficult term to express with one English word. Uncommon in classical Greek, the New Testament uses the word frequently to refer to remaining strong in unwelcome toil and hardship (cf. Rom. 5:3–4; 12:12; 2 Cor. 1:6; 2 Thess. 1:4; James 1:12; 1 Peter 2:20; Rev. 2:2–3), the kind that can make life extremely difficult, painful, grievous, and shocking—even to the point of death (cf. Rev. 1:9; 3:10; 13:10; 14:12). Barclay again offers helpful insight:

> [*Hupomonē*] is usually translated patience, but patience is too passive a word. Cicero defines *patientia,* its Latin equivalent, as: "The voluntary and daily suffering of hard and difficult things, for the sake of honour and usefulness." Didymus of Alexandria writes on the temper of Job: "It is not that the righteous man must be without feeling, although he must patiently bear the things which afflict him; but it is true virtue when a man deeply feels the things he toils against, but nevertheless despises sorrows for the sake of God."
>
> *Hupomonē* does not simply accept and endure; there is always a forward look in it. It is said of Jesus . . . that for the joy that was set before him, he endured the Cross, despising the shame (Hebrews 12:2). That is *hupomonē,* Christian steadfastness. It is the courageous acceptance of everything that life can do to us and the transmuting of even the worst event into another step on the upward way. (*Letters of James and Peter,* 303)

At the heart of spiritual pursuit is a fifth virtue, **godliness,** from a term (*eusebeia*) meaning reverence for God (1:3; 3:11; 1 Tim. 2:2; 6:6; cf.

1 Cor. 10:31). It could also be translated "true religion," or "true worship" and conveys the idea that one who has it properly honors and adores God (1 Tim. 3:16; Titus 1:1; cf. John 4:24; Phil. 3:3). In Greek thought *eusebeia* encompassed all the rituals related to worship and loyalty given to the pagan gods—respect toward all that is divine. The early Christians sanctified the Greek definitions of the word and directed them at the one true God and Father of the Lord Jesus Christ. The apostle Paul instructed Timothy that such reverence toward God is the highest priority because of its eternal value. "Godliness," Paul wrote, "is profitable for all things, since it holds promise for the present life and also for the life to come" (1 Tim. 4:8; cf. Acts 2:25–28).

Flowing out of the vertical reverence for God in every area of life is the horizontal virtue of **brotherly kindness.** The companion of affection for God is affection for others (cf. Rom. 13:8–10; Gal. 5:14; 1 Thess. 1:3; Heb. 6:10; James 2:8). Peter undoubtedly recalled what Jesus had told the religious leaders:

> One of them, a lawyer, asked Him a question, testing Him, "Teacher, which is the great commandment in the Law?" And He said to him, "'You shall love the Lord your God with all your heart, and with all your soul, and with all your mind.' This is the great and foremost commandment. The second is like it, 'You shall love your neighbor as yourself.' On these two commandments depend the whole Law and the Prophets." (Matt. 22:35–40; cf. 1 John 4:20–21)

The saints' pursuit of devotion to one another flows from the highest virtue of all—**love.** For believers, **love** for others (especially fellow believers) has always been inseparable from love for God (John 13:34; 15:12; 1 Thess. 4:9; 1 John 3:23; 4:7, 21). This is the familiar *agapē,* the sacrificial, selfless love of the will (Matt. 5:43–44; 19:19; Mark 10:21; Luke 6:35; John 14:21, 23; 15:12–13; Rom. 12:9; 1 Cor. 8:1; 16:14; 2 Cor. 8:8; Gal. 5:13–14; Eph. 1:15; Phil. 1:9; 2:2; Col. 1:4; 1 Thess. 3:6; Heb. 10:24; 1 John 2:5; 4:7–12). (For further discussion of the biblical concept of love, see chapter 7 of John MacArthur, *1 Peter,* MacArthur New Testament Commentary [Chicago: Moody, 2004].)

THE OPTIONS PRESENTED

For if these qualities are yours and are increasing, they render you neither useless nor unfruitful in the true knowledge of our Lord Jesus Christ. For he who lacks these qualities is blind or short-sighted, having forgotten his purification from his former sins. (1:8–9)

God certainly does not want His children miserable and doubt-ing His gift of salvation; instead He desires and delights in their joy and confidence (cf. Pss. 5:11; 16:11; 33:1; 90:14; 105:43; John 15:11; Acts 13:52; Rom. 15:13). If Christians are to fully enjoy their assurance as God desires for them, they must consider the two options Peter presents in this pas-sage and choose the positive one rather than the negative.

Positively, Peter calls for pursuing **these qualities** (the preceding list of virtues) and sets forth the result of doing so. The phrase rendered **are yours and are increasing** is a strong expression drawn from two present participles (*huparchonta* and *pleonazonta*). The first denotes owning property in an abiding sense, and the second refers to possessing more than enough, even too much, of something. If the virtues are abun-dantly present in a believer's life and actually on the increase, that reality will **render** ("make," "set in order") him as **neither** spiritually **useless nor unfruitful.**

Useless (*argos*), meaning "inactive," or "idle" when employed in the New Testament, always describes something inoperative or unser-viceable (cf. Matt. 12:36; 20:3, 6; 1 Tim. 5:13; Titus 1:12; James 2:20). **Unfruitful** (*akarpos*) or "barren" is sometimes used in connection with unbelief or apostasy. For example, Paul warned against the "unfruitful deeds of darkness" (Eph. 5:11). Jude described apostates as "autumn trees without fruit, doubly dead, uprooted" (Jude 12). Matthew 13:22 and Mark 4:19 use it as they record Jesus' description of superficial believers in the parable of the soils. It can refer even to true believers who are for a time unproductive (Titus 3:14; cf. 1 Cor. 14:14). If Christians pursue the virtues Peter outlined, their lives will be increasingly productive spiritu-ally. But if those qualities are not present, believers are likely to be indis-tinguishable from the superficial professors Jesus described in His parable.

Use of the identifying expression **the true knowledge of our Lord Jesus Christ** demonstrates that Peter is addressing genuine Chris-tians. Real believers to whom God has granted **true** saving **knowledge** (1:3; Luke 1:77; 2 Cor. 2:14; 4:6; 8:7; Col. 2:2–3; 3:10; cf. Prov. 1:7; 2:5–6; 9:10; Isa. 33:6) therefore possess the capacity to pursue and fruitfully apply the virtues mentioned. If those virtues are present in one's life, then he has and enjoys this **true knowledge.**

On the other hand, Peter presents a negative option for his readers to avoid. If one who professes faith in Christ fails to pursue virtues and fruitfulness, and thus **lacks these qualities,** he is **blind or short-sighted,** unable to discern his true spiritual condition (cf. Isa. 59:10; Rev. 3:17).

The believer who is not experiencing an increase in the virtues will forfeit assurance, **having forgotten his purification from his for-mer sins.** Literally the phrase here means "to receive [*lambanō*] forget-fulness [*lēthē*]." **Purification** translates *katharismos*, from which the

English *catharsis* ("cleansing") derives. Such a believer's sin makes him unable to be confident that he was cleansed and rescued from his former life (Eph. 2:4–7; 5:8, 26; Titus 3:5–6; James 1:18; 1 Peter 1:23; 1 John 1:7). He cannot be certain if he has been truly saved because he does not see an increase of virtue and usefulness in his life. Once blind before salvation, then made to see, these saints can experience a kind of spiritual blindness again.

That kind of spiritual forgetfulness leads to the repeating of old sins, and it robs such Christians of their assurance. Assurance of salvation is directly related to present spiritual service and obedience, not merely to a past salvation event made dim in the disobedient believer's memory.

THE BENEFITS PROMISED

Therefore, brethren, be all the more diligent to make certain about His calling and choosing you; for as long as you practice these things, you will never stumble; for in this way the entrance into the eternal kingdom of our Lord and Savior Jesus Christ will be abundantly supplied to you. (1:10–11)

Peter urges believers to select the positive option already stated in verse 8. Reiterating verse 5 ("applying all diligence"), the apostle commands believers to **be all the more diligent** spiritually, so as to know and enjoy the reality of their eternal salvation. **Be . . . diligent** (*spoudasate*) is the verb form of the noun *spoudē* ("diligence") used in verse 5 and again conveys urgency and eagerness. To emphasize the right believers have to enjoy assurance, the apostle speaks not of their faith, but God's sovereign choice. Believers are able **to make certain**—in Hebrews 9:17 the word for **certain** [*bebaios*] is used in the sense of a legal validity or confirmation—God's **calling and choosing** of them. **To make** (*poieisthai*) is reflexive, indicating believers are to assure themselves. **Calling and choosing** are inseparable realities indicating God's effectual call of believers to salvation (Rom. 11:29; 2 Thess. 2:14; 2 Tim. 1:9; cf. Matt. 4:17; Acts 2:38; 3:19; 17:30) based on His sovereign election of them in eternity past (Rom. 8:29; Eph. 1:4, 11; Titus 1:2; 1 Peter 2:9). Peter's concern is that believers have confidence and assurance that they are included in the elect. God knows His elect (cf. 2 Tim. 1:9, and the discussion of 1 Peter 1:1–5 in John MacArthur, *1 Peter*, MacArthur New Testament Commentary [Chicago: Moody, 2004], 13–38), and His elect should enjoy the knowledge that they are His.

As long as Christians **practice these things**—increasingly pursue the moral virtues essential to holy living—they give evidence to themselves and enjoy assurance that God has granted them eternal life (cf. Heb. 6:11). **Practice** refers to the pattern of daily conduct (cf. Rom. 12:9–13; Gal. 5:22–25; Eph. 5:15; Col. 3:12–17). If it is in keeping with the moral virtues Peter described, believers **will never stumble** into doubt, despair, or fear, which allows them to confidently enjoy an abundant and productive spiritual life (cf. Ps. 16:11; John 10:10; Eph. 1:18; 2:7; 1 Tim. 6:17).

In this way, again referring to the constant pursuit of holiness, the blessings of assurance and perseverance come to believers. As a result, **the entrance into the eternal kingdom of their Lord and Savior Jesus Christ will be abundantly supplied to** them. Assurance of one's having entered into **the eternal kingdom** is the experience of the Christian who practices what Peter has listed. That was great encouragement to the apostle's weary readers. No believer needs to live with doubt regarding salvation, but he may have assurance **abundantly supplied** in the present. A rich heavenly reward in the future may also be implied (cf. 2 Tim. 4:8; Heb. 4:9; 12:28; 1 Peter 5:4; Rev. 2:10; 22:12).

The Lord will reward His children based on their faithful pursuit of righteousness (see again 1 Cor. 3:11–14; 2 Cor. 5:10). Assurance in this life and riches in heaven are the benefits of spiritual diligence and fruitfulness.

Peter's Legacy Statement (2 Peter 1:12–15)

3

Therefore, I will always be ready to remind you of these things, even though you already know them, and have been established in the truth which is present with you. I consider it right, as long as I am in this earthly dwelling, to stir you up by way of reminder, knowing that the laying aside of my earthly dwelling is imminent, as also our Lord Jesus Christ has made clear to me. And I will also be diligent that at any time after my departure you will be able to call these things to mind. (1:12–15)

Any good teacher realizes the value of repetition. Research has shown that within an hour after hearing a spoken message, people forget up to ninety percent of it. Certainly God knew that when He said to Israel:

> Hear, O Israel! The Lord is our God, the Lord is one! You shall love the Lord your God with all your heart and with all your soul and with all your might. These words, which I am commanding you today, shall be on your heart. You shall teach them diligently to your sons and shall talk of them when you sit in your house and when you walk by the way and when you lie down and when you rise up. You shall bind them as a sign on your hand and they shall be as frontals on your forehead. You

shall write them on the doorposts of your house and on your gates. (Deut. 6:4–9; cf. v. 12; 7:18; 8:2, 18–20; 9:7; 2 Kings 17:38; 1 Chron. 16:12; Pss. 78:7,11,42; 103:2; 106:7,13; 119:16,153; Isa. 51:13–15; Mark 12:29–30, 32–33)

In spite of all the warnings and reminders through the centuries, Israel has had a great memory for the wrong things and a poor memory for God's truth, as when Isaiah indicted her:"For you have forgotten the God of your salvation and have not remembered the rock of your refuge" (Isa. 17:10a; cf. 51:13a; Hos. 8:7–14). Similarly, God gave the Passover to be an annual reminder of His redemption, grace and mercy, judgment and justice, and covenant (Ex. 13:3–10). But today when Jews observe Passover, they remember the Exodus from Egypt, even while rejecting the God who delivered them (cf. Rom. 2:28–29; 10:2–4).

Even believers tend to remember things that are better forgotten and to forget things that should be remembered (cf. Rom. 7:15, 18–19; Heb. 12:5). Thus Peter writes the words in this text and later tells his readers, "This is now, beloved, the second letter I am writing to you in which I am stirring up your sincere mind by way of reminder" (3:1). And not long after Peter wrote, Jude called on his readers "to remember the words that were spoken beforehand by the apostles of our Lord Jesus Christ" (Jude 17; cf. Acts 20:35; 2 Tim. 2:8; James 1:25). Because Jude's letter is so similar to 2 Peter, he must have had Peter's epistle in mind. They were following the Lord's example when He admonished the apostles to "remember the word that I said to you" (John 15:20).

In this passage Peter digresses from his subject of salvation and drops in a statement about the importance of reminding people of essential truth. Christ had called Peter to pastor (John 21:15–19), and his words reveal his pastoral passion in four motivations: urgency, kindness, faithfulness, and brevity.

URGENCY

Therefore, I will always be ready to remind you of these things, (1:12a)

Therefore refers back to the greatness of salvation (1:1–4) and the blessedness of assurance (1:5–11), themes so crucial they must never be forgotten. Peter did not want his readers to forget they were saved (v. 9), nor the blessings of their salvation (v. 3). When Peter used the future tense, **will always be ready,** he was first indicating that he would **remind** his listeners of truth whenever given the opportunity, including when writing this Spirit-inspired epistle. But he also anticipated all who, in the ages to come, would read this letter and be reminded **of** the great **things** God gave him to say.

The apostle Paul, like Peter, knew the necessity of repeating the truth: "Finally, my brethren, rejoice in the Lord. To write the same things again is no trouble to me, and it is a safeguard for you" (Phil. 3:1; cf. Rom. 15:15; 2 Thess. 2:5). Jude also sought to remind his readers of what they once knew (v. 5).

Contrary to the beliefs of some, there is no such thing as brand-new spiritual truth, only a clearer understanding of the timeless truths (Isa. 40:8; 1 Peter 1:23–25; cf. Matt. 5:18) in God's Word. People do not always know the truths of Scripture, nor do they always hear true and accurate interpretations of it. Therefore, some in that condition may think certain truth is new—and it is to them. But there is no new revelation from God (cf. Jude 3). All who preach and teach the Scriptures are reminding people of what God has said in His Word so constantly that His repetition and theirs makes truth stick.

Certainly 2 Peter 2 and Jude's letter vividly illustrate this principle of divine repetition in Scripture. The New Testament epistles deal with the same gospel in all its richness by revealing it in different terms and analogies. The Synoptic Gospels tell the same story three ways. Jesus repeated His message in sermons, parables, and object lessons everywhere He went, exposing His followers to the truth again and again. That was critical in the training of the Twelve.

Even the messages of the Old Testament prophets are essentially the same as they preach law, judgment, and forgiveness. The Psalms repeat the attributes and works of God. The books of Chronicles rehearse material from 1 and 2 Samuel and 1 and 2 Kings. Deuteronomy 5:1–22 is a second giving of the Law at Sinai (Exodus 20), which reminded the people of it and readied them to enter the Promised Land.

KINDNESS

even though you already know them, and have been established in the truth which is present with you. (1:12*b*)

Peter was a kind shepherd who understood and exhibited sensitivity for his flock. Scripture extols gentleness (cf. 2 Cor. 10:1; Gal. 5:23; 6:1; 1 Thess. 2:7; 2 Tim. 2:25), meekness (cf. Matt. 5:5, NKJV; 1 Tim. 6:11, KJV; James 3:13 KJV), and tenderness (cf. Eph. 4:32), characteristics Peter displayed when he acknowledged that his readers **already** possessed godly virtue. He was encouraging, not condescending or indifferent to their devotion to Christ (cf. 1 Peter 5:2–3).

The recipients of this letter undoubtedly had heard other inspired New Testament letters read and preached (cf. 3:15–16), so they knew and believed **the truth,** so as to be **established in** it. The verb rendered **established** (*stērizō*), meaning "to firmly establish," or "to strengthen," is a perfect passive participle indicating a settled condition. They had given evidence by their faithfulness that the true gospel was strongly **present with** them. Peter affirmed them without doubt as genuine, maturing believers. He could have echoed Paul's words to the Colossians, "You previously heard in the word of truth, the gospel which has come to you, just as in all the world also it is constantly bearing fruit and increasing, even as it has been doing in you also since the day you heard of it and understood the grace of God in truth" (Col. 1:5*b*–6; cf. 1 Thess. 2:13; 1 John 2:27; 2 John 2). When anyone comes to know Christ, the truth abides in him (2 Peter 1:12; 1 John 2:14, 27; 2 John 2; cf. John 17:19; 2 Cor. 11:10; Eph. 4:24; 6:14). It was still imperative that Peter's readers receive this reminder, in view of the threat they faced from the powerful infiltration of false teachers (chapter 2 of this letter).

FAITHFULNESS

I consider it right, as long as I am in this earthly dwelling, to stir you up by way of reminder, (1:13)

Because he was an intimate confidant of Jesus as the recognized leader of the Twelve, the apostle Peter lived in closer and more constant proximity to divine truth than any man. Yet he and his fellow apostles still did not fully understand or appreciate that truth, even at the end of Christ's earthly ministry, as the Lord's question to them indicates: "Have I been so long with you, and yet you have not come to know Me?" (John 14:9).

Peter monumentally defected from his Master for a time—despite Jesus' warning (see Luke 22:31–34, 54–62). The apostle therefore knew firsthand that even though believers are grounded in the truth, they need constant shepherding to protect them from wandering into sin. The biblical shepherd exhibits faithfulness in teaching the people God has given him.

It is not just that such loyal instruction is beneficial, helpful, and strengthening, though it surely is. Beyond the benefits, Peter **consider**ed **it right,** that is, "righteous" (*dikaios*). His devotion as a shepherd made him faithful to his people because he was loyal to his Lord in doing what was **right, as long as** he was **in this earthly dwelling.** The term rendered **earthly dwelling** (*skēnōma*) is the word for "tent," drawing from the familiar image of Middle Eastern nomads living in portable tents. Peter, too, was in a temporary house and knew that one day God would fold up that tent to free his eternal soul to enter heaven.

As long as God gave him earthly life, Peter would be faithful **to stir up** those the Lord put in his life **by way of reminder. To stir you up** is a compound form of the verb *diegeirō*, meaning "to arouse completely," or "to thoroughly awaken" from lethargy, drowsiness, or sleep. Nothing short of spiritual alertness would satisfy this loyal pastor. Believers can become sluggish (cf. Mark 13:35–37; Rom. 13:11; 1 Thess. 5:6; Heb. 6:12), failing to be alert and clear-minded regarding spiritual issues or other duties (cf. Prov. 13:4; 24:30–31). That word may have caused Peter to recall his own inability to stay awake in Gethsemane the night before Jesus' death (Matt. 26:36–46).

The godly shepherd stimulates his flock primarily **by way of reminder.** He consistently and tirelessly keeps teaching and reviewing all the major themes, doctrines, and commands of Scripture. No matter how much divine truth believers have heard or how spiritually mature they are, they still need reminders to apply that truth (cf. Rom. 12:1–13:10; 1 Cor. 3:5–23; Gal. 5:1–6; Eph. 4:11–16). Wanting them to remember, the true shepherd constantly feeds his flock spiritual food in all its scriptural dress. Realizing that familiarity can breed contempt, he employs all the passages on all the themes, so there is freshness instead of familiarity.

BREVITY

knowing that the laying aside of my earthly dwelling is imminent, as also our Lord Jesus Christ has made clear to me. And I will also be diligent that at any time after my departure you will be able to call these things to mind. (1:14–15)

Finally, Peter's passion and motivation for ministry includes a clear understanding of the brevity of his life itself (cf. Job 7:6–7; 9:25–26; 14:1–2; Pss. 39:5; 89:47*a*; 90:5–6, 10; James 4:13–17). Thus he wrote of **knowing** for certain **that the laying aside of** his **earthly dwelling** was **imminent.** Clearly, Peter believed that his death was near. He described death in the analogy of **laying aside** his tent, the same imagery Paul used in his second letter to the Corinthians:

For we know that if the earthly tent which is our house is torn down, we have a building from God, a house not made with hands, eternal in the heavens. For indeed in this house we groan, longing to be clothed with our dwelling from heaven. (2 Cor. 5:1–2)

The term **imminent** carried a dual meaning in that it can denote "soon," or "swift." Perhaps here it conveys both. When he wrote this he was already in his seventies; thus it was reasonable for Peter to expect that his death was not far off. He also knew that his death would be sudden or swift, **as also . . . Christ . . . made clear to me.** The Lord Jesus had clearly indicated to the apostle that his death would be rather sudden, about forty years before, during Peter's restoration and recommissioning, between the Lord's resurrection and ascension:

"Truly, truly, I say to you, when you were younger, you used to gird yourself and walk wherever you wished; but when you grow old, you will stretch out your hands and someone else will gird you, and bring you where you do not wish to go." Now this He said, signifying by what kind of death he would glorify God. And when He had spoken this, He said to him, "Follow Me!" (John 21:18–19)

Jesus' words were a prediction of Peter's martyrdom. That He predicted Peter would be executed, specifically by crucifixion, is evidenced by the expression "you will stretch out your hands." So Peter had lived another four decades or more, being faithful to feed the Lord's sheep, knowing all the while that at any moment his life could swiftly end. (Tradition—recorded by Eusebius [*Ecclesiastical History*, 3:1, 30]—attests that he was crucified, and upside down at his request because he felt unworthy to die exactly as Christ had died.)

In view of the brevity of his life and ministry, Peter was relentlessly **diligent** to remind believers of the truth, so **that at any time after** his **departure** they would **be able to call these things to mind.** There is no reason to restrict his words, **these things,** to what he wrote just prior (vv. 1–11), as some do. All that is in this letter is part of essential doctrine, to be imbedded unforgettably in believers' minds.

The apostle used the term **departure** (*exodos*) to refer to his death because the word connotes the leaving from one place (earth) to go to another (heaven)—the exodus that every believer will enjoy (1 Cor. 15:50–57; Heb. 4:9–10). Peter, like Paul (Acts 20:24), was not concerned that his audience remember him or his death, but that they would remember the truth he taught them.

That Peter truly understood the urgency, kindness, faithfulness, and brevity of ministry is clear from this epistle, especially as summarized in the legacy statement of this passage. The leader of the Twelve wanted believers to avoid the hazards of spiritual negligence; therefore, he labored diligently through his preaching and writing to reiterate the important issues. He desired to leave a final will and testament to remind saints of the greatness of salvation, the blessedness of assurance, and to make certain that false doctrine did not rob them of their rich spiritual heritage.

The Sure Word
(2 Peter 1:16–21)

4

For we did not follow cleverly devised tales when we made known to you the power and coming of our Lord Jesus Christ, but we were eyewitnesses of His majesty. For when He received honor and glory from God the Father, such an utterance as this was made to Him by the Majestic Glory, "This is My beloved Son with whom I am well-pleased"—and we ourselves heard this utterance made from heaven when we were with Him on the holy mountain. So we have the prophetic word made more sure, to which you do well to pay attention as to a lamp shining in a dark place, until the day dawns and the morning star arises in your hearts. But know this first of all, that no prophecy of Scripture is a matter of one's own interpretation, for no prophecy was ever made by an act of human will, but men moved by the Holy Spirit spoke from God. (1:16–21)

Through the centuries the Bible has had many formidable critics and detractors. Attacks on its veracity arguably reached a watershed during the time of the Enlightenment. Hayden V. White articulated the climate of that era as follows:

The Enlightenment attitude of mind was complex and internally varied, but it can be characterized roughly as a dedication of human reason, science, and education as the best means of building a stable society for free men on earth. This meant that the Enlightenment was inherently suspicious of religion, hostile to tradition, and resentful of any authority based on custom or faith alone. Ultimately the Enlightenment was nothing if not secular in its orientation; it offered the first program in the history of mankind for the construction of a human community out of natural materials alone. ("Editor's Introduction," in Robert Anchor, *The Enlightenment Tradition* [New York: Harper & Row, 1967], ix; cited in Norman L. Geisler and William E. Nix, *A General Introduction to the Bible,* revised and expanded [Chicago: Moody, 1968, 1986], 139)

Through their writings and the promotion of their secular ideas, philosophers such as Thomas Hobbes (1588–1679; materialism), Benedict de Spinoza (1632–1677; rationalistic pantheism and naturalism), David Hume (1711–1776; skepticism and antisupernaturalism), Immanuel Kant (1724–1804; philosophical agnosticism), Friedrich Schleiermacher (1768–1834; romanticism and positive theology), and Georg W. F. Hegel (1770–1831; philosophical idealism and the dialectical process [thesis, antithesis, and synthesis]) did much to undermine and destroy confidence in the infallibility of Scripture and a biblical understanding of the nature of truth. Those Enlightenment philosophies also paved the way for theological liberalism (Albrecht Ritschl, 1822–1899; Adolf von Harnack, 1851–1930), present-day existentialism and postmodern relativism (Soren Kierkegaard, 1813–1855; Friedrich W. Nietzsche, 1844–1900; Rudolf Bultmann, 1884–1976; Martin Heidegger, 1889–1976), and higher criticism (F. C. Baur, 1792–1860; Julius Wellhausen, 1844–1918).

However, conservative, orthodox, evangelical scholars such as Francis Turretin (1623–1687), Jonathan Edwards (1703–1758), Charles Hodge (1797–1878), Benjamin B. Warfield (1851–1921), and J. Gresham Machen (1881–1937) tirelessly and consistently defended Scripture's sufficiency and trustworthiness. Those men and other God-honoring teachers firmly supported the Reformation's view of the supremacy of God's Word, which is summarized by Bush and Nettles:

The Reformers believed Scripture to be God's Word written. It was trusted, not doubted. It was studied, not ignored. It was taken as the final authority with regard to those matters on which it spoke or made affirmations. God had not revealed everything. The Bible did not expressly contain all the truth that could be known. But what the Bible did teach was believed to be completely trustworthy. Truth in any other area would not contradict biblical truth. Starting from Scripture, one could find the true knowledge of reality. (L. Russ Bush and Tom J. Nettles, *Baptists and the Bible* [Chicago: Moody, 1980], 175)

What the apostle Peter wrote in 2 Peter 1:16–21 is foundational to the Reformers' understanding of Scripture and clearly declares that in the Bible believers have an accurate, written revelation of God's truth. Peter echoed the psalmist's declaration: "The testimony of the Lord is sure, making wise the simple" (Ps. 19:7*b*; cf. 93:5; 111:7). God, through the prophet Isaiah, said this about both the reliability and impact of His Word:

> For as the rain and snow come down from heaven, and do not return there without watering the earth and making it bear and sprout, and furnishing seed to the sower and bread to the eater; so will My word be which goes forth from My mouth; it will not return to Me empty, without accomplishing what I desire, and without succeeding in the matter for which I sent it. (Isa. 55:10–11; cf. 40:8; Ps. 119:89; Matt. 5:18; 24:35; John 10:35*b*; 2 Tim. 2:19*a*)

In his second epistle, Peter wrote to believers barraged by false teaching that sought to undermine their trust in Scripture and thus destroy the Christian faith. In chapter 2 he would describe in vivid terms the proponents of such error so his readers could understand and better recognize the danger they posed. But it is not enough merely to be aware of false teachers; believers need to know how to defend against their errors. The weapon in that defense is God's sure Word (cf. 2 Cor. 10:3–5). In the present passage, the apostle references both his own eyewitness experience of revelation and God's supernatural, written revelation.

PETER'S EYEWITNESS EXPERIENCE

For we did not follow cleverly devised tales when we made known to you the power and coming of our Lord Jesus Christ, but we were eyewitnesses of His majesty. For when He received honor and glory from God the Father, such an utterance as this was made to Him by the Majestic Glory, "This is My beloved Son with whom I am well-pleased"—and we ourselves heard this utterance made from heaven when we were with Him on the holy mountain. (1:16–18)

For is the causal term linking this passage to the previous one and explaining why Peter reminded his hearers of the truth. He was absolutely convinced of the truth he taught because he had personally experienced it. He also spoke for the other apostles and New Testament authors when he asserted, **we did not follow cleverly devised tales.** All of them received supernatural revelation (John 1:51; 1 John 1:1–3) verifying that what they were taught and were subsequently preaching was the truth (Matt. 13:11, 16–17; cf. Matt. 11:25–26; 1 Cor. 2:10).

Peter's opening assertion answers the accusation of his critics that he taught carefully crafted lies only to attract gullible followers and make money off them. False religious teachers commonly sought the power and popularity that brought not only money (cf. Mic. 3:11), but also sexual favors (cf. Jer. 23:14). However, Peter refuted his accusers by saying he and his fellow apostles **did not follow** the deceptive approach of false teachers.

Cleverly devised stems from *sophizō* ("to make wise") and connotes sophisticated, subtly concocted ideas. The expression also refers to anything clandestine or deceitful. Seeking to devour the sheep, the false teachers would disguise their lies (cf. 2:1) to make them appear as divine truth (Jer. 6:14; 14:14; 23:16, 21, 26; cf. Matt. 7:15).

Tales (*muthos*, from which the English *myths* derives) refers to legendary stories of gods and heroic figures participating in miraculous events and performing extraordinary feats. Those tales characterized pagan mythology and its worldview. Paul used *muthos*, which always has a negative connotation in the New Testament, much as Peter did, to refer to the lies, fabrications, and deceptions of all false teachers (1 Tim. 1:4; 4:7; 2 Tim. 4:4; Titus 1:14). Peter flatly denied that he was drawing upon such fictitious stories **when** he **made known** his teaching. Undoubtedly, false teachers had told his readers that Christian faith and doctrine was just another set of myths and fables.

Made known (*gnōrizō*) is often used in the New Testament to speak of imparting new revelation (John 17:26; Rom. 16:26; Eph. 1:9; 3:3, 5, 10; cf. Luke 2:15; John 15:15; Acts 2:28; Rom. 9:22–23; 2 Cor. 8:1; Col. 1:27; 4:7, 9). In this instance, the revelation concerned **the power and coming of** the **Lord Jesus Christ**—His second coming in glory and dominion (Matt. 25:31; Luke 12:40; Acts 1:10–11; Titus 2:13; 1 Peter 1:13; Rev. 1:7). Apparently the false teachers were not only undermining Peter's teaching in general, but also specifically denying what he said about the return of Christ. Peter's reference to that line of attack later in this letter (3:3–4) confirms that fact.

Because Peter connected the phrase **power and coming** with the appearance of the **Lord Jesus Christ,** it is a sure indicator that he referred to His return (cf. Matt. 24:30; 25:31; Rev. 19:11–16). The description certainly does not fit His first coming in meekness and humility (cf. Luke 2:11–12; Rom. 1:3; 2 Cor. 8:9; Phil. 2:6–7).

Coming is the familiar New Testament word *parousia,* which also means "appearing," or "arrival." The term, whenever used in the New Testament of Jesus Christ, always refers to His return. W. E. Vine elaborated on this aspect of the meaning:

> When used of the return of Christ . . . it signifies, not merely His momentary coming for His saints, but His presence with them from that moment until His revelation and manifestation to the world. In some passages the word gives prominence to the beginning of that period, the course of the period being implied, 1 Cor. 15:23; 1 Thess. 4:15; 5:23; 2 Thess. 2:1; Jas. 5:7, 8; 2 Peter 3:4. In some, the course is prominent, Matt. 24:3, 37; 1 Thess. 3:13; 1 John 2:28; in others the conclusion of the period, Matt. 24:27; 2 Thess. 2:8. (*An Expository Dictionary of New Testament Words,* 4 vols. [London: Oliphants, 1940; reprint, Chicago: Moody: 1985], 1:209)

In his first letter, Peter had declared the truth of Christ's second coming (1 Peter 1:7, 13; 4:13; 5:4). But here he stresses that he and the other apostles were eyewitnesses of the very majesty Christ will fully display when He returns. Certainly all the apostles had seen Christ's majesty in His life and ministry (John 2:11; 17:6–8), and in His death (John 19:25–30), resurrection (Luke 24:33–43), and ascension (Acts 1:9–11), so that those who were New Testament writers (e.g., Matthew, John, Peter) were eyewitnesses to much of what they wrote. Peter's point is that the false teachers denied his claims about Jesus, but unlike him, they were not eyewitnesses to His life and ministry.

Eyewitnesses (*epoptai*) originally meant "general observers" or "spectators," but over the years its meaning evolved. Barclay explains:

> In the Greek usage of Peter's day this was a technical word. We have already spoken about the Mystery Religions. These Mystery Religions were all of the nature of passion plays, in which the story of a god who lived, suffered, died, and rose again, never to die again, was played out. It was only after a long course of instruction and preparation that the worshipper was finally allowed to be present at the passion play, and to be offered the experience of becoming one with the dying and rising God. When he reached the stage of being allowed to attend the actual passion play, he was an initiate, and the technical word to describe him was in fact *epoptēs;* he was a prepared and privileged eye-witness of the experiences of God. (*The Letters of James and Peter,* rev. ed. [Philadelphia: Westminster, 1976], 367)

With that usage in mind, it is clear that Peter saw himself and his fellow apostles as preeminently privileged spectators who had reached the highest and truest level of spiritual experience in being with Christ. Peter had in mind one event in particular that dramatically previewed Christ's second coming **majesty.**

Majesty (*megaleiotēs*), which can also be translated "splendor," "grandeur," or "magnificence," is elsewhere in the New Testament used to identify "the greatness of God" (Luke 9:43). Jesus had predicted that some of the apostles would see the manifestation of His divine greatness: "Truly I say to you, there are some of those who are standing here who will not taste death until they see the Son of Man coming in His kingdom" (Matt. 16:28; cf. Luke 9:27). God the Father was present at that special event, at which Christ **received honor** (*timē*, "exalted status") **and glory** (*doxa*, "radiant splendor") **from** Him. The first term gives Jesus the highest respect and recognition (John 5:23; 1 Tim. 1:17; Heb. 2:9; Rev. 4:9, 11; 5:12–13), and the second accords divine, unparalleled brightness to Him (Matt. 24:30; Luke 9:32; cf. John 1:14; 17:22; 2 Thess. 1:9).

At that extraordinary event **God the Father,** also called **the Majestic Glory** (a beautiful substitute name for God; cf. Deut. 33:26, LXX), gave an extremely significant **utterance** (audible announcement) to Christ. The Father's **utterance** was **"This is My beloved Son with whom I am well-pleased,"** which could refer to one of two different occasions—the Lord's baptism or His Transfiguration (Matt. 3:17; 17:5). The apostle's further description of the episode precisely identifies it as the Transfiguration since the **utterance** was **made from heaven when we were with Him on the holy mountain.** The mountain was most likely Mount Hermon, the highest mountain near Caesarea Philippi (cf. Mark 8:27), where Peter, James, and John saw the cloud of divine glory surround them and Jesus and heard the voice of God (Matt. 17:5; Mark 9:7; Luke 9:35).

The announcement **"This is My beloved Son with whom I am well-pleased"** is the Father's affirmation that the Son is both of identical nature and essence with Him (cf. John 5:17–20; Rom. 1:1–4; Gal. 1:3; Col. 1:3; 2:9) and that He is perfectly righteous (cf. 2 Cor. 5:21; Heb. 7:26). Thus in one concise statement God declared a relationship of both divine nature and divine love with Christ—the perfect bond of love and holiness within the Godhead—and His complete satisfaction with everything Jesus said and did. By clear implication, the Father's pronouncement also confirmed Christ's right to come again, at the ordained time, and receive His own and possess the kingdom that is rightfully His. As Revelation 5:9–13 says:

> And they sang a new song, saying, "Worthy are You to take the book and to break its seals; for You were slain, and purchased for God with Your blood men from every tribe and tongue and people and nation. You have made them to be a kingdom and priests to our God; and they will reign upon the earth." Then I looked, and I heard the voice of many

> angels around the throne and the living creatures and the elders; and the number of them was myriads of myriads, and thousands of thousands, saying with a loud voice, "Worthy is the Lamb that was slain to receive power and riches and wisdom and might and honor and glory and blessing." And every created thing which is in heaven and on the earth and under the earth and on the sea, and all things in them, I heard saying, "To Him who sits on the throne, and to the Lamb, be blessing and honor and glory and dominion forever and ever."

(For a complete commentary on the Transfiguration and Matthew 17:1–13, see John MacArthur, *Matthew 16–23*, MacArthur New Testament Commentary [Chicago: Moody, 1988], 61–72.)

There is no reason for Peter's audience then or now to believe false teachers who deny the glorious future return of Jesus Christ. Whereas those heretics were not present on the Mount of Transfiguration, Peter was an eyewitness to second coming majesty. He, James, and John saw Moses and Elijah affirm Christ (Luke 9:30–32), and above all, the apostles heard God Himself honor His Son.

GOD'S SUPERNATURAL REVELATION

So we have the prophetic word made more sure, to which you do well to pay attention as to a lamp shining in a dark place, until the day dawns and the morning star arises in your hearts. But know this first of all, that no prophecy of Scripture is a matter of one's own interpretation, for no prophecy was ever made by an act of human will, but men moved by the Holy Spirit spoke from God. (1:19–21)

As accurate as they were, in declaring the truth God did not merely depend on the oral, eyewitness accounts of the apostles. Through the agency of the Holy Spirit He superintended the recording of those experiences and thoughts in the inspired revelation of Scripture (2 Tim. 3:16). Peter's reply to those who would question the validity of his experiences is that believers have even a better source—**the prophetic word made more sure**—the Word of God. Some commentators contend the phrase indicates that the apostles' experiences validated the Scripture, that glimpsing Jesus' kingdom glory on the Mount of Transfiguration somehow confirmed the prophets' predictions concerning His second coming. That is a possible interpretation, but the phrase's literal rendering, "we have more sure the prophetic word," recommends another interpretation. That is, as reliable and helpful as Peter's experience was, the **prophetic word** of Scripture is **more sure.** Throughout redemptive history, God

Himself has repeatedly emphasized that His inspired Word is inerrant, infallible, and the all-sufficient source of truth, which does not require human confirmation (Pss. 19:7; 119:160; John 17:17; 1 Cor. 2:10–14; 1 Thess. 2:13; cf. Prov. 6:23; Dan. 10:21, NKJV).

We in verse 19 is not an emphatic pronoun as it is in verse 18, where it refers to Peter, James, and John. Instead, this second usage refers generically to all believers. As a group they possess the Word, the source of God's truth that is far more reliable than their collective experience, even as apostles. Second Corinthians 12:1 is a helpful example of the limitations of human experience as a source of truth: "Boasting is necessary, though it is not profitable; but I will go on to visions and revelations of the Lord." The apostle Paul desired to defend his apostleship, but he appears to admit that personal visions and experiences—even of heaven—are not helpful, not substantial as defenses of God's truth. That is because they are unverifiable, unrepeatable, and incomprehensible (vv. 2–4). Paul actually preferred to defend his apostleship with his suffering rather than with his supernatural visions (vv. 5–10). When the New Testament writers wrote about Christ and His promised return, they confirmed the truth of Old Testament Scripture (cf. Matt. 4:12–16; 12:19–20; 21:1–5; Luke 4:16–21; Rom. 15:3; Heb. 5:5–6; 1 Peter 2:6–7, 22; Rev. 19:10). Thus it was not the apostles' experience but the inspired and inscripturated record of Christ's life and words, penned by the Spirit-directed authors and contained in the New Testament, which validated the Old. That validation fit the Jews' beliefs regarding the supremacy of written revelation, as Michael Green explains:

> The Jews always preferred prophecy to the voice from heaven. Indeed they regarded the latter, the *bath qōl*, "daughter of the voice", as an inferior substitute for revelation, since the days of prophecy had ceased. And as for the apostles, it is hard to overemphasize their regard for the Old Testament. One of their most powerful arguments for the truth of Christianity was the argument from prophecy (see the speeches in Acts, Rom. XV, I Peter II, or the whole of Heb. or Rev.). In the word of God written, they sought absolute assurance, like their Master, for whom "it is written" sufficed to clinch an argument. . . . [Peter] is saying "If you don't believe me, go to the Scriptures". "The question", says Calvin, "is not whether the prophets are more trustworthy than the gospel." It is simply that "since the Jews were in no doubt that everything that the prophets taught came from God, it is no wonder that Peter says that their word is more sure". (*The Second General Epistle of Peter and the Epistle of Jude* [Grand Rapids: Eerdmans, 1968], 87)

The expression **the prophetic word** in Peter's day embraced the entire Old Testament. The expression extends beyond the passages of predictive prophecy to include all the inspired Word, which in general anticipated the coming of Messiah, as Paul made clear when he wrote:

> Now to Him who is able to establish you according to my gospel and the preaching of Jesus Christ, according to the revelation of the mystery which has been kept secret for long ages past, but now is manifested, and by the Scriptures of the prophets, according to the commandment of the eternal God, has been made known to all the nations, leading to obedience of faith; to the only wise God, through Jesus Christ, be the glory forever. Amen. (Rom. 16:25–27)

Jesus Himself affirmed that reality, saying, "You search the Scriptures because you think that in them you have eternal life; it is these that testify about Me" (John 5:39; cf. Luke 24:27, 44–45). While the Lord was primarily speaking of Old Testament Scripture, the words are not limited to that. Scripture is Scripture, and what is true of the Old Testament is also true of New Testament Scripture (cf. 2 Peter 3:15–16, in which Peter calls the writings of Paul Scripture).

Peter asserts that his readers would **do well to pay attention** to the **prophetic word.** If they were going to be exposed to the subtle errors of the false teachers, it was imperative that they know and carefully heed Scripture so that they could reject false teachings (Ps. 17:4; Acts 18:28; Eph. 6:11, 17; cf. Matt. 4:4; 22:29; 1 Cor. 10:11; Rev. 22:19). To make his point even more direct, Peter offered a simple metaphor, comparing God's Word **to a lamp shining in a dark place.** That figure of speech recalls the psalmist's familiar words, "Your word is a lamp to my feet and a light to my path" (Ps. 119:105; cf. v. 130; 43:3; Prov. 6:23). **Dark** (*auchmēros*) is the meaning that came from the original idea of this word, "dry," or "parched," then "dirty," or "murky." The phrase **dark place** encompasses the murky blackness of the fallen world that prevents people from seeing the truth until the **lamp** of divine revelation shines forth.

Thus Peter likens Scripture to a lantern that provides light to a dark and sinful world. The calendar of redemptive history moves toward a **day** God has designated for the glorious event when Jesus Christ returns in full, blazing splendor and majesty (Matt. 24:30; 25:31; Titus 2:13; Rev. 1:7; cf. Col. 3:4). When that **day dawns,** Christ will terminate the temporary earthly night of sin and spiritual darkness, returning in glory to establish His kingdom. The apostle John describes this in Revelation 19:11–16:

> And I saw heaven opened, and behold, a white horse, and He who sat on it is called Faithful and True, and in righteousness He judges and wages war. His eyes are a flame of fire, and on His head are many diadems; and He has a name written on Him which no one knows

except Himself. He is clothed with a robe dipped in blood, and His name is called The Word of God. And the armies which are in heaven, clothed in fine linen, white and clean, were following Him on white horses. From His mouth comes a sharp sword, so that with it He may strike down the nations, and He will rule them with a rod of iron; and He treads the wine press of the fierce wrath of God, the Almighty. And on His robe and on His thigh He has a name written, "King of Kings and Lord of Lords."

The bittersweet event marks the climax of God's salvation purpose and His judgment on the wicked (cf. Isa. 2:12; 13:6; Zeph. 1:14; 1 Cor. 1:8; 3:13; 4:5; Eph. 4:30; 1 Thess. 3:13; 2 Thess. 1:7; 2 Tim. 4:1; 1 Peter 2:12).

Morning star (*phōsphoros*), which literally means "light bringer," was the name for the planet Venus, which precedes the morning sun in the sky, and is used here for Christ, whose coming inaugurates the promised millennial kingdom and the establishment of His kingdom. Scripture in several places refers to Christ as a star (Num. 24:17; Rev. 2:28; 22:16; cf. Matt. 2:2). Peter adds the fact that the star **arises in** believers' **hearts.** Christ will return in a blaze of physically visible, all-encompassing light that will affect everyone for blessing or cursing and change the millennial earth (3:10–13), eventually destroying the universe and replacing it with the new heavens and new earth (Rev. 20:11; 21:1). The reference to the **hearts** indicates His return will also transform believers into perfect reflections of the truth and righteousness of Christ and make them into the image of His glory (Rom. 8:29; Phil. 3:20–21; 1 John 3:1–2). At His second coming, Christ will replace the perfect temporal revelation of Scripture with the perfect eternal revelation of His person. He will fulfill the written Word and write it forever on the hearts of the glorified saints.

From considering the end of Scripture, when it completely rules the perfected heart, Peter went back to the start of Scripture—its divine inspiration. As Paul wrote, "All Scripture is inspired by God" (2 Tim. 3:16); therefore, **no prophecy of Scripture is a matter of one's own interpretation.** The phrase **is a matter of** translates *ginetai*, which more precisely means "comes into being," "originates," or "arises." No portion of the holy writings, Old Testament or New, came into existence in the manner all false prophecies did (cf. Jer. 14:14; 23:32; Ezek. 13:2). For example, the prophet Jeremiah explained how God viewed the false prophets of his time:

> Thus says the Lord of hosts, "Do not listen to the words of the prophets who are prophesying to you. They are leading you into futility; they speak a vision of their own imagination, not from the mouth of the Lord. They keep saying to those who despise Me, 'The Lord has said, "You will have peace"'; and as for everyone who walks in the stub-

bornness of his own heart, they say, 'Calamity will not come upon you.' But who has stood in the council of the Lord, that he should see and hear His word? Who has given heed to His word and listened? Behold, the storm of the Lord has gone forth in wrath, even a whirling tempest; it will swirl down on the head of the wicked. The anger of the Lord will not turn back until He has performed and carried out the purposes of His heart; in the last days you will clearly understand it. I did not send these prophets, but they ran. I did not speak to them, but they prophesied. But if they had stood in My council, then they would have announced My words to My people, and would have turned them back from their evil way and from the evil of their deeds. "Am I a God who is near," declares the Lord, "and not a God far off? Can a man hide himself in hiding places so I do not see him?" declares the Lord. "Do I not fill the heavens and the earth?" declares the Lord. "I have heard what the prophets have said who prophesy falsely in My name, saying, 'I had a dream, I had a dream!'" (Jer. 23:16–25; cf. Ezek. 13:3)

False prophets spoke of their own things, from their own ideas, but no true message from God ever arose from a human **interpretation. Interpretation** (*epiluseōs*) is an unfortunate translation because in English it indicates how one understands Scripture, whereas the Greek noun is a genitive, indicating source. Thus Peter is not referring to the explanation of the Scripture, but to its origin. The next statement in verse 21, **for no prophecy was ever made by an act of human will, but** (*alla,* "just the opposite," "quite the contrary") **men moved by the Holy Spirit spoke from God,** further supports the point of source. What human beings might think or want has absolutely nothing to do with divine prophecy. (See John MacArthur, *1 Peter,* MacArthur New Testament Commentary [Chicago: Moody, 2004, 51–57].)

Moved (*pheromenoi*) is a present passive participle that means "continually carried," or "borne along." Luke twice used this verb (Acts 27:15, 17) to describe how the wind blows a sailing ship across the waters. For Peter, it was as if the writers of Scripture raised their spiritual sails and allowed the Spirit to fill them with His powerful breath of revelation as they penned its divine words (cf. Luke 1:70). When Jeremiah said, "The word of the Lord came to me saying" (Jer. 1:4), he spoke for all the Old Testament writers and, by extension, all the New Testament writers who followed them. The only one who knows the mind of God is the Spirit of God (1 Cor. 2:10–13; cf. John 15:26; Rom. 8:27; 11:34; cf. John 3:8), so only He could have inspired the Scripture.

If believers are going to stand against the errors of false teachers, they must seek to know, accept, and obey the totality of Scripture, even as the apostle Paul did in testifying before the Roman governor Felix, "But this I admit to you, that according to the Way which they [the Jews] call a sect I do serve the God of our fathers, believing *everything* that is in accordance with the Law and that is written in the Prophets" (Acts 24:14, emphasis added).

A Portrait of False Teachers (2 Peter 2:1–3*a*)

5

But false prophets also arose among the people, just as there will also be false teachers among you, who will secretly introduce destructive heresies, even denying the Master who bought them, bringing swift destruction upon themselves. Many will follow their sensuality, and because of them the way of the truth will be maligned; and in their greed they will exploit you with false words; (2:1–3*a*)

There is nothing more offensive to God than the distortion of His Word (cf. Rev. 22:18–19). To falsify the facts about who God is and what He said—even promoting Satan's lies as if they were God's truth—is the basest form of hypocrisy. With eternity at stake, it is hard to believe that anyone would intentionally deceive other people, teaching them something that is spiritually catastrophic. Yet, such atrocious arrogance is exactly what characterizes the pseudo-ministries of false teachers.

As the father of lies (John 8:44), Satan is constantly using deception and false doctrine to attack the church—employing false teachers to infiltrate the true flock. Claiming to teach truth, these purveyors of demonic error disguise themselves as angels of light (cf. 2 Cor. 11:14), attempting to creep into the fold unnoticed. As a result, throughout redemptive history, God has repeatedly warned believers to be on the alert against such men (and women).

Deuteronomy 13, for example, contains an early warning from Moses against false prophets. He prescribes a severe punishment for these men, along with all those who endorse their falsehood:

> If a prophet or a dreamer of dreams arises among you and gives you a sign or a wonder, and the sign or the wonder comes true, concerning which he spoke to you, saying, "Let us go after other gods (whom you have not known) and let us serve them," you shall not listen to the words of that prophet or that dreamer of dreams; for the Lord your God is testing you to find out if you love the Lord your God with all your heart and with all your soul. You shall follow the Lord your God and fear Him; and you shall keep His commandments, listen to His voice, serve Him, and cling to Him. But that prophet or that dreamer of dreams shall be put to death, because he has counseled rebellion against the Lord your God who brought you from the land of Egypt and redeemed you from the house of slavery, to seduce you from the way in which the Lord your God commanded you to walk. So you shall purge the evil from among you. (Deut. 13:1–5; cf. 18:20–22)

This same sobriety is echoed in the New Testament by Christ and the apostles, who carefully warn believers about false teachers and their deceptions (Matt. 24:11; Luke 6:26; 2 Cor. 11:13–15). In light of this satanic threat, the New Testament writers emphasize the importance of being armed with the truth (cf. Eph. 6:14–17) for the purpose of discernment (1 Thess. 5:20–22). For them, doctrinal purity was a very high priority (1 John 4:1) and a heartfelt concern (2 Cor. 11:28). In fact, the apostles reserve their harshest criticism for those who distort the truth (cf. Gal. 1:9; Phil. 3:2).

The verdict from both Old and New Testaments is unmistakable: God does not tolerate false prophets (cf. Isa. 9:15; Mic. 3:5–7; Matt. 7:15–20; 1 Tim. 6:3–5; 2 Tim. 3:1–9; 1 John 4:1–3; 2 John 7–11). Ironically, many in today's church do exactly the opposite—tolerating any teacher who claims to be Christian, regardless of the *content* of his teaching. Such mindless acceptance, in the name of love and unity, has tragically produced a careless indifference to the truth. As a result, some Christians view biblical absolutes as an embarrassment, preferring to embrace false teachers despite the Bible's clear protest (Jer. 28:15–17; 29:21, 32; Acts 13:6–12; 1 Tim. 1:18–20; 3 John 9–11).

To be sure, Satan's attacks are often external, through the propagation of false religions and cults. But he also uses internal tactics, seeking to destroy God's people from within. Hence, his servants, as wolves in sheep's clothing (Matt. 7:15), do their best to infect the flock with the doctrine of demons (1 Tim. 4:1). Because this false teaching comes in subtle forms, the undiscerning are often deceived, being unable to distinguish the error from the truth.

Peter understood the danger that false doctrine posed for his readers. In his first epistle, he had already warned them to be aware of the devil's tactics (1 Peter 5:8). In this passage, he again addresses the strategies of the Evil One—exposing Satan's servants for who they really are. In fact, he gives us a clear portrait of false teachers—looking specifically at the sphere, secrecy, sacrilege, success, sensuality, stigma, and sustaining motive of their operations. As a result, Peter's insights are as relevant today as they were two millennia ago, since they address a problem that continues to plague the contemporary church (cf. 2 John 7).

THEIR SPHERE

But false prophets also arose among the people, just as there will also be false teachers among you, (2:1*a*)

Having just discussed the sure word of truth (1:19–21), Peter now shifts his focus to the deceptive words of false prophets (chapter 2). The coordinate conjunction **but** marks this contrasting transition. Through genuine prophets, God has spoken the truth to His people, **but,** through false prophets, Satan has always tried to obscure or contaminate God's message. As servants of the Deceiver, false prophets propagate lies and falsehood in their systematic attack on the truth.

Throughout history, these spiritual mercenaries have always plagued God's flock. Even in Old Testament times they **arose among the people** of Israel, spreading their deceptions and causing devastation (1 Kings 22:1–28; Jer. 5:30–31; 6:13–15; 23:14–16, 21, 25–27; 28:1–17; Ezek. 13:1–7, 15–19). That Old Testament Israel is in view here is evidenced both by Peter's terminology (cf. Matt. 2:4; Luke 22:66; Acts 7:17; 13:17; 26:17, 23, where similar usages of **the people** clearly refer to the Jewish people) and his Old Testament illustrations (Noah—2:5; Sodom and Gomorrah—2:6; Lot—2:7; and Balaam—2:15).

Even during Jesus' ministry, false prophets were still a serious problem for the Jewish people (Matt. 7:15–20). For that matter, the entire religious establishment was corrupt, with the Pharisees providing the quintessential example of false religion. Here is Christ's indictment of those spiritual pretenders:

> But the Lord said to him, "Now you Pharisees clean the outside of the cup and of the platter; but inside of you, you are full of robbery and wickedness. You foolish ones, did not He who made the outside make the inside also? But give that which is within as charity, and then all

things are clean for you. But woe to you Pharisees! For you pay tithe of mint and rue and every kind of garden herb, and yet disregard justice and the love of God; but these are the things you should have done without neglecting the others. Woe to you Pharisees! For you love the chief seats in the synagogues and the respectful greetings in the market places. Woe to you! For you are like concealed tombs, and the people who walk over them are unaware of it." One of the lawyers said to Him in reply, "Teacher, when You say this, You insult us too." But He said, "Woe to you lawyers as well! For you weigh men down with burdens hard to bear, while you yourselves will not even touch the burdens with one of your fingers. Woe to you! For you build the tombs of the prophets, and it was your fathers who killed them. So you are witnesses and approve the deeds of your fathers; because it was they who killed them, and you build their tombs. For this reason also the wisdom of God said, 'I will send to them prophets and apostles, and some of them they will kill and some they will persecute, so that the blood of all the prophets, shed since the foundation of the world, may be charged against this generation, from the blood of Abel to the blood of Zechariah, who was killed between the altar and the house of God; yes, I tell you, it shall be charged against this generation.' Woe to you lawyers! For you have taken away the key of knowledge; you yourselves did not enter, and you hindered those who were entering." (Luke 11:39–52; cf. 12:1; Matt. 23:13–36; Mark 12:38–40)

Just as he knew false prophets had assaulted Israel, Peter understood that **there will also be false teachers among** the church. Years before, Jesus had predicted that in the last days the church would have to endure a variety of false teachers: "See to it that no one misleads you. For many will come in My name, saying, 'I am the Christ,' and will mislead many" (Matt. 24:4–5; cf. vv. 11, 24).

In a similar vein, Paul warned Timothy:

Preach the word. . . . For the time will come when they will not endure sound doctrine; but wanting to have their ears tickled, they will accumulate for themselves teachers in accordance to their own desires, and will turn away their ears from the truth and will turn aside to myths. (2 Tim. 4:2–4; cf. Acts 15:24; 20:29–30; Rom. 16:17–18; Gal. 1:6–9; 1 Tim. 4:1–3; 2 Tim. 3:1–9; Jude 4, 12–13)

False teachers arise when the church begins to embrace the worldly culture around it. As a result, congregations no longer desire to "endure [hold to] sound [healthy] doctrine." God-centered worship and preaching is replaced by man-centered antics and entertainment. A biblical emphasis on sin, repentance, and holiness is replaced by an emphasis on self-esteem and felt needs. People look for teachers who proclaim only pleasant, positive ideas "in accordance to their own desires" because they want "to have their ears tickled." As a result, these popular teachers (whom "they will accumulate for themselves") will "turn" the minds of the people from the truth, leaving them vulnerable to Satan's deceptive influence.

The warning from Scripture is clear: false teachers *will* arise in the church. In fact, the church is one of Satan's primary spheres of operation. For that reason, the true shepherd must continually be on guard—constantly studying, proclaiming, and defending the truth, "so that he will be able both to exhort in sound doctrine and to refute those who contradict" (Titus 1:9*b*).

THEIR SECRECY

who will secretly introduce destructive heresies, (2:1*b*)

False teachers are never honest and straightforward about their operations. After all, the church would never embrace them if their schemes were unmasked. Instead, they **secretly** and deceptively enter the church, posing as pastors, teachers, and evangelists. That is why Jude describes them as "certain persons [who] have crept in unnoticed" (Jude 4). The verb "to creep in" (*pareisduō*) means to "slip in without being seen," or "to sneak in under false pretenses." The term refers to a clever defendant attempting to fool a judge, or a criminal secretly returning to a place from which he was banished.

Posing as true shepherds, false teachers **introduce destructive heresies** (or literally, "heresies of destruction"). **Destructive** (*apōleias*) means "utter ruin" and speaks of the final and eternal condemnation of the wicked. In this context, the term indicates that the antics of these men have disastrous eternal consequences, both for them and their followers. That this Greek word has the sense of damnation can be seen by its use to describe those who go through the wide gate in Matthew 7:13, its use to describe the fate of Judas in John 17:12, its application to unbelievers' doom in Romans 9:22, its use to describe the judgment of the man of sin in 2 Thessalonians 2:3, and its use by Peter in 3:7 of this letter to describe the destruction of the ungodly. Peter marked those **heresies** as contrary to the gospel—they damn rather than save.

The term **heresies** (*haireseis*) denotes "an opinion, especially a self-willed opinion, which is substituted for submission to the power of truth, and leads to division and the formation of sects" (W. E. Vine, *An Expository Dictionary of New Testament Words,* 4 vols. [London: Oliphants, 1940; reprint, Chicago: Moody, 1985], 2:217). By using this word, Peter indicated that those false teachers had exchanged the truth of God's Word for their own self-styled opinions. As a result, they distorted the truth to their own ends, convincing the gullible to believe their lies. Their teaching, then, was nothing more than a religious counterfeit—a pseudo-Christian knockoff. While *haireseis* can simply refer to a sect or division (Acts 24:14; cf. 5:17; 15:5; 24:5; 26:5; 28:22; 1 Cor. 11:19), here it refers to the worst kind of deviation and deception—teaching that claims to be biblical but is actually the very opposite.

False teachers do not always openly oppose the gospel. Some claim to believe it, to have the true interpretation of it; but in truth they misrepresent it, or offer a shallow, inadequate message that cannot save. Because their teaching is as lethal as it is subtle, the self-styled opinions of false teachers can damn the souls of unsuspecting, professed believers (cf. Matt. 13:20–22, 36–42, 47–50). Unless they repent, believe the truth, and turn to Christ, those who embrace these heretical doctrines will be eternally lost.

Their Sacrilege

even denying the Master who bought them, bringing swift destruction upon themselves. (2:1c)

The conjunction **even** underscores the unthinkable magnitude of the false teachers' arrogance—a pride that evidenced itself by **denying the Master. Denying** is a strong term meaning "to refuse," "to be unwilling," or "to firmly say no." The same verb appears in Hebrews 11:24 to describe Moses' refusal to be called the son of Pharaoh's daughter. Here in this passage, Peter used the present tense participle (*arnoumenoi*) to denote a habitual pattern of refusal, indicating that false teachers characteristically reject divine authority (cf. Jude 8).

Master (*despotēs,* from which the English *despot* derives) means "sovereign," "ruler," or "lord." The word appears ten times in the New Testament and always refers to one who has supreme authority. In four occurrences (1 Tim. 6:1, 2; Titus 2:9; 1 Peter 2:18) it refers to the master of a household or estate, who has full authority over all the servants. Here and in the other five occurrences (Luke 2:29; Acts 4:24; 2 Tim. 2:21; Jude 4; Rev. 6:10) it directly refers to Christ or God.

Thus for Peter the supreme sacrilege of false teachers is that they deny the sovereign lordship of Jesus Christ. Granted, they may not outwardly deny Christ's deity, atonement, resurrection, or second coming. But internally, they adamantly refuse to submit their lives to His sovereign rule (Prov. 19:3; cf. Ex. 5:2; Neh. 9:17). As a result, their immoral and rebellious lifestyles will inevitably give them away.

The phrase **who bought them** fits Peter's analogy perfectly. He is alluding to the master of a house who would purchase slaves and put them in charge of various household tasks. Because they were now regarded as the master's personal property, they owed their complete allegiance to him. While false teachers maintain that they are part of Christ's household, they deny such professions through their actions— refusing to become servants under His authority. **Bought** (*agorazō*) means "to purchase," or "to redeem out of the marketplace," and in this context is parallel to Deuteronomy 32:5–6 (cf. Zeph. 1:4–6). The false teachers of Peter's day claimed Christ as their Redeemer, yet they refused to accept His sovereign lordship, thus revealing their true character as unregenerate enemies of biblical truth.

Many take this statement **the Master who bought them** to mean that Christ actually has purchased redemption in full for all people, even for false teachers. It is commonly thought that Christ died to pay in full the penalty for everyone's sins, whether they ever believe or not. The popular notion is that God loves everyone, wants everyone saved, so Christ died for everyone.

This means His death was a potential sacrifice or atonement that becomes an actual atonement when a sinner repents and believes the gospel. Evangelism, according to this view, is convincing sinners to receive what has already been done for them. All can believe and be saved if they will, since no one is excluded in the atonement.

This viewpoint, if taken to its logical conclusion, has hell full of people whose salvation was purchased by Christ on the cross. Therefore the lake of fire is filled with those damned people whose sin Christ fully atoned for by bearing their punishment under God's wrath.

Heaven will be populated by people who had the same atonement provided for them, but they are there because *they* received it. Christ, in this view, died on the cross for the damned in hell the same as He did for the redeemed in heaven. The only difference between the redeemed's fate and that of the damned is the sinner's choice.

This perspective says that the Lord Jesus Christ died to make salvation possible, not actual. He did not absolutely purchase salvation for anyone. He only removed a barrier for everyone, which merely makes salvation potential. The sinner ultimately determines the nature of the atonement and its application by what he does. According to this perspective, when Jesus cried, "It is finished," it really should be rendered, "It is stated."

Of course, the preceding interpretational difficulties and fallacies arising from this view stem from the misunderstanding of two very important biblical teachings: the doctrine of absolute inability (often called total depravity) and the doctrine of the atonement itself.

Rightly understood, the doctrine of absolute inability says that all people are dead in trespasses and sins (Eph. 2:1), alienated from the life of God (Rom. 1:21–22), doing only evil from terminally deceitful hearts (cf. Jer. 17:9), incapable of understanding the things of God (1 Cor. 2:14), blinded by love of sin, further blinded by Satan (2 Cor. 4:4), desiring only the will of their father the devil, unable to seek God, and unwilling to repent (cf. Rom. 3:10–23). So how is the sinner going to make the right choice to activate the atonement on his behalf?

Clearly, salvation is solely from God (cf. Ps. 3:8; Jonah 2:9)—He must give light, life, sight, understanding, repentance, and faith (John 1:12–13; 1 Cor. 1:30; Eph. 2:8–9). Salvation comes to the sinner from God, by His will and power. Since that is true, and based on the doctrine of sovereign election (1 Peter 1:1–3; 2 Peter 1:3; cf. Rom. 8:26–30; 9:14–22; Eph. 1:3–6), God determined the extent of the atonement.

For whom did Christ die? He died for all who would believe because they were chosen, called, justified, and granted repentance and faith by the Father. The atonement is limited to those who believe, who are the elect of God. Any believer who does not believe in universal salvation knows Christ's atonement is limited (cf. Matt. 7:13; 8:12; 10:28; 22:13; 25:46; Mark 9:43, 49; John 3:17–18; 8:24; 2 Thess. 1:7–9). Anyone who rejects the notion that the whole human race will be saved believes necessarily in a limited atonement—either limited by the sinner who is sovereign, or by God who is sovereign.

One should forget the idea of an unlimited atonement. If he asserts that sinners have the power to limit its application, then the atonement by its nature is limited in actual power and effectiveness. With that understanding, it is less than a real atonement and is, in fact, merely potential and restricted by the volitions of fallen human beings. But in truth, only God can set the atonement's limits, which extend to every believing sinner without distinction.

Adherents to the unlimited view must affirm that Christ actually atoned for no one in particular but potentially for everyone without exception. Whatever He did on the cross was not a full and complete payment for sin, because sinners for whom He died are still damned. Hell is full of people whose sins were paid for by Christ—sin paid for, yet punished forever.

Of course, such thinking is completely unacceptable. God limits the atonement to the elect, for whom it was not a potential but an actual and real satisfaction for sin. God provided the sacrifice in His Son, which actually paid for the sins of all who would ever believe, the ones chosen by Him for salvation (cf. Matt. 1:21; John 10:11, 27–28; Eph. 5:25–26).

Charles Spurgeon once gave a pointedly accurate and convincing perspective on the argument about the extent of the atonement:

> We are often told that we limit the atonement of Christ, because we say that Christ has not made a satisfaction for all men, or all men would be saved. Now, our reply to this is, that, on the other hand, our opponents limit it; we do not. The Arminians say, Christ died for all men. Ask them what they mean by it. Did Christ die so as to secure the salvation of all men? They say, "No, certainly not." We ask them the next question—Did Christ die so as to secure the salvation of any man in particular? They answer, "No." They are obliged to admit this, if they are consistent. They say, "No, Christ has died that any man may be saved if"—and then follow certain conditions of salvation. Now, who is it that limits the death of Christ? Why, you. You say that Christ did not die so as infallibly to secure the salvation of anybody. We beg your pardon, when you say we limit Christ's death; we say, "No, my dear sir, it is you that do it." We say that Christ so died that he infallibly secured the salvation of a multitude that no man can number, who through Christ's death not only may be saved, but are saved and cannot by any possibility run the hazard of being anything but saved. You are welcome to your atonement; you may keep it. We will never renounce ours for the sake of it. (Cited by J. I. Packer, "Introductory Essay," in John Owen, *The Death of Death in the Death of Christ* [n.p., n.d.; reprint, London: Banner of Truth, 1959], 14.)

Contemporary writer David Clotfelter adds these observations:

> From the Calvinist point of view, it is Arminianism that presents logical impossibilities. Arminianism tells us that Jesus died for multitudes that will never be saved, including millions who never so much as heard of Him. It tells us that in the case of those who are lost, the death of Jesus, represented in Scripture as an act whereby He took upon Himself the punishment that should have been ours (Isa. 53:5), was ineffective. Christ has suffered once for their sins, but they will now have to suffer for those same sins in hell.

> The Arminian atonement has the initial appearance of being very generous, but the more closely we look at it, the less we are impressed. Does it guarantee the salvation of any person? No. Does it guarantee that those for whom Christ died will have the opportunity to hear of Him and respond to Him? No. Does it in any way remove or even lessen the sufferings of the lost? No. In reality, the Arminian atonement does not *atone*. It merely clears the way for God to accept those who are able to lift themselves by their own bootstraps. The Calvinist does not believe that any fallen person has such power, and so he views the Arminian atonement as unsuited to the salvation of sinners and insulting to

Christ. (*Sinners in the Hands of a Good God* [Chicago: Moody, 2004], 165; emphasis in original)

Therefore, false teachers' sins were not paid for in the atonement of Christ.

Contrary to what some Christians believe today, people who reject Christ's lordship are not merely to be designated as second-class Christians (as *believers* but not *disciples*). Instead, those who reject Christ's sovereign lordship will face **swift destruction** if they do not repent from such rebellion (cf. Heb. 10:25–31). **Swift** (*tachinos*) means "quick," or "imminent," and **destruction** (*apōleia*) refers to perdition or eternal damnation in hell (cf. Matt. 7:13; John 17:12; 2 Thess. 2:3). This horrible fate, coming either at death or at Christ's return (John 12:48; 2 Thess. 1:7–10) awaits false teachers and all who follow their unrepentant path.

THEIR SUCCESS

Many will follow (2:2*a*)

The Bible is clear that **many** more people **follow** the broad way that leads to destruction than adhere to the narrow way that leads to life (Matt. 7:13–14; cf. 24:10–12). In part, credit is due to false teachers for the popularity of the "wide road," as they usher people onto the broad way and encourage them not to look back. Their message of independence, personal freedom, and self-exaltation is inherently appealing to fallen human hearts, who would rather serve themselves than submit to Christ.

In His Sermon on the Mount, Jesus declared, "Not everyone who says to Me, 'Lord, Lord,' will enter the kingdom of heaven, but he who does the will of My Father who is in heaven will enter" (Matt. 7:21). Superficial, insincere claims to be followers of Christ are meaningless; only those who fully submit to His lordship and obey His will demonstrate that they truly belong to Him (cf. John 15:14–16; James 1:22–25; 1 John 2:3–6; 5:1–5).

THEIR SENSUALITY

their sensuality (2:2*b*)

Sensuality is a strong word referring to habitual sexual immorality and unrestrained, debauched conduct. By using the plural form of the noun *(aselgeiais)*, Peter emphasizes that the false teachers' sexual lewdness came in many forms and extremes. Because they had rejected the lordship of Christ, their lives were characterized by unrestrained indulgence and lawlessness (cf. Matt. 23:28; 2 Thess. 2:7; 1 John 3:4). They intentionally refused to place any restraints on their fleshly desires or their sexual escapades. Their decadent behavior caused Jude to compare their sins with those of Sodom and Gomorrah:

> For certain persons have crept in unnoticed, those who were long beforehand marked out for this condemnation, ungodly persons who turn the grace of our God into licentiousness and deny our only Master and Lord, Jesus Christ . . . just as Sodom and Gomorrah and the cities around them, since they in the same way as these indulged in gross immorality and went after strange flesh, are exhibited as an example in undergoing the punishment of eternal fire. (Jude 4, 7; cf. Gen. 18:16–19:29)

Peter certainly agreed with Jude's assessment of the false teachers, as is seen later in this chapter of his epistle (2:7, 10, 13–14, 18–19, 22). As he repeatedly addressed their sinful behavior, Peter made it clear that unmitigated **sensuality** is a distinguishing mark of these spiritual counterfeits. A teacher may claim to be God's spokesman, but if his life is characterized by corruption, lust, and immorality, it proves that he is actually a fraud.

THEIR STIGMA

and because of them the way of the truth will be maligned; (2:2c)

The way of the truth refers to right doctrine and the accurate proclamation of the gospel (Acts 9:2; 19:9, 23; 22:4; 24:14, 22; cf. Matt. 7:14; John 14:6; Acts 16:17; 18:25–26). But **because of** false teachers, and the spiritual wreckage they leave behind, the biblical message has often been reproached in the eyes of the world. As Lenski wrote:

> True Christianity is blasphemed, reviled, cursed, condemned by outsiders who see professed Christians running to all manner of excesses. "If that is Christianity," they will say, "curse it!" When many follow such excesses, outsiders are unable to distinguish and so blaspheme the whole "way." These false exponents seem true products of the way to them. (R. C. H. Lenski, *The Interpretation of the Epistles of St. Peter, St. John, and St. Jude* [reprint, Minneapolis: Augsburg, 1966], 307)

By their deceptive teaching and immoral behavior, false teachers have **maligned** (literally "blasphemed," "slandered," or "defamed") the gospel. Of course, their mode of operation is consistent with Satan's mission. On the one hand, he seeks to undermine the church from the inside, by introducing deceptive heresies and false doctrines. On the other hand, he seeks to tarnish the church's reputation from the outside, by periodically unmasking false teachers before a watching world. When unbelievers associate the conduct of false teachers with the practice of the true church, the name of Christ is inevitably defamed.

To counter these relentless, satanic efforts, the church must be doctrinally pure, and Christians must live the kind of righteous lives that make the transforming power of Christ believable. With this in mind, the apostle Paul exhorted the Philippians, "Prove yourselves to be blameless and innocent, children of God above reproach in the midst of a crooked and perverse generation, among whom you appear as lights in the world" (Phil. 2:15; cf. Matt. 5:16; Eph. 2:10; 5:8; 1 Thess. 2:12; Titus 2:5, 7, 14; 1 Peter 2:9–12).

THEIR SUSTAINING MOTIVE

and in their greed they will exploit you with false words; (2:3*a*)

False teachers are not ultimately motivated by a fascination with false doctrine, rebelliousness, or even a penchant for sexual immorality. To be sure, they actively participate in each of those activities. But people can do all such sins without being teachers. Instead, the primary motivation driving false teachers is an unbridled love of money. The term for **greed** (*pleonexia*) connotes an uncontrolled, covetous desire for money and wealth. Later in this chapter Peter describes false teachers as "having a heart trained in greed" (v. 14). They crave as much money as possible (cf. 1 Tim. 6:3–5, 10) and are experts at bilking people in the church out of their wealth. This is a standard biblical indictment and characterization of religious charlatans (see Jer. 6:13; 8:10; 1 Tim. 6:3, 5, 9–11; Titus 1:7, 11; 1 Peter 5:1–3; Jude 11, 16).

To accomplish their materialistic goals, false teachers **will exploit** people **with false words. Exploit** (*emporeuomai*) means "to traffic in," or "to realize gain from." Such men want to get rich from the people to whom they "minister." Although they claim to serve others, they are only interested in serving themselves, using **false words** to enrich their own pockets.

Interestingly, the English word *plastic* is derived from the term **false** (*plastos*). In keeping with its etymological roots, *plastic* originally had the connotation of something not completely authentic. After all, plastic items often look as if they are manufactured from another substance, such as wood, metal, china, and so forth. Thus plastic at first glance "deceives" consumers. In a similar way, false teachers deal in phony doctrine. Their theology is not really based on biblical truth, but only molded by false reasoning to appear genuine (cf. Col. 2:8, 20–23; 2 Tim. 2:14–18).

Satan's goal, then, is to deceive as many people as possible, both inside and outside the church, by means of false teachers. In contrast, God's goal is to identify and expose such hypocrites. Through Peter's warning, the Holy Spirit makes it clear that false teachers are everywhere and have been since the dawn of redemptive history. In response, believers need to be vigilant and discerning, taking to heart the apostolic admonition of Paul to the Ephesian elders:

> Be on guard for yourselves and for all the flock, among which the Holy Spirit has made you overseers, to shepherd the church of God which He purchased with His own blood. I know that after my departure savage wolves will come in among you, not sparing the flock; and from among your own selves men will arise, speaking perverse things, to draw away the disciples after them. Therefore be on the alert, remembering that night and day for a period of three years I did not cease to admonish each one with tears. And now I commend you to God and to the word of His grace, which is able to build you up and to give you the inheritance among all those who are sanctified. (Acts 20:28–32)

Divine Judgment on False Teachers
(2 Peter 2:3*b*–10*a*)

6

their judgment from long ago is not idle, and their destruction is not asleep. For if God did not spare angels when they sinned, but cast them into hell and committed them to pits of darkness, reserved for judgment; and did not spare the ancient world, but preserved Noah, a preacher of righteousness, with seven others, when He brought a flood upon the world of the ungodly; and if He condemned the cities of Sodom and Gomorrah to destruction by reducing them to ashes, having made them an example to those who would live ungodly lives thereafter; and if He rescued righteous Lot, oppressed by the sensual conduct of unprincipled men (for by what he saw and heard that righteous man, while living among them, felt his righteous soul tormented day after day by their lawless deeds), then the Lord knows how to rescue the godly from temptation, and to keep the unrighteous under punishment for the day of judgment, and especially those who indulge the flesh in its corrupt desires and despise authority. (2:3*b*–10*a*)

God is truth.

Time and time again, the Scripture reiterates this simple yet indispensable fact (Pss. 25:10; 31:5; 57:10; 86:15; 108:4; 117:2; John 1:9, 14, 17; 3:33; 7:28; 14:17; 15:26; 16:13; 17:3; 1 Thess. 1:9; 1 John 5:6, 20; Rev. 3:7, 14; 6:10; 15:3; 19:11). The psalmist declares of Him, "Righteousness and justice are the foundation of Your throne; lovingkindness and truth go before You" (Ps. 89:14). The prophet Isaiah concurs: "He who is blessed in the earth will be blessed by the God of truth; and he who swears in the earth will swear by the God of truth" (Isa. 65:16). And the Lord Jesus Christ, as God in human flesh, proclaims: "I am the way, the truth, and the life" (John 14:6*a*).

As the God of truth, He cannot lie. Even the wicked prophet Balaam recognized this: "God is not a man, that He should lie, nor a son of man, that He should repent; has He said, and will He not do it? Or has He spoken, and will He not make it good?" (Num. 23:19; cf. Rom. 3:4; Titus 1:2). And the author of Hebrews agrees, "It is impossible for God to lie" (Heb. 6:18).

Thus, when God speaks, He always speaks truth. This means that His infallible Word is perfectly without error and completely trustworthy. Put simply, the Bible—like its Author—is truth (Pss. 12:6; 19:7; 119:151, 160; cf. Neh. 8:3; Pss. 119:42, 130; Matt. 22:29; John 17:17; Acts 18:28; 20:32; Rom. 1:2; 15:4; 16:26; Eph. 5:26; 2 Tim. 3:15–17; Heb. 4:12; James 1:18; 2 Peter 1:19–21). In light of this, it is not surprising that God wants His servants to proclaim and explain His Word in a truthful way (2 Cor. 4:2; 2 Tim. 2:15)—accurately and completely, with no deviation or manipulation (cf. Deut. 4:2; 12:32; Rev. 22:19). To do anything less is to misrepresent both the intended meaning and the inherent character of God Himself.

In stark contrast, Satan is the archliar and the father of lies (John 8:44; cf. Gen. 3:1; 2 Cor. 11:14; 2 Thess. 2:9). His primary goal, as God's adversary, is to deceive—having "blinded the minds of the unbelieving so that they might not see the light of the gospel of the glory of Christ, who is the image of God" (2 Cor. 4:4). In other words, Satan and his servants are antithetically opposed to God's saving purposes; they distort the truth in order to obscure God's message.

Of course, in the end, all of Satan's plans will be thwarted (Rev. 20:10–15; cf. Isa. 24:21–23). After all, God is sovereign over the Evil One and his minions (cf. Job 1:12, 2:6; Luke 8:31; 22:31). And, as the God of truth, the Lord opposes all of Satan's lying deceivers (cf. Prov. 6:16–19; 19:5, 9; Matt. 4:1–11), promising to ultimately punish them forever (cf. Rev. 21:8; 22:15).

In fact, the Bible makes it clear that God hates all lying (Prov. 6:16, 17; 12:22), especially lies about Him and His Word. James 3:1 warns that all spiritual teachers (including believers) are subject to "a stricter judgment" (a higher level of accountability before God) because of the influence they wield (cf. 1 Cor. 3:9–15). When unbelieving false teachers propagate spiritual fabrications and heresies, they are simultaneously increasing the severity of their future punishment. While destroying themselves they deceive others also—which is why God has always responded to false teaching so acutely.

> Therefore, thus says the Lord God, "Because you have spoken falsehood and seen a lie, therefore behold, I am against you," declares the Lord God. So My hand will be against the prophets who see false visions and utter lying divinations. They will have no place in the council of My people, nor will they be written down in the register of the house of Israel, nor will they enter the land of Israel, that you may know that I am the Lord God." (Ezek. 13:8–9; cf. Isa. 9:13–17; 28:14–17; Jer. 14:14–15; 23:13–15)

As Peter continues his description of false teachers, he underscores just how serious God is about truth, and also how hostile He is toward those who distort it. The apostle has already given his readers a general portrait of false teachers (vv. 1–3*a*). Later in this chapter, he will enlarge that portrait, adding detailed descriptions and vivid word pictures. But first, in this section (vv. 3*b*–10*a*), he elaborates on the "swift destruction" (v. 1), or certain and imminent judgment, that God will bring on spiritual deceivers. Such judgment, guaranteed to befall every unrepentant false teacher, unfolds under three headings: the promise of judgment, the precedent for judgment, and the pattern of judgment.

THE PROMISE OF JUDGMENT

their judgment from long ago is not idle, and their destruction is not asleep. (2:3*b*)

Although false teachers will not face their eternal **judgment** until death, their sentence was decreed by God **from long ago.** (The phrase **from long ago** translates one word, *ekpalai,* which simply means "from a long time.") Throughout history, from the first pronouncement of judgment on the serpent in the Garden (Gen. 3:13–15), God has condemned all those who distort divine truth (cf. Isa. 8:19–21; 28:15; Jer. 9:6–9; 14:14–15; Zeph. 3:1–8; Rev. 21:8, 27). The expression **is not idle** strengthens the sobering reality of divine retribution; God's sentence against every lying teacher is actively accumulating wrath until each perishes in hell. (See the discussion on Jude 4's phrase "long beforehand marked out for this condemnation" in chapter 11 of this volume.)

With the words **destruction is not asleep,** Peter personifies eternal damnation as if it were an executioner, who remains fully awake, ready to administer God's just sentence of condemnation on those who falsify His Word.

THE PRECEDENT FOR JUDGMENT

For if God did not spare angels when they sinned, but cast them into hell and committed them to pits of darkness, reserved for judgment; and did not spare the ancient world, but preserved Noah, a preacher of righteousness, with seven others, when He brought a flood upon the world of the ungodly; and if He condemned the cities of Sodom and Gomorrah to destruction by reducing them to ashes, having made them an example to those who would live ungodly lives thereafter; and if He rescued righteous Lot, oppressed by the sensual conduct of unprincipled men (for by what he saw and heard that righteous man, while living among them, felt his righteous soul tormented day after day by their lawless deeds), (2:4–8)

Peter continues his denouncement of false teachers by referencing three well-known accounts of divine judgment from the book of Genesis. It may have been tempting for some of Peter's original readers to doubt whether or not the false teachers would really ever be punished. For the moment, they seemed to be flourishing—circulating their spiritual lies and basking in their popularity, sensuality, and wealth. So Peter reminded his readers of biblical history, noting that just as God judged faithfully in the past, so He will also uphold justice in the present.

As the apostle gives an overview of three Old Testament examples, he highlights the height of God's wrath (in the case of fallen angels), the breadth of God's wrath (in the case of the ancient world at the time of the Flood), and the depth of God's wrath (in the case of Sodom and Gomorrah). In other words, there are no creatures too lofty, too numerous, or too base to escape divine judgment—His vengeance will be meted out on all who oppose Him. And, as Peter points out in this passage, the false teachers of his day were no exception.

THE CASE OF THE FALLEN ANGELS

For if God did not spare angels when they sinned, but cast them into hell and committed them to pits of darkness, reserved for judgment; (2:4)

The short phrase **for if** introduces a conditional sentence that extends through verse 8. **If,** however, does not imply uncertainty here and is probably better rendered "since." Since **God did not spare** the **angels** of heaven **when they sinned** against Him (nor did He provide any means for their salvation), humans who pervert His truth should not expect to escape His vengeance either. Angels, like mankind (Matt. 24:45–51; 25:14–30; Luke 12:48; 16:1–8; 19:12–27; 1 Cor. 4:2), were responsible to honor God and obey His truth. Those who rebelled were sentenced to eternal punishment.

The spiritual dynamics of how and why angels **sinned** remains, in many ways, a theological mystery. The highest ranking of all the angels, Lucifer, wanted to exalt himself to a position of equality with God. As depicted in the dramatic language of Revelation 12:3–9, one-third of the angels joined Lucifer's heavenly revolt, arrogantly opposed God, and were expelled from heaven (cf. Isa. 14:12–21; Ezek. 28:12–19; Luke 10:18).

But Peter is probably not referring here to the angels who originally fell, since they were not immediately incarcerated in **hell** nor confined permanently **to pits of darkness** to await their final judgment. In fact, they are the demons who are now loose in the world, securing Satan's unholy purposes. The apostle Paul identified them when he wrote, "For our struggle is not against flesh and blood, but against the rulers, against the powers, against the world forces of this darkness, against the spiritual forces of wickedness in the heavenly places" (Eph. 6:12; cf. 2:1–2; 1 Peter 5:8). When the Lord returns, the demons (along with Satan) will be bound during Christ's millennial reign (Isa. 24:21–23; Rev. 20:1–3) and eventually cast into the lake of fire (Rev. 20:10).

Cast them into hell is actually the translation of a single word, *tartarōsas.* The verb, used only here in the New Testament, is derived from Tartarus, which in Greek mythology identified a subterranean abyss that was even lower than Hades (hell). Tartarus came to refer to the abode of the most wicked spirits, where the worst rebels and criminals received the severest divine punishment. Much like Jesus used the term *gehenna* (the name for Jerusalem's garbage dump, where fires burned continuously) to illustrate the inextinguishable torments of eternal anguish (Matt. 5:22, 29–30; 10:28; 18:9; 23:15, 33; Mark 9:43, 45, 47; Luke 12:5), Peter used a familiar word from popular Greek thought to designate hell. The pseudepigraphal book of *1 Enoch,* a well-known work to most New Testament Jews (cf. Jude 14), also mentions Tartarus (1:9). Peter must have been confident that his readers understood exactly what he meant, since he offered them no additional explanation of the term.

Further, Peter describes this demonic incarceration by saying that God **committed** the fallen angels **to pits of darkness. Committed** (*paredōken*), as in Acts 8:3 and 12:4, means to turn over for imprisonment.

Pits of darkness (cf. Matt. 8:12) is the best translation, even though some ancient manuscripts read "chains" (hence the King James translation). Whether the rendering is **pits** or "chains," the idea is the same—it refers to loss of freedom in a place of confinement, a fate demons feared (cf. Matt. 8:29; Luke 8:31). Those who were sent there were **reserved for judgment,** like guilty prisoners awaiting final sentencing and execution at the last day (cf. Rev. 20:10).

But two important questions still arise from the text: To which fallen angels does this action refer? And what did they do to deserve such severe imprisonment? What Peter does not expand on, Jude does:

> And angels who did not keep their own domain, but abandoned their proper abode, He has kept in eternal bonds under darkness for the judgment of the great day, just as Sodom and Gomorrah and the cities around them, since they in the same way as these indulged in gross immorality and went after strange flesh, are exhibited as an example in undergoing the punishment of eternal fire. (Jude 6–7)

Those demons "did not keep their own domain," meaning that they moved out of their proper sphere of existence and behavior—"their proper abode." Jude 6 is a reference to the events of Genesis 6:1–4 in which certain fallen angels possessed mortal men and then cohabited with women. The egregious transgression of those demons was a clear violation of the boundaries God had set for them. Jude 7 compares their "gross immorality" to that of Sodom and Gomorrah who "went after strange flesh" (i.e., practiced homosexuality, a perversion which God wholly condemns—Lev. 18:22; 20:13; Rom. 1:26–27; 1 Cor. 6:9). (For a complete discussion of Jude's text, see the section in chapter 11 of this volume on Jude 6–7. It should be noted that Peter also referred to those same demons in his first epistle—1 Peter 3:18–20. For an extended discussion of that passage, see John MacArthur, *1 Peter,* MacArthur New Testament Commentary [Chicago: Moody, 2004], 208–16.)

Of course, Peter's primary purpose here was not to get lost in the details of this account about fallen angels, especially since his readers were apparently already familiar with it. Instead, he used this illustration to emphasize the main thrust of his argument—namely, that God severely judges all those who oppose Him and His truth. Like those angels, rebellious false teachers will face divine wrath.

THE CASE OF THE ANCIENT WORLD

and did not spare the ancient world, but preserved Noah, a preacher of righteousness, with seven others, when He brought a flood upon the world of the ungodly; (2:5)

Not only did God judge certain fallen angels, but He also **did not spare the ancient world.** In fact, He wiped out the full breadth of earth's population by drowning all **of the ungodly** in the Flood. **The ancient world** refers to the people living at the time of the Flood, all of whom were wicked. The world was destroyed because:

> The Lord saw that the wickedness of man was great on the earth, and that every intent of the thoughts of his heart was only evil continually. The Lord was sorry that He had made man on the earth, and He was grieved in His heart. The Lord said, "I will blot out man whom I have created from the face of the land, from man to animals to creeping things and to birds of the sky; for I am sorry that I have made them." (Gen. 6:5–7)

God, however, **preserved Noah,** who was righteous, a true worshiper of God immersed in a wicked and corrupt society. Resisting the suffocating evil around him, Noah walked with God, along with his wife, his sons, and their wives, who constituted the **seven others** whom the Lord **preserved** from destruction in the ark. More than a century before the Flood actually came, God revealed to Noah His plan to send judgment:

> But Noah found favor in the eyes of the Lord. These are the records of the generations of Noah. Noah was a righteous man, blameless in his time; Noah walked with God. Noah became the father of three sons: Shem, Ham, and Japheth. Now the earth was corrupt in the sight of God, and the earth was filled with violence. God looked on the earth, and behold, it was corrupt; for all flesh had corrupted their way upon the earth. Then God said to Noah, "The end of all flesh has come before Me; for the earth is filled with violence because of them; and behold, I am about to destroy them with the earth." (Gen. 6:8–13)

While building the ark, Noah also labored as **a preacher of righteousness,** warning people of impending death and divine retribution and calling them to repent. Years earlier, Enoch had preached a similar message:

> It was also about these men that Enoch, in the seventh generation from Adam, prophesied, saying, "Behold, the Lord came with many thousands of His holy ones, to execute judgment upon all, and to convict

all the ungodly of all their ungodly deeds which they have done in an ungodly way, and of all the harsh things which ungodly sinners have spoken against Him." (Jude 14–15; see the commentary on this passage in chapter 13 of this volume)

Flood translates *kataklusmos,* from which the English *cataclysm* derives. The Genesis account, along with current geological evidence, indicates that the Flood truly was *cataclysmic* in every sense (cf. Gen. 7:10–24). Because of man's sinfulness, God destroyed every person and every land animal (except those in the ark), covering the entire planet with water—even the peaks of the highest mountains (Gen. 7:19–20). (For a detailed biblical and scientific examination of the Flood, see John C. Whitcomb, Jr., and Henry M. Morris, *The Genesis Flood* [Grand Rapids: Baker, 1961]; for a concise defense of the biblical doctrine of a world-wide flood, see Morris, *Science and the Bible,* rev. ed. [Chicago: Moody, 1986], chap. 3, "Science and the Flood.")

Ungodly (cf. 2:6; 3:7; Jude 4, 15, 18), from the Greek *asebeia,* is the one-word characterization of ancient humanity—a term that refers to a complete lack of reverence, worship, or fear of God (cf. Matt. 24:11, 24; 1 John 4:1–3; 2 John 7). The early church fathers used it to describe atheists and heretics. Like the false teachers of Peter's time, the **ungodly** of Noah's day—through their rebellious immorality—eventually brought God's judgment upon themselves.

THE CASE OF SODOM AND GOMORRAH

and if He condemned the cities of Sodom and Gomorrah to destruction by reducing them to ashes, having made them an example to those who would live ungodly lives thereafter; and if He rescued righteous Lot, oppressed by the sensual conduct of unprincipled men (for by what he saw and heard that righteous man, while living among them, felt his righteous soul tormented day after day by their lawless deeds), (2:6–8)

For his third historical illustration of divine judgment, the apostle descended to the perverted depths **of Sodom and Gomorrah.** At one time, they were the main cities of the Jordan plain or basin (Gen. 13:12; 14:8; Deut. 29:23), located in the Valley of Siddim or Salt Sea, near the southeast corner of the Dead Sea. Before the destruction of Sodom and Gomorrah, Genesis favorably describes the area as fertile—an ideal place for raising crops and animals (13:8–10).

Because of their gross sin, God **condemned** both cities **to destruction.** The judgment described in Genesis 19:1–28 was a small-scale parallel to the worldwide Flood (which occurred about 450 years earlier). Like Noah and his family, Lot and his daughters were the only inhabitants to escape. All of the other citizens **of Sodom and Gomorrah** were obliterated, this time by incineration and asphyxiation rather than drowning. Genesis 19:24–25 sums up the account like this:

> Then the Lord rained on Sodom and Gomorrah brimstone and fire from the Lord out of heaven, and He overthrew those cities, and all the valley, and all the inhabitants of the cities, and what grew on the ground.

The word rendered **destruction** (*katastrophē*, of which the English word *catastrophe* is a transliteration) indicates complete overthrow and total ruin. The devastation was so thorough that it reduced those cities to nothing more than **ashes.** (The phrase **reducing them to ashes** is described by one word in the original—*tephrōsas*—an aorist participle from a root verb that can also be translated "covered with ashes.") In fact, God's judgment was so complete that the ruins remain undiscovered, and the cities' precise location is still unknown. It is possible, but not substantiated, that they were buried under what is now mineral-dense water in the southern portion of the Dead Sea. That this **destruction** refers to more than physical death is clear from the parallel text in Jude 7, which says the people of those cities are "an example in undergoing the punishment of eternal fire." Divine judgment not only buried the people's bodies under the ashes, but it plunged their souls into eternal judgment. It is because of eternal punishment that the cities are examples, as are the angels.

Although the citizens of Sodom and Gomorrah would probably have known the message of righteousness and judgment Noah preached after the Flood (as passed on by Noah and his family), they rejected it nonetheless. Instead, they chose to live in sin and perversion, most notably homosexuality (Gen. 19:4–11). More than twenty times in Scripture these cities are used as **an example to those who would live ungodly lives thereafter** (see Matt. 10:14, 15; 11:23, 24; Luke 17:28–32). God used them and their holocaust to send an unmistakable warning to future generations of rebellious sinners—namely, that depraved people cannot pursue ungodliness and also escape God's vengeance and everlasting judgment (cf. 3:7, 10; Matt. 25:41; Rom. 1:18; 2:5, 8; Eph. 5:6; 1 Thess. 2:16; 2 Thess. 1:8; Heb. 10:26–27; Rev. 6:17).

Prior to their destruction, God revealed the wickedness of Sodom and Gomorrah to Abraham (Gen. 18:20–21; cf. 13:13). In response, the patriarch expressed his sincere concern for any righteous people who might still be living there. He implored the Lord to withhold His judgment for their sakes (Gen. 18:23–33). The Lord was willing to spare the city if as few as ten righteous inhabitants could be found. But when even that minimum could not be met, the Lord destroyed the wicked populace.

As in the previous illustration of the Flood, Peter comforted his readers by reminding them of those who escaped punishment. During the Flood, God graciously preserved Noah and his family. In this instance, during the demolition of Sodom and Gomorrah, God **rescued righteous Lot,** along with his two daughters.

Those who are familiar with the Genesis account may wonder why **Lot** is designated as **righteous** no less than three times in verses 7–8. After all, when he first appears in Scripture, Lot is described as implicitly superficial, selfish, and worldly (Gen. 13:5–13). During the events of Genesis 19, he displayed unambiguous moral weakness and incredibly poor judgment when, in place of the visiting angels, he offered his daughters to the lusting Sodomites (vv. 6–8). Later, he hesitated when the angels urged him to leave the city immediately (vv. 15–22). Even after he escaped God's wrath, he displayed shockingly sinful behavior, including drunkenness and incest (vv. 30–35).

There are, nonetheless, reasons to designate Lot as **righteous** (i.e., a believer). For instance, like his uncle Abraham (cf. Gen. 15:6; Rom. 4:3, 20–24), Lot was righteous in the sense of being a believer to whom God had credited righteousness by his faith. This did not mean that either Lot or Abraham was free from sin (see Gen. 16:1–6 for an example of Abraham's disobedience), but they were righteous in the forensic sense. God imputed His own righteousness to them because they were true believers (cf. Ps. 24:3–5; Phil. 3:9). Thus Lot, like Abraham, is an Old Testament illustration of justification.

To be sure, Lot also showed several signs of the Holy Spirit's work in his heart. For example, his reverence toward the holy angels who visited him provided a stark contrast to the perverted advances of his neighbors (Gen. 19:1–8). And, although he was initially hesitant to leave the city, he ultimately obeyed God's command and even warned his sons-in-law about the impending doom (19:14). Furthermore, when he finally left, he obediently refused to look back (cf. 19:17).

Peter, then, is pointing out that Lot was righteous in heart, as is clear from the fact that he was **oppressed by the sensual conduct of unprincipled men.** His abhorrence for the sin of those around him was a sure indicator that he was a believer (cf. Pss. 97:10; 119:7, 67–69, 77, 101, 106, 121, 123; Prov. 8:13; Rom. 12:9). At times, Lot might have been materialistic and morally weak, but he did not want any part of the **sensual conduct** that characterized Sodom's **unprincipled** culture. The term **sensual** (*aselgeia*) means "outrageous behavior," while

unprincipled (*athesmos*) denotes actions that are "unrestrained," and "without lawful standards"—violating both the conviction of conscience and the commandment of God. The blatant immorality of his fellow citizens greatly **oppressed** Lot; the Greek word (*kataponeō*) conveys the idea of exhausting someone by wearing him down and deeply troubling his soul.

The depth of Lot's dismay is found in Peter's parenthetical statement: **for by what he saw and heard that righteous man, while living among them, felt his righteous soul tormented day after day by their lawless deeds.** The word **tormented** (*basanizō*) literally means "to torture," and demonstrates the sheer excruciation Lot experienced as he was exposed to the lewdness all around him. Peter knew his readers, living in the midst of their corrupt culture, could identify with Lot's difficult position. Their own situations were equally soul-distressing as they witnessed the immoral excesses of the false teachers and their followers (cf. 2:18–20).

Like Noah and his family, Lot stood against the sin of his day and refused to follow the demonic doctrines and immoral practices that permeated ancient society. By recalling the account of God's judgment on Sodom and Gomorrah, Peter warns his readers of the doom that all of God's enemies (and, specifically, false teachers) will face. But, by highlighting the salvation of Lot, the apostle simultaneously comforts the righteous, reminding them that they have nothing to fear.

THE PATTERN OF JUDGMENT

then the Lord knows how to rescue the godly from temptation, and to keep the unrighteous under punishment for the day of judgment, and especially those who indulge the flesh in its corrupt desires and despise authority. (2:9–10*a*)

Earlier in this section (in verse 4), Peter began a lengthy conditional clause. Now, in verses 9 and 10, he provides the conclusion—*if* (or *since*) God knew whom to judge and whom to rescue in the past, **then** He certainly **knows how** to do the same in the present and the future.

Centuries before Peter's time, Scripture established God's pattern of judgment. The prophet Malachi wrote:

> Then those who feared the Lord spoke to one another, and the Lord gave attention and heard it, and a book of remembrance was written before Him for those who fear the Lord and who esteem His name. "They will be Mine," says the Lord of hosts, "on the day that I prepare My own possession, and I will spare them as a man spares his own son

> who serves him. So you will again distinguish between the righteous and the wicked, between one who serves God and one who does not serve Him. For behold, the day is coming, burning like a furnace; and all the arrogant and every evildoer will be chaff; and the day that is coming will set them ablaze," says the Lord of hosts, "so that it will leave them neither root nor branch. But for you who fear My name, the sun of righteousness will rise with healing in its wings; and you will go forth and skip about like calves from the stall. You will tread down the wicked, for they will be ashes under the soles of your feet on the day which I am preparing," says the Lord of hosts. (Mal. 3:16–4:3)

Put simply, **the Lord knows how** to judge the wicked while simultaneously preserving His own (cf. Matt. 13:36–43; 1 Thess. 4:13–18; 5:1–5).

For Peter, then, the pattern of divine judgment is clear. First, there is comfort in the fact that **the Lord knows how to rescue the godly from temptation.** God knows how to save those who belong to Him; therefore they have absolutely nothing to fear (Ps. 27:1; Prov. 1:33; John 14:27; 2 Tim. 1:7; cf. Isa. 8:12). In this context, the word rendered **temptation** (*peirasmos*, which usually conveys the concept of testing) connotes the idea of an attack with intent to destroy. (See Mark 8:11; Luke 4:12; Acts 20:19; and Rev. 3:10 for other instances where *peirasmos* is used in this same way.) Believers, then, are called to trust in the infinite wisdom and sovereign power of their divine protector (cf. Rom. 8:28, 38–39).

God not only knows how to rescue His children but how **to keep the unrighteous under punishment for the day of judgment.** He is holding them **for the day of** final reckoning while continuing their **punishment** in the meantime. **The unrighteous** are like prisoners in jail who await final sentencing and transfer to their final fate. While they wait, they continue to accumulate more guilt (cf. Rom. 2:3–6). They will then face **judgment** at the Great White Throne, the future tribunal where God condemns all the ungodly from all the ages to eternal hell, the lake of fire (Rev. 20:11–15; cf. Matt. 11:22, 24; 12:36; John 12:48; Acts 17:31).

The Lord **especially** targets **those who indulge the flesh in its corrupt desires and despise authority.** Thus Peter brings the discussion full circle, again recounting the false teachers' two primary characteristics. Like the wicked contemporaries of Noah and Lot, false teachers are slaves to sin. The Greek indicates that their lives are characterized by a continual "going after flesh in defiling lust." They are dishonest, disrespectful, and displeasing to God—actively pursuing their sensual fantasies (as mentioned earlier in 2:2; cf. Jude 6, 7) and eagerly parading their irreverent blasphemies (cf. 2:1). **Corrupt** translates *miasmou*, meaning "pollution." The English word *miasma*, meaning unpleasant and unwholesome, is derived from this term. **Authority** (*kuriotēs*) means "lordship" (cf. Eph. 1:21; Col. 1:16; Jude 8), and in this context indicates that the false teachers rejected the sovereign lordship of Jesus Christ over their lives. As discussed in verse 1, they superficially identified with Him but refused to live by His commands.

In keeping with God's unmistakable promise, divine judgment will ultimately come upon all His enemies (cf. 1 Cor. 15:25–26). The historical precedent leaves no room for doubt. As in the past, God will finally destroy any who oppose Him—including the false teachers and their followers. At the same time, however, He will rescue believers from such a terrifying end. This passage thus echoes Paul's words to the Thessalonians:

> We ought always to give thanks to God for you, brethren, as is only fitting, because your faith is greatly enlarged, and the love of each one of you toward one another grows ever greater; therefore, we ourselves speak proudly of you among the churches of God for your perseverance and faith in the midst of all your persecutions and afflictions which you endure. This is a plain indication of God's righteous judgment so that you will be considered worthy of the kingdom of God, for which indeed you are suffering. For after all it is only just for God to repay with affliction those who afflict you, and to give relief to you who are afflicted and to us as well when the Lord Jesus will be revealed from heaven with His mighty angels in flaming fire, dealing out retribution to those who do not know God and to those who do not obey the gospel of our Lord Jesus. These will pay the penalty of eternal destruction, away from the presence of the Lord and from the glory of His power, when He comes to be glorified in His saints on that day, and to be marveled at among all who have believed—for our testimony to you was believed. (2 Thess. 1:3–10)

Creatures Born to Be Killed
(2 Peter 2:10*b*–22)

7

Daring, self-willed, they do not tremble when they revile angelic majesties, whereas angels who are greater in might and power do not bring a reviling judgment against them before the Lord. But these, like unreasoning animals, born as creatures of instinct to be captured and killed, reviling where they have no knowledge, will in the destruction of those creatures also be destroyed, suffering wrong as the wages of doing wrong. They count it a pleasure to revel in the daytime. They are stains and blemishes, reveling in their deceptions, as they carouse with you, having eyes full of adultery that never cease from sin, enticing unstable souls, having a heart trained in greed, accursed children; forsaking the right way, they have gone astray, having followed the way of Balaam, the son of Beor, who loved the wages of unrighteousness; but he received a rebuke for his own transgression, for a mute donkey, speaking with a voice of a man, restrained the madness of the prophet. These are springs without water and mists driven by a storm, for whom the black darkness has been reserved. For speaking out arrogant words of vanity they entice by fleshly desires, by sensuality, those who barely escape from the ones who live in error, promising them freedom while they

themselves are slaves of corruption; for by what a man is over-come, by this he is enslaved. For if, after they have escaped the defilements of the world by the knowledge of the Lord and Savior Jesus Christ, they are again entangled in them and are overcome, the last state has become worse for them than the first. For it would be better for them not to have known the way of righteous-ness, than having known it, to turn away from the holy command-ment handed on to them. It has happened to them according to the true proverb, "A dog returns to its own vomit," and, "A sow, after washing, returns to wallowing in the mire." (2:10b–22)

Faithful shepherds protect their sheep. They work hard, day after day, to instruct, reprove, correct, and train God's people (cf. 2 Tim. 3:16–17)—leading their flocks on the path of truth (Ps. 119:105). Like the Good Shepherd Himself, they stand guard even when spiritual enemies threaten (Acts 20:28–32; cf. John 10:13–14). Cowardice is not a consideration for them; neither is compromise. After all, they have received a divine commission, to "shepherd the flock of God [until] the Chief Shepherd appears" (1 Peter 5:2, 4).

Because they love the truth and genuinely care for the health of their congregations, genuine shepherds are always leery of false teaching. They recognize the deadly nature of Satan's lies—spiritual fabrications designed to deceive, divide, and ultimately destroy God's people. That's why faithful pastors proclaim truth and expose error with such tenacity. They realize eternity is at stake.

Along these lines, the Puritan John Owen wrote:

> It is incumbent on them [pastors] to preserve the truth or doctrine of the gospel received and professed in the church, and to defend it against all opposition. This is one principal end of the ministry. . . . And the sinful neglect of this duty is that which was the cause of most of the pernicious heresies and errors that have infested and ruined the church. Those whose duty it was to preserve the doctrine of the gospel entire in the public profession of it have, many of them 'spoken perverse things, to draw away disciples after them'. Bishops, presbyters, public teachers, have been the ringleaders in heresies. Wherefore this duty, especially at this time, when the fundamental truths of the gospel are on all sides impugned, from all sorts of adversaries, is in an especial manner to be attended unto. (*Works*, ed. William Goold [Johnstone and Hunter: Edinburgh, 1850–53], XVI:81f. Cited in J. I. Packer, *A Quest for Godliness* [Wheaton, Ill.: Crossway, 1990], 64)

In other words, godly church leaders take an aggressive stand against false teachers and their doctrines. They cannot embrace or tolerate error in the name of love, nor can they simply ignore it. Instead, they are called to "refute those who contradict" (Titus 1:9).

Peter himself was a concerned pastor (1 Peter 5:1–4), responding to false teachers with rhetorical fury. In fact, many years earlier, Jesus had charged him specifically to feed God's people (John 21:15–17). Now, in penning his second epistle, Peter reserved the strongest words of divine rebuke for those who would substitute spiritual poison for the pure milk of the Word (cf. 1 Peter 2:2). His pointed description completes the portrait of false teachers begun in 2:1–3. (As the previous section did, so this one closely parallels Jude's epistle.)

In this passage, the Holy Spirit does not specifically identify the targets of Peter's criticism. The text does not even give a detailed description of the exact errors being refuted. It follows, then, that the apostle's diatribe was intended to be applied generally to false teaching in any form and at any time. Those who propagate doctrinal deception invite the highest levels of divine denunciation—condemnation that is deserved for at least five reasons: their presumption, their practices, their premium, their prophecies, and their perversion.

THEIR PRESUMPTION

Daring, self-willed, they do not tremble when they revile angelic majesties, whereas angels who are greater in might and power do not bring a reviling judgment against them before the Lord. But these, like unreasoning animals, born as creatures of instinct to be captured and killed, reviling where they have no knowledge, will in the destruction of those creatures also be destroyed, suffering wrong as the wages of doing wrong. (2:10b–13a)

Ever since Satan's initial rebellion (cf. Ezek. 28:17), pride has been the primary characteristic of God's enemies (cf. 1 Tim. 3:6). False teachers, of course, can be no exception to this. Both their words and their actions betray attitudes of self-centered arrogance and **self-willed** presumption typical of the unregenerate who are the devil's children. They are brazen and audacious, **daring** (*tolmētai*—literally "darers" or "reckless ones") to defy God in exalting themselves, no matter the consequences (e.g., 2 Chron. 32:25; Est. 3:5; Dan. 4:30; 5:20, 22–23; Acts 12:21–23). They are determined to have their own way at any cost, being stubborn and **self-willed** (*authadeis*)—a term that connotes a self-pleasing conceit and obstinacy.

To illustrate the extent of their unshakeable presumption, Peter notes that these false teachers **do not tremble when they revile**

angelic majesties. Revile (*blasphēmeō*), of which the English word *blaspheme* is a transliteration, means "to slander" or "to speak lightly or profanely of sacred things" (cf. 2 Kings 19:4, 22; Ps. 74:18; 1 Tim. 1:20; Rev. 16:10–11). And **angelic majesties** in this context refers to demons (cf. Jude 8), who are **majesties** (*doxa*, "glories") in that they possess a transcendent, supernatural being, beyond the human level (Eph. 6:12). Although these false teachers were mere mortals, who were by nature "lower than the angels" (Ps. 8:5 NKJV), they arrogantly considered themselves superior to angelic beings.

The Bible indicates that even fallen angels retain the imprint of divine majesty, a shadow of their pre-Fall glory. In this sense, they are like sinful men—who still retain the divine image (Gen. 1:26; Ps. 8:5)—and post-Fall creation—which still evidences its God-given magnificence (1 Cor. 15:40–41). Thus there remains a transcendant amount of dignity for demons, even though they are fallen. The apostle Paul implied this when he referred to demons as principalities, powers, and rulers (cf. 2 Cor. 10:3–5)—delineating at least three levels of majesty and authority within the demonic realm. Although they are certainly subservient to God, fallen angels (under the leadership of Satan) wield extensive influence and power in this world (John 12:31; cf. Eph. 2:2). A powerful demon hindered the mighty angel Gabriel for twenty-one days from doing God's work until the archangel Michael and the most powerful angels came to help him (Dan. 10:13). Yet, the false teachers of Peter's day simply mocked demons fearlessly, presuming that they (as fallen men) were somehow greater than fallen angels.

It should be recognized that many modern false prophets in the extreme sectors of the charismatic movement make their fortunes supposedly binding and flippantly damning demons, as if they had real power over them. They are actually false exorcists like the "sons of one Sceva" (Acts 19:13–16) and perfectly fit Peter's description. Pagans develop elaborate schemes to appease their demonic gods. Yet, pseudo-Christian teachers and preachers brashly declare their authority over the forces of hell.

In contrast, even righteous **angels who are greater in might and power do not bring a reviling judgment against them** (the angelic majesties of v. 10) **before the Lord.** Since there is no modifier, the term **angels** refers to the holy ones who are certainly **greater in might and power** than either fallen men or demons. But even from their exalted position, holy angels do not disrespect their fallen counterparts like the false teachers do. For example, the preeminently powerful Michael, "when he disputed with the devil and argued about the body of Moses, did not dare pronounce against him a railing judgment, but said, 'The Lord rebuke you!'" (Jude 9). Like Michael, believers should not confront Satan and his minions alone. Instead, they should seek God's intervening power against demons. Yet false teachers, by stark contrast, are so self-confident, brazen, and reckless that they did what even Michael "did not dare" to do—directly reviling angelic majesties as though they had authority over them. (For more on the struggle between Michael and Satan, see the comments on Jude 8–9 in chapter 12 of this volume.)

The reckless blasphemies of God and angels by false teachers demonstrate that they are like **unreasoning animals** (cf. Jude 10). They are comparable to beasts that have no rational capability, operating solely on self-indulgence and unthinking passion. **Animals** are **born as creatures of instinct,** meaning that their responses to stimuli are preprogrammed, having been built into their genetic makeup by God (cf. Gen. 1:30). Because they operate on instinct, animals are not rational; thus they make no intellectual contributions to society. In fact, for most of them, their primary role in the ecological system is **to be captured and killed,** thereby providing meat for other members up the food chain.

Spiritual pretenders, dishonestly presenting themselves as true teachers, exhibit an animal-like ignorance, **reviling where they have no knowledge.** They ridicule divine truth and heavenly authority, including things they do not even understand. Like animals, they make no positive contribution and would actually serve others best by being dead. Hence the end of verse 12 predicts that they **will . . . be destroyed;** they will not escape God's future wrath. When God's fire consumes the entire world and all its creatures (3:7, 12), false teachers will **also** be finally wiped out **in the destruction of those creatures.** Jude adds that false teachers' instinctive evil programs them to be destroyed (v. 10). As God's enemies, having intentionally distorted the message of His Word, they will all face eternal punishment in the lake of fire (Rev. 20:9–15).

In fact, the lake of fire is where false teachers will forever endure the fury of God's wrath, **suffering wrong as the wages of doing wrong.** (**Suffering wrong** is not the best translation, since it might be misunderstood that it is wrong for God to judge them. The Greek is *adikoumenoi,* a present middle or passive verb form best understood as meaning "to be damaged," "to be harmed," or "to be injured" [cf. Rev. 2:11].) In that way they epitomize the law of sowing and reaping: "Do not be deceived, God is not mocked; for whatever a man sows, this he will also reap" (Gal. 6:7; cf. Hos. 10:12–13). Those who dedicate themselves to false doctrine, exhibiting a presumptuous approach to spiritual things, will eternally be punished for their transgressions (cf. Jer. 8:1–2; 14:15; 29:32).

Their Practices

They count it a pleasure to revel in the daytime. They are stains and blemishes, reveling in their deceptions, as they carouse with you, having eyes full of adultery that never cease from sin, enticing unstable souls, having a heart trained in greed, accursed children; (2:13b–14)

As a general rule, sinners tend to engage in debauchery at night: "For those who sleep do their sleeping at night, and those who get drunk get drunk at night" (1 Thess. 5:7). According to historians, pagan Roman society tolerated dissipation and revelry as long as it was discreetly confined to the cover of darkness. But it frowned on and disapproved of debauchery during the daytime when it could be viewed by everyone. Because of its public nature, such behavior was considered inappropriate, even by Roman unbelievers. Nonetheless, the false teachers of Peter's day were so consumed with lust, greed, and vice that they considered **it a pleasure to revel in the daytime,** not wanting to wait until nightfall.

In light of their passion for perversion, Peter likened these spiritual charlatans to **stains and blemishes**—two terms that speak of filthy spots, defects, scabs, and things diseased. Like malignant sores, the false teachers were **reveling in their deceptions** and openly enjoying the fruit of their sin. At the same time, they deceived those under their teaching influence (Rom. 16:18; 2 Tim. 3:13; Jude 16–19; cf. Jer. 23:26; 2 Cor. 11:13; 2 Thess. 2:10) by actively promoting wickedness in the lives of their followers.

To make matters worse, the false teachers brought their lewdness into the church, purposefully choosing to **carouse with** the saints. The word translated **carouse** (*suneuōcheomai*) means "to eat together," or "entertain together," as in a public meal. Here it may refer to the church's love feast that accompanied the Lord's table (cf. comments on Jude 12a in chapter 12 of this volume). By feigning faith in Christ, the false teachers pretended to have a rightful place at the table. But in fact they were a polluting influence. Elsewhere in the New Testament, as a safeguard against such intrusions, the Holy Spirit warns believers to conduct special church meals with propriety (1 Cor. 11:20–22), to beware of false teachers who might want to infiltrate them (Matt. 7:15; cf. Acts 20:28–31; 1 Cor. 16:13), and to turn such men away (2 John 9–11).

In verse 14, Peter shifts the focus from the false teachers' public behavior to their private thoughts and actions. **Having eyes full of adultery** indicates that these spiritual frauds no longer possessed any moral self-control; they could not even look at a woman without viewing her as a potential object of their adultery or fornication (cf. Matt. 5:28).

Put simply, their lust was overpowering and insatiable—an appalling form of lasciviousness that was brimming with sinful desire.

Yet, even as menacing predators, the false teachers still gained a following within the church. As agents of Satan, they were **enticing unstable souls**—preying upon the spiritually weak (cf. James 1:6), convincing them to believe doctrinal lies, and enticing them into debauched lifestyles. The word **enticing** (*deleazō*) literally means "to catch with bait," and the apostle's word picture is unmistakable. The false teachers, like fishermen using a lure, tricked their victims to believe their deceptions. Under the guise of authentic ministry, they targeted the unsuspecting (cf. 2 Tim. 3:6–8)—the spiritually immature, undiscerning, or unbelieving. Peter knew that the only sure defense against their tactics was a strong foundation in God's Word (1 Peter 2: 1–3; cf. Eph. 4:14; 1 John 2:13).

Beyond sexual favors, the false teachers of Peter's day were also interested in accumulating wealth. The phrase **having a heart trained in greed** indicates that their immorality was always accompanied by avarice. **Trained** (*gumnazō*), from which the English word *gymnasium* is derived, is an athletic term meaning "exercise," or "discipline." As a verb, it presents a disturbing description of the false teachers. William Barclay explains:

> The picture is a terrible one. The word which is used for *trained* is the word which is used for an athlete, exercising and training himself for the games. These people have actually trained and equipped and taught their minds and hearts to concentrate on nothing but the forbidden desire. They have deliberately fought with conscience until they have destroyed it; they have deliberately wrestled with God until they have thrown God out of life; they have deliberately struggled with their finer feelings until they have strangled them; they have deliberately trained themselves to concentrate on the forbidden things. Their lives have been a dreadful battle to destroy virtue and to train themselves in the techniques of sin. (*The Letters of James and Peter*, rev. ed. [Philadelphia: Westminster, 1976], 392–93; italics in the original)

Without question, Peter understood that their actions were not accidental. Their offenses were crimes of premeditation, not momentary lapses of judgment. As masterminds of sin, the false teachers had planned their attacks and purposed their hearts toward sensual and materialistic ends.

With understandable disgust, the apostle responds with a blunt but appropriate appellation, **accursed children.** As liars and hypocrites, the false teachers epitomized those whom God has cursed to hell. Peter's phrase is a Hebraism expressing the idea that people are "children" of whatever influences most dominate their lives (cf. Gal. 3:10, 13;

Eph. 2:1–3; 1 Peter 1:14). As servants of Satan and slaves to sin, they were rightly denounced as children of hell's curse.

THEIR PREMIUM

forsaking the right way, they have gone astray, having followed the way of Balaam, the son of Beor, who loved the wages of unrighteousness; but he received a rebuke for his own transgression, for a mute donkey, speaking with a voice of a man, restrained the madness of the prophet. (2:15–16)

The dictionary defines *premium* as an inducement to doing something, or a motivator to accomplishing a task. In the case of false teachers, Peter revealed that their primary incentive was and is personal gain. Put simply, their premium was really a price tag—they were motivated by money, as has already been noted in verses 3 and 14. In order to further illustrate his point, Peter compared false teachers to the Old Testament false prophet Balaam (Num. 22–24; cf. Jude 11).

The false teachers, like Balaam before them, were **forsaking the right way. The right way** is an Old Testament metaphor indicating obedience to God's Word (Gen. 18:19; 1 Sam. 12:23; Job 8:19; Pss. 18:30; 25:9; 119:14, 33; Prov. 8:20, 22; cf. Acts 13:10). **Forsaking** describes a direct, deliberate rebellion against Scripture. By rejecting God's Word, the false teachers of Peter's day refused to walk in obedience, choosing instead to wander away in spite of the eternal consequences (cf. Jude 13). In so doing, they foolishly **followed the way of Balaam, the son of Beor.**

The story of **Balaam** is a classic example of a prophet who was motivated by financial gain. Having been hired by Balak, the king of Moab, Balaam attempted to curse the people of Israel as they wandered in the wilderness (Num. 22:1–6). Balak saw the Israelites as a military threat and hoped to defeat them with Balaam's help. Having garnered a reputation as a prophet-for-hire, Balaam was from a city along the Euphrates River where scholars have found evidence of a cult of prophets whose activities resembled Balaam's practices.

In the first half of Numbers 22, Balaam appears to be a faithful prophet (vv. 7–21). Yet, even in this passage, Balaam's stall tactics imply that he hoped to negotiate a higher payment from Balak before performing his prophetic service (v. 13). Of course, in the end, Balaam did not curse Israel but rather blessed her. Nonetheless, he was more than willing to accept Balak's riches (vv. 18, 40; 24:13) because he **loved the wages of unrighteousness** (cf. Prov. 11:18). If God had not intervened on Israel's behalf, Balaam would have willfully sinned for his own material profit (cf. Deut. 23:4–5).

Even though Balaam claimed to speak only the words of God, the Lord knew that he wanted to curse Israel in exchange for money. Because of his greed, Balaam **received a rebuke for his own transgression.** While he was riding on his **mute donkey,** the Lord miraculously caused the animal to speak (Num. 22:22–35) and **the madness of the prophet** was **restrained.** The term translated **madness** (*paraphronia*) literally means "beside one's own mind." In other words, Balaam was so greedy that he was "beside himself." His love of money had caused him to act irrationally (cf. 2 Cor. 11:23).

In addition to his greed, Balaam was also motivated by sexual immorality. When his attempt to curse Israel failed, **the prophet** tried to ruin the Hebrews through moral corruption. He used his influence to promote relationships that God had strictly forbidden (Ex. 34:12–16; Deut. 7:1–4; Josh. 23:11–13; Ezra 9:12; cf. Ex. 23:32)—namely, marriages between the Israelites and their pagan neighbors, the Moabites and Midianites (Num. 25; 31:9–20). In Numbers 31:16, Moses identifies Balaam as a primary corrupting influence: "Behold, these [pagan women] caused the sons of Israel, through the counsel of Balaam, to trespass against the Lord in the matter of Peor" (cf. Num. 25:1–3). Balaam encouraged the Israelites to practice idolatry, immorality, and intermarriage in a second attempt to destroy them—this time by assimilating them into pagan Canaanite society. The prophet's apostasy not only assaulted God's holiness, but it also threatened the very existence of His chosen people. Although Balaam knew better, he allowed fleshly impulses to guide his choices. And, as a result, he suffered the ultimate penalty of death (Num. 31:8; cf. Prov. 13:15).

THEIR PROPHECIES

These are springs without water and mists driven by a storm, for whom the black darkness has been reserved. For speaking out arrogant words of vanity they entice by fleshly desires, by sensuality, those who barely escape from the ones who live in error, promising them freedom while they themselves are slaves of corruption; for by what a man is overcome, by this he is enslaved. (2:17–19)

Three main features have always characterized the ministry style of false teachers. First, they are authoritarian (Jer. 5:31), invariably ruling over their churches in a domineering fashion (cf. 3 John 9–10), and strongly denouncing any who question their authority. To make matters worse, they almost always lack formal training or reputable ordination, operating beyond any legitimate biblical or theological accountability.

Second, false teachers minister in a man-centered way (Jer. 23:16, 26; Ezek. 13:2), pandering to what they think people want to hear and accept (cf. Isa. 30:10; 2 Tim. 4:3–4). As a result, they preach their own visions (Lam. 2:14; Ezek. 13:9; Zech. 10:2; Col. 2:18) of health, wealth, prosperity, and false peace (Jer. 6:14; 23:17; Ezek. 13:10, 16). The true teacher emphasizes God's holiness, man's sinfulness, and the desperate condition that results. But false teachers prefer messages of their own making—syrupy deceptions that appeal to the carnal appetites of their listeners.

Third, they treat the historic, Scripture-based doctrines of the church with contempt (cf. Jer. 6:16). Instead of proclaiming biblical orthodoxy, they promote their own self-styled novelties, methods, and doctrines. They purposefully distance themselves from the past, arrogantly endorsing some new-fangled approach to ministry, and often claiming private revelation from God in its defense.

To be sure, all three of these characteristics matched the false teachers of Peter's day. But the apostle was not fooled by their glamour or their gimmicks. He knew them for who they really were—**springs without water and mists driven by a storm** (cf. Jude 12*b*).

In describing the false teachers, Peter chose two metaphors that represent water, the most essential natural commodity of the arid Middle East. Due to its relative scarcity and vital importance, water provided the perfect illustration of spiritual sustenance. In fact, the Lord Jesus Christ had used this same metaphor years earlier when he promised His disciples: "If anyone is thirsty, let him come to Me and drink. He who believes in Me, as the Scripture said, 'From his innermost being will flow rivers of living water'" (John 7:37–38).

Thus, like mirages in the hot desert sand, Peter describes the false teachers as those who promise what they do not deliver. They are **springs without water,** offering the spiritually thirsty nothing more than false hopes of relief. They are also **mists driven by a storm.** In the eastern Mediterranean region, sea breezes periodically bring in mist and fog that appear to signal rain. But sometimes the atmospheric moisture stays only briefly and produces no significant rainfall. The land is left dry and parched; the inhabitants are left disappointed. Like those **mists,** false teachers are without substance and provide no life-changing refreshment (cf. Jude 12).

Peter again did not hesitate to announce the terrible judgment that awaits false teachers, **for whom the black darkness has been reserved** (cf. Jude 13). The **black darkness** mentioned here refers to hell—the place of eternal punishment where both fire (Matt. 13:42; 25:41) and darkness (Matt. 8:12; 22:13) coexist.

Despite the fact that they have no spiritual substance to offer, false teachers invariably claim great wisdom and knowledge—**speaking out arrogant words of vanity.** Through their flamboyant verbosity and high-sounding rhetoric, they fool their followers into believing that they possess deep theological scholarship, profound spiritual insight, and even direct revelations from God. With such "truths" they dazzle their victims (Jude called such men "wandering stars," v. 13), while in reality they say nothing that is truly divine and, like a meteor, fade into blackness (cf. Jude 13*b*). In today's church, these **words of vanity** (cf. 1 Tim. 1:5–6; 6:3–5; 2 Tim. 2:14–18; Titus 3:9) include the flowery vocabulary of religious ritualism, the convoluted doctrines of pseudo-Christian cults, and the academic arguments of mainstream liberalism.

As in Peter's day, contemporary false teachers use their empty, haughty speech to **entice** their listeners **by fleshly desires, by sensuality.** They do not care about bringing the truth to people's minds; instead, they target people's lusts—offering a carnal, feelings-oriented message that feeds the sensual instincts of its hearers. Often such teachers possess a personal charm and charismatic appeal that other people, especially vulnerable women, find attractive (cf. 2 Tim. 3:1–6; 4:3–4).

Individuals who follow false teachers are **those who barely escape from the ones who live in error.** In other words, they are men and women who through moral resolution are trying to better themselves. They include people who struggle with broken relationships, wrestle with emotional "felt needs" and spiritual problems, and desperately desire relief from guilt, anxiety, and stress. They are dissatisfied with the lifestyle of **the ones who live in error**—the average mass of unregenerate humanity—and seek some better way to live (cf. Mark 10:17–22) or some form of religious experience (cf. Acts 8:18–24). But that does not mean they are truly redeemed. In fact, in their dissatisfaction, loneliness, and self-betterment attempts, they are highly vulnerable to the seductive exploitations of false teachers.

In appealing to these people, false teachers promise freedom and victory while **they themselves are slaves of corruption.** Their empty guarantees include liberation, purpose, prosperity, peace, and happiness. Yet, they do not even possess those blessings themselves. In fact, they are slaves to their lust, **for by what a man is overcome, by this he is enslaved.** They are so thoroughly dominated and controlled by their sinful nature (John 8:34; Rom. 6:16) that their teaching is void of any divine power. Although they offer freedom, they are slaves to sin, utterly unable to bestow true spiritual freedom because they reject Jesus

Christ—the only One who can truly liberate the soul (John 8:31–32, 36; Rom. 8:2; Gal. 5:1; Heb. 2:14–15; cf. James 1:25).

For if, after they have escaped the defilements of the world by the knowledge of the Lord and Savior Jesus Christ, they are again entangled in them and are overcome, the last state has become worse for them than the first. For it would be better for them not to have known the way of righteousness, than having known it, to turn away from the holy commandment handed on to them. It has happened to them according to the true proverb, "A dog returns to its own vomit," and, "A sow, after washing, returns to wallowing in the mire." (2:20–22)

To be sure, the false teachers of Peter's day were outwardly religious people. They had professed faith in Jesus Christ and probably convinced the people that they knew far more about Him than they actually did. Otherwise they would not have been able to infiltrate the church so effectively.

In pursuing religion, specifically Christianity, **they** in a sense **escaped the defilements of the world. Defilements,** or "pollution," is *miasma,* a transliterated word in English that conveys the same meaning as it does in Greek: "a vaporous exhalation formerly believed to cause disease . . . an influence or atmosphere that tends to deplete or corrupt." The debauched system **of the world** produces, as it were, poisonous vapors, infectious evils, and moral pollutions in every conceivable form. Unsaved humanity is heavily contaminated by the world's immorality and vanity, and some, such as those who become false teachers, seek to escape it. They do so **by the knowledge of the Lord and Savior Jesus Christ,** finding provisional shelter in the church. Such **knowledge** is an accurate awareness *about* Christ, but it is not a saving knowledge *of* Him (Matt. 7:21–23; Heb. 6:4–6; 10:26–29). Thus, their efforts ultimately result in nothing more than temporary and superficial moral reform through religion—the religion of nominal Christianity, devoid of genuine faith and repentance.

It is evident that false teachers are not really in Christ because **they are again entangled in** the world's defilements **and are overcome.** They are not the "overcomers" the apostle John wrote about in his first epistle (1 John 5:4–5) or the book of Revelation (2:7, 11, 17, 26; 3:5, 12, 21). Since there is no real salvation for them—no grace received to overcome the power of sin (Eph. 1:7), walk by the Holy Spirit (1 Cor.

2:12–13; Eph. 2:8–10), and persevere in the faith (Phil. 2:12–13; 2 Thess. 1:11–12)—they sink back into the pollution of the world and completely reject the gospel of salvation. **This last state** is much **worse for them than the first.** After all, those who understand the truth and still turn away will face far greater judgment than those who have never heard (cf. Matt. 10:14–15; 11:22–24; Mark 6:11; Luke 12:47–48).

In light of this, **it would be better for them not to have known the way of righteousness, than having known it, to turn away from the holy commandment handed on to them** (cf. Matt. 26:24). **The way of righteousness** is the Christian faith (see the discussion of 2:2 in chapter 5 of this volume). Because of the greater condemnation they face, false teachers would be better off not hearing about Scripture and doctrine than, having contemplated it, to reject it. Their insincere consideration of the gospel gives them access to divine teaching in God's Word, **the holy commandment** (cf. Ex. 24:12; Deut. 6:1, 25; Josh. 22:5; 2 Kings 17:37; Pss. 19:8; 119:96; Prov. 6:23; Matt. 15:3; John 12:50; Rom. 7:12; 16:26; 1 John 2:7). But they ultimately renounce Christ and His saving truth. Thus, they spurn the only true way of salvation and are subsequently left without any hope of eternal life. The writer of Hebrews gives a similar warning against apostasy:

> For in the case of those who have once been enlightened and have tasted of the heavenly gift and have been made partakers of the Holy Spirit, and have tasted the good word of God and the powers of the age to come, and then have fallen away, it is impossible to renew them again to repentance, since they again crucify to themselves the Son of God and put Him to open shame. (Heb. 6:4–6; cf. Matt. 13:3–7; John 6:60–66)

Later in that letter, the writer reiterates the same truth in different words:

> For if we go on sinning willfully after receiving the knowledge of the truth, there no longer remains a sacrifice for sins, but a terrifying expectation of judgment and the fury of a fire which will consume the adversaries. Anyone who has set aside the Law of Moses dies without mercy on the testimony of two or three witnesses. How much severer punishment do you think he will deserve who has trampled under foot the Son of God, and has regarded as unclean the blood of the covenant by which he was sanctified, and has insulted the Spirit of grace? For we know Him who said, "Vengeance is Mine, I will repay." And again, "The Lord will judge His people." It is a terrifying thing to fall into the hands of the living God. (Heb. 10:26–31)

(For commentary on the Hebrews passages, see John MacArthur, *Hebrews*, MacArthur New Testament Commentary [Chicago: Moody, 1983], 142–49, 276–80.)

Apostate teachers, as Peter describes them, actually develop from within the church where, partially exhumed from the muck of society's wickedness, they hear the truth but ultimately reject it. Like Judas Iscariot, they breed in close proximity to Jesus Christ and His Word—cloaking themselves in the feigned righteousness of hypocrisy. Ultimately, they use the church solely for their own selfish purposes, like spiritual parasites, seductively seeking to drag as many as possible down with them, to the fiendish satisfaction of the hosts of Satan (cf. 1 Tim. 4:1–2).

In a final portrayal of their despicable nature, Peter described the false teachers by using graphic imagery from the animal kingdom. His first analogy of what **happened to them** is **according to the true proverb,** Proverbs 26:11, **"A dog returns to its own vomit."** The second is probably borrowed from an ancient secular adage, **"A sow, after washing, returns to wallowing in the mire."** In biblical times, dogs and swine were both contemptible animals (cf. Job 30:1; Ps. 22:16; Matt. 7:6; Luke 16:21). Dogs, for instance, were rarely kept as household pets because they were usually half-wild mongrels—often dirty, diseased, and dangerous (cf. 1 Kings 14:11; 21:19, 23–24; Isa. 56:11; Rev. 22:15). They lived on garbage and refuse, and were even willing to eat their **own vomit.** It is not surprising, then, that the Jews treated dogs with contempt and disgust. Swine similarly represented filth, being the ultimate in uncleanness to the Jews (cf. Luke 15:15–16). This was primarily because the Mosaic law declared them ceremonially unclean (Lev. 11:7; Deut. 14:8). Peter's comparison, then, is unmistakable: False teachers are the epitome of spiritual uncleanness and smut.

Contemporary Christianity, sadly, contains many people like the ones Peter describes in this passage. They have sought personal improvement and moral reformation in their quests for spiritual and religious experience. Many of them have become teachers, preachers, and self-styled prophets within the professed church. Tragically, like dirty dogs or unclean pigs, they eventually return to their old lifestyles—rejecting the only One who can truly reform them. Those who become spiritual leaders are in reality false teachers, motivated by their own selfish pursuits and sensual desires. In view of their appalling character and damning influence, Peter's warning is clear: Stay away from false teachers and expose them! Believers are to listen to the true apostles and prophets, not the false ones (3:1–2).

The Certainty of the Second Coming (2 Peter 3:1–10)

8

This is now, beloved, the second letter I am writing to you in which I am stirring up your sincere mind by way of reminder, that you should remember the words spoken beforehand by the holy prophets and the commandment of the Lord and Savior spoken by your apostles. Know this first of all, that in the last days mockers will come with their mocking, following after their own lusts, and saying, "Where is the promise of His coming? For ever since the fathers fell asleep, all continues just as it was from the beginning of creation." For when they maintain this, it escapes their notice that by the word of God the heavens existed long ago and the earth was formed out of water and by water, through which the world at that time was destroyed, being flooded with water. But by His word the present heavens and earth are being reserved for fire, kept for the day of judgment and destruction of ungodly men. But do not let this one fact escape your notice, beloved, that with the Lord one day is like a thousand years, and a thousand years like one day. The Lord is not slow about His promise, as some count slowness, but is patient toward you, not wishing for any to perish but for all to come to repentance. But the day of the Lord will come like a thief, in which the heavens

**will pass away with a roar and the elements will be destroyed
with intense heat, and the earth and its works will be burned up.**
(3:1–10)

Jesus Christ *is* coming back.

Throughout the centuries, the reality of that wonderful promise
has formed the crux of Christian expectation. It is the church's blessed
hope (Titus 2:11–14), her utmost longing (cf. Rom. 8:23), and the great climax of salvation history (Matt. 25:31–46)—a time of redemption for
believers (Eph. 4:30) and a time of judgment for God's enemies (2 Thess.
2:1–12). It also marks the inauguration of Christ's earthly kingdom (Rev.
20:6), during which the saints will reign with Him in holiness (2 Tim. 2:12;
Rev. 5:10). The hope of bodily resurrection (1 Thess. 4:13–18), spiritual
reward (cf. Matt. 25:21, 23), and a righteous world system (Isa. 9:6–7) are
all tied to Jesus' return. It is no wonder, then, that the early church found
tremendous comfort in the second coming. After all, the readers of this
epistle had already endured much persecution from outside the church
(cf. 1 Peter 4:12–14). Now they were experiencing internal turmoil from
false teachers. Thus, they longed for the return of their Savior—the Judge
who would make all things right (cf. 2 Tim. 4:7–8). As one author explains:

> The hope of Christ's coming was of paramount importance for the
> early church. In fact, its certainty was so real that first-century believers
> would greet one another with the term "maranatha," meaning "Lord,
> come quickly." Instead of being frightened by the possibility, they clung
> to it as the culmination of everything they believed. Not surprisingly,
> the New Testament reflects this intense anticipation by referencing
> Jesus' return, whether directly or indirectly, in every New Testament
> book except Philemon and 3 John. (Nathan Busenitz, *Living a Life of
> Hope* [Ulrichsville, Ohio: Barbour Books, 2003], 122)

Of course, the devil also recognizes how important this doctrine
is to the church. When Christians live in anticipation of Christ's promised
return, they demonstrate spiritual zeal and enthusiasm, recognizing that
they will soon give an account to their Master (Rom. 13:11; 1 Tim. 6:14;
2 Tim. 4:5). As the apostle John wrote, it is a purifying hope (1 John 3:3).
But, when believers forget about the second coming and begin focusing
instead on the things of this world, they become absorbed in the temporal and grow apathetic and cold toward the eternal. Satan knows that if
he can get the church to discount the importance of Christ's return, or
even completely deny its reality, he can remove a very significant source
of Christian hope and motivation. To that end the devil continually
places skeptics and false teachers within the church, men who reject,

minimize, or alter Jesus' promise. Such cynics who plague Christendom today were also around in Peter's time. (For a more detailed treatment of the Lord's coming and those who deny it, see John MacArthur, *The Second Coming* [Wheaton, Ill.: Crossway, 1999].)

In 3:1–10, Peter responds directly to the false teachers' attacks. First, he considers the fallacious arguments they made against the second coming. Second, he answers those allegations, providing counter-arguments which support Christ's return. Finally, he concludes by assuring his readers that, no matter what the heretics say, God's future judgment is certain.

THE ARGUMENTS AGAINST THE SECOND COMING

Know this first of all, that in the last days mockers will come with their mocking, following after their own lusts, and saying, "Where is the promise of His coming? For ever since the fathers fell asleep, all continues just as it was from the beginning of creation." (3:3–4)

In their brazen rejection of Christ's return, the false teachers of Peter's day began by denying the Word of God. Although they recognized **the promise of His coming** (see the discussion of vv. 1–2 below; 3:15–16; cf. Matt. 10:23; 24:29–31, 42; 25:31; Mark 8:38; Acts 1:10–11; 3:20–21; 1 Cor. 4:5; Phil. 3:20; 1 Thess. 1:10; 5:23; 2 Tim. 4:1; Titus 2:13; Heb. 9:28; 1 Peter 5:4; 1 John 2:28; Rev. 16:15), they simply discounted it as false. Instead of submitting to God's self-revelation, the false teachers flatly rejected the reality of Jesus' second coming—simultaneously, and to their own sinful satisfaction, disregarding any thought of future accountability (cf. 1 Peter 5:1–4). As a result, they ridiculed those who were righteous, flaunted their own immorality, and foolishly clung to a uniformitarian worldview. The apostle addressed each of these three factors (their ridicule, immorality, and uniformitarian worldview) for his readers as he unmasked the true motivation of the false teachers' hearts.

RIDICULE

Know this first of all, that in the last days mockers will come with their mocking, (3:3a)

Throughout church history, false teachers have commonly tried to intimidate people through contemptuous **mocking** and sarcastic ridicule. In this case, the hope of Jesus' coming bore the brunt of their derision.

Without question, the early church believed Christ's return was imminent. The apostle Paul, for example, thought it could occur even within his lifetime (cf. 1 Thess. 4:17)—a view that was probably shared by all of the disciples. As followers of Christ, they longed to be reunited with their Lord and to see His kingdom established on the earth.

But the passage of time soon threatened the church's sense of expectancy. Apparently, some of the Christians to whom Peter wrote were beginning to doubt if Jesus was even coming back at all. They worried that their hope was not as sure as they had first believed.

The false teachers, of course, were quick to capitalize on such fears—planting seeds of further doubt and nurturing apocalyptic anxiety. As a first line of defense, Peter exhorted his readers to **know this first of all.** The phrase **first of all** is not speaking about chronological sequence, but rather about first priority. Before developing his counterarguments, Peter's primary goal was to warn his readers about the false teachers' tactics—namely, that they were purposefully denying the return of Christ in order to indulge their own sinful exploits without facing consequences. (For a discussion on how Paul responded to similar concerns about Christ's return, see the exposition of 1 Thessalonians 4:13–18 and 2 Thessalonians 2:1–5 in John MacArthur, *1 & 2 Thessalonians,* MacArthur New Testament Commentary [Chicago: Moody, 2002], 123–38, 263–74).

The apostle continued with the common New Testament expression **in the last days,** a phrase that refers to the entire time between Christ's first and second comings (cf. Acts 2:17; 2 Tim. 3:1; Heb. 1:2; James 5:3; 1 Peter 1:20; 1 John 2:18; Jude 18). All throughout that long period **mockers will come,** seeking to undermine the church's confidence in Christ's return. Although Peter used the future tense form of *erchomai* (**will come**), he was not limiting the mockers' activities to some far-off future day. Instead, he was indicating the certainty of their presence within the church. There have always been those who mocked the promise of judgment or deliverance (cf. Isa. 5:18–19; Jer. 17:15; Ezek. 12:21–24; Mal. 2:17). And such blasphemies will continue until the end of redemptive history (cf. Jude 18–19).

To further emphasize his point, Peter used the repetitive expression **mockers will come with their mocking.** By their senseless ridicule, false teachers—even today—attack Christ's promise and any who believe it. Their argument is neither sound nor logical; rather it is a vicious form of intimidation that derides hope-filled Christians as silly and uninformed.

IMMORALITY

following after their own lusts, (3:3*b*)

Whether or not they admit it, immorality is the real reason that false teachers deny the second coming. The word rendered **following after** is a form of the verb *poreuomai,* which literally means "travel" or "go." It denotes a course of conduct or long-term behavior (cf. Luke 1:6; Acts 9:31; 14:16). For false teachers, their lifestyles focus on **their own lusts** and sensuality (cf. 2:10, 13–14, 18). Thus they deny Christ's return because they hate the thought of divine retribution (cf. Rom. 1:18). They want the freedom to pursue all kinds of lustful pleasures without any fear of future punishment. In the words of Michael Green:

> Anthropocentric hedonism [man-centered pleasure-seeking] always mocks at the idea of ultimate standards and a final division between saved and lost. For men who live in the world of the relative, the claim that the relative will be ended by the absolute is nothing short of ludicrous. For men who nourish a belief in human self-determination and perfectibility, the very idea that we are accountable and dependent is a bitter pill to swallow. No wonder they mocked! (*The Second Epistle of Peter and the Epistle of James* [Grand Rapids: Eerdmans, 1968], 127)

In contrast, believers embrace the fact that the Lord will return (Acts 1:10–11), that they will give account for their lives (Rom. 14:12; 2 Cor. 5:10), and that He will bestow rewards based on faithfulness (1 Cor. 3:12–15). They also believe that when Christ comes He will reveal the secret things of the heart (1 Cor. 4:5). Those who truly hope in His return have an incentive for holy living (Phil. 3:20–21; 4:1; 1 John 3:2–3) because they realize that "each one of us will give an account of himself to God" (Rom. 14:12).

UNIFORMITARIANISM

and saying, "Where is the promise of His coming? For ever since the fathers fell asleep, all continues just as it was from the beginning of creation." (3:4)

The taunting question **"Where is the promise of His coming?"** introduced a denial of the Lord's return based on a revisionist view of history. To support their misguided view, the false teachers claimed that, **"ever since the fathers fell asleep, all continues just**

as it was from the beginning of creation." Although **the fathers** could refer to the fathers of the Christian faith or to first-generation believers who had died, neither one of those meanings is likely. Rather, in keeping with other New Testament references (e.g., Rom. 9:5; Heb. 1:1), it is probably a reference to the Old Testament patriarchs (cf. Gen. 25:8–10; 35:28–29; 49:33). **Fell asleep** is a New Testament euphemism for death (John 11:11, 13; 1 Cor. 11:30; 15:51).

The heretics' argument was simple. If everything **continues just as it was from the beginning of creation** (meaning that the universe is a divinely created but closed, naturalistic system of cause and effect), then divine intervention—including the return of Christ—must be ruled out *a priori*. In modern times, that view is known as uniformitarianism. Contending that the present is the key to the past, uniformitarianism asserts that the only natural processes that have ever operated in the past are the same processes at work today. It categorically denies divine intervention throughout world history, most notably opposing both six-day creation and the global Flood.

The rise of modern uniformitarianism occurred largely because of the efforts of the nineteenth-century British lawyer and geologist Charles Lyell. His book *Principles of Geology* had a profound impact on the scientific community of his day. In fact, Lyell's uniformitarianism was a primary pillar on which Charles Darwin established his theory of evolution. (Darwin took a copy of *Principles of Geology* with him during his famous voyage on the *Beagle* to the Galapagos and other islands off the Pacific coast of South America in 1831–32.) As a result of Lyell's hypothesis, catastrophism—which had previously been the dominant view among geologists—was largely abandoned for more than a century.

In recent decades, however, there has been a resurgence of interest in catastrophism among secular geologists. It became apparent that there is far too much evidence of catastrophism in the earth's geologic features to support Lyell's tranquil, uniformitarian view. But instead of embracing the biblical account of a catastrophic six-day creation and another worldwide catastrophe—namely, Noah's Flood—the "new catastrophists" opt for countless smaller catastrophes.

To be sure, there is an element of general uniformity in the universe; it is a manifestation of God's providential care for His creation. After all, if the natural laws and universal processes did not normally function in a consistent manner, chaos would ensue. A biblical view of the universe, then, sees creation as an *open* system—in which God has ordained a uniform operation of natural causes, but also a universe in which He has intervened and still does intervene. Those who go beyond this, advocating a uniformitarianism so rigid as to preclude God's involvement in history, have foolishly deceived themselves. Like the false teachers of Peter's day, they deny the promises of Scripture (including Christ's return) on the basis of their conveniently devised worldview.

THE ARGUMENTS FOR THE SECOND COMING

This is now, beloved, the second letter I am writing to you in which I am stirring up your sincere mind by way of reminder, that you should remember the words spoken beforehand by the holy prophets and the commandment of the Lord and Savior spoken by your apostles. . . . For when they maintain this, it escapes their notice that by the word of God the heavens existed long ago and the earth was formed out of water and by water, through which the world at that time was destroyed, being flooded with water. But by His word the present heavens and earth are being reserved for fire, kept for the day of judgment and destruction of ungodly men. But do not let this one fact escape your notice, beloved, that with the Lord one day is like a thousand years, and a thousand years like one day. The Lord is not slow about His promise, as some count slowness, but is patient toward you, not wishing for any to perish but for all to come to repentance. (3:1-2, 5-9)

In refuting the blasphemous allegations presented by the false teachers, Peter relied on four primary sources—Scripture, history, eternity, and the character of God.

SCRIPTURE

This is now, beloved, the second letter I am writing to you in which I am stirring up your sincere mind by way of reminder, that you should remember the words spoken beforehand by the holy prophets and the commandment of the Lord and Savior spoken by your apostles. (3:1-2)

Peter's opening words of this section, **This is now, beloved, the second letter,** indicate that the apostle also wrote other letters to this same audience. In fact, this expression is probably an implicit reference to 1 Peter, his other canonical **letter.** The apostle's pastoral heart and genuine concern for his readers is expressed in the term **beloved** (cf. 3:8), used so frequently by the apostles Paul and John in their New Testament writings.

Peter wrote both of his inspired letters in part to remind his readers of certain basic doctrinal and spiritual truths (1:12–15; 1 Peter 1:13–16,22–25). The expression **stirring up** indicates his effort to disturb any complacency and make clear the spiritual urgency with which he warned his audience about false teachers. The apostle actively and aggressively opposed the heretics, hoping to protect his flock from menacing wolves. To do that, he had to alert the sensibilities of those to whom he wrote, revealing the truth to their **sincere mind by way of reminder.** At salvation, the Holy Spirit gives each believer a **sincere mind,** a new understanding that is purified and uncontaminated by the seductive influences of the world and the flesh (Rom. 8:9, 11, 13–16; cf. 1 Cor. 2:12; 3:16; 6:11; Eph. 1:12–14; 2 Tim. 1:7, 14). By reiterating spiritual truths that his readers already knew, the apostle armed them with renewed conviction and rebuttal against false teaching.

Peter's first reminder concerns the truth of Old Testament Scripture, **the words spoken beforehand by the holy prophets** (cf. 1:20–21). (Peter's use of the adjective **holy** provided a sharp contrast between the unrighteousness of the false prophets and the righteousness of the true ones [cf. Jude 14–15].)

Throughout the Old Testament, the **prophets** continually predict God's eschatological judgment. For example, Isaiah proclaims:

> For behold, the Lord will come in fire and His chariots like the whirlwind, to render His anger with fury, and His rebuke with flames of fire. For the Lord will execute judgment by fire and by His sword on all flesh, and those slain by the Lord will be many. (Isa. 66:15–16; cf. 13:10–13; 24:19–23; 34:1–4; 51:6)

And the prophet Malachi echoes this theme, announcing:

> "For behold, the day is coming, burning like a furnace; and all the arrogant and every evildoer will be chaff; and the day that is coming will set them ablaze," says the Lord of hosts, "so that it will leave them neither root nor branch. But for you who fear My name, the sun of righteousness will rise with healing in its wings; and you will go forth and skip about like calves from the stall. You will tread down the wicked, for they will be ashes under the soles of your feet on the day which I am preparing," says the Lord of hosts. (Mal. 4:1–3)

Thus, from Isaiah to Malachi—from the beginning of the Old Testament prophets to the end—the theme of God's final wrath (often called "the day of the Lord") is clearly heralded (cf. Ezek. 30:3; Joel 2:31; Mic. 1:3–4; Zeph. 1:14–18; 3:8; Mal. 4:5).

The commandment of the Lord and Savior spoken by the **apostles** refers to the New Testament (cf. a similar use of *entolē* [commandment] in 1 Tim. 6:14) and its subject, Jesus Christ. (Peter calls them **your apostles** in order to denote the special relationship they had with the church.) Twenty-three of the twenty-seven books in the New Testament explicitly refer to the Lord's return. Of those four that do not (Galatians, Philemon, 2 John, and 3 John), Galatians 5:5 does allude to it: "For we through the Spirit, by faith, are waiting for the hope of righteousness." And 2 John 8 speaks of the believer's future reward, a doctrine that finds its ultimate fulfillment after the second coming. In reality, then, only Philemon and 3 John are completely silent on the subject. In the two hundred sixty chapters of the New Testament, there are about three hundred instances in which Christ's apostles make reference to His second coming.

In proclaiming their great hope, the apostles were merely reflecting the promise of their Savior, "For the Son of Man is going to come in the glory of His Father with His angels, and will then repay every man according to his deeds" (Matt. 16:27; cf. 25:31; 26:64; Mark 13:3–27; Luke 12:40). The apostle Paul, for example, repeatedly confirmed his belief in Christ's glorious return (1 Cor. 4:5; 15:23–28; 1 Thess. 3:13; 2 Thess. 1:7–8, 10; 2 Tim. 4:1, 8; Titus 2:13; cf. Heb. 9:27–28)—an event that the apostle John described like this:

> And I saw heaven opened, and behold, a white horse, and He who sat on it is called Faithful and True, and in righteousness He judges and wages war. His eyes are a flame of fire, and on His head are many diadems; and He has a name written on Him which no one knows except Himself. He is clothed with a robe dipped in blood, and His name is called The Word of God. And the armies which are in heaven, clothed in fine linen, white and clean, were following Him on white horses. From His mouth comes a sharp sword, so that with it He may strike down the nations, and He will rule them with a rod of iron; and He treads the wine press of the fierce wrath of God, the Almighty. And on His robe and on His thigh He has a name written, King of Kings, and Lord of Lords." (Rev. 19:11–16; cf. 1:7; 16:15; Isa. 24:23)

From Matthew to Revelation, Jesus' return is reiterated time and time again. Peter understood the weight of this inspired apostolic testimony. As a result, he affirmed the second coming with unwavering confidence.

HISTORY

For when they maintain this, it escapes their notice that by the word of God the heavens existed long ago and the earth was

formed out of water and by water, through which the world at that time was destroyed, being flooded with water. But by His word the present heavens and earth are being reserved for fire, kept for the day of judgment and destruction of ungodly men. (3:5–7)

The New Testament writers often appealed to Old Testament history to make a point (e.g., 1 Cor. 10:1–13; Heb. 11; cf. Rom. 15:4), as did Jesus on several occasions (Luke 11:29–32; 17:26–32). Thus, it is not surprising that Peter would do the same. In this case, he appealed to Old Testament history to further defend the second coming.

When the false teachers **maintain**ed their uniformitarian view of history (see the discussion of v. 4 above), they ignored historical facts. The word translated **escapes their notice** (*lanthanō*) actually carries a more negative connotation, expressed better by the King James rendering, "willingly are ignorant of." The facts did not merely elude such mockers. Rather, those individuals had purposefully shut their eyes to the truth. They willfully ignored the historical evidence, choosing to disregard the biblical accounts of divine retribution. Because they loved their sin, wanting to live as they pleased (cf. Job 20:12–13; Pss. 36:1–4; 73:5–12; Prov. 13:19; 14:9; 16:30; 26:11; John 3:20; Rom. 1:21–32; Eph. 4:17–19; 2 Tim. 3:2–4), they made conscious decisions not to consider the final consequences (cf. Num. 15:31; Deut. 7:9–10; Job 36:12, 17; Pss. 34:16; 78:49–50; Matt. 10:28; 13:41–42, 49–50; Rom. 1:18; 1 Cor. 6:9–10; Gal. 6:8; 2 Thess. 2:8–10; Rev. 21:8, 27).

As a result of their self-induced blindness, the false teachers discounted two monumental events in history that disprove their uniformitarian views. The first is the creation when, **by the word of God,** the Lord instantly brought the universe, or **heavens,** into being (Gen. 1:1). He needed no preexisting materials (Gen. 1:1–2:1; cf. Isa. 40:28; 45:8, 12, 18; 48:13; Acts 17:24) and no long periods of time. Although God has always existed (Pss. 90:2; 102:25–27; Rom. 1:20; Rev. 16:5), creation marked the beginning of the universe in time and space. Scripture, most notably Genesis 1–2, supports a relatively recent creation and a young earth—one specially created out of nothing in six consecutive, twenty-four-hour days. The phrase **existed long ago** does not imply a creation billions of years old. Several thousand years would certainly have been sufficient for Peter's use of that phrase. Moreover, a young-earth view (in which the universe is not more than ten thousand years old) is clearly supported by the larger context of Genesis (see, for example, the genealogies in chaps. 5, 10–11).

As God created the heavens, **the earth was** divinely **formed out of water and by water.** God shaped the earth between two areas of watery mass (Gen. 1:6–9; cf. Prov. 8:27–29). On the second day of creation, He collected the upper waters into something like a vapor canopy around the entire earth, and the lower waters into underground reservoirs, rivers, lakes, and seas. Then, on the third day, He separated the land from the water, allowing dry earth to appear (Gen. 1:10). (For a complete treatment of biblical creation and many of the major issues involved, see John MacArthur, *The Battle for the Beginning* [Nashville: W Publishing, 2001].)

As Adam and Eve lived on that pre-Flood world, underneath the vapor canopy that God had created, they were shielded from the sun's harmful radiation. As a result, they lived much longer than human beings do today (cf. Gen. 5:5). Yet, despite the ideal environment they enjoyed, the spiritual climate of the pre-Flood world quickly worsened. In fact, the wickedness of their descendants grew so great that God decided to judge the world and drown all but eight of its inhabitants (Gen. 6:5–7, 11–13). Therefore **the world at that time was destroyed, being flooded with water.** Peter's reference to **world** is not primarily to the physical earth, because the planet itself was not obliterated, but rather to the sinful world order (1 John 2:15–17; cf. 1 Cor. 1:20–21; 2 Cor. 4:4; Gal. 4:3; Col. 2:8, 20; 1 Tim. 6:17; Heb. 11:7; Rev. 11:15; 18:2–20). The term **flooded** (*katakluzō*, from which the English word *cataclysm* derives) means "to flood," or "inundate," implying complete, destructive overflow.

Contrary to the objections of certain skeptics, there would have been more than enough water to cover the entire earth. In addition to the water already on the earth's surface (which even in today's post-Flood world covers nearly three-fourths of the planet), two other vast sources of water existed: subterranean reservoirs (the "fountains of the great deep" [Gen. 7:11; cf. 8:2]), and the canopy created on day two (the "waters which were above the expanse" [Gen. 1:7]). Together, those two sources provided enough water to encompass the entire globe with rain for forty days and nights (Gen. 7:12). The language of Genesis 7, where the Flood is described in detail, can be explained only if a global Flood is in view. (For additional commentary on the Flood, see notes on Genesis 7:11–8:4 in John MacArthur, ed., *The MacArthur Study Bible* [Nashville: Word, 1997], 25–27.)

The false teachers of Peter's time refused to view world history properly. Due to their self-centered hedonism, they provide a classic example of willful ignorance. Like today's revisionist historians, the false teachers deliberately denied both the creation story and the Flood—the two catastrophic events that easily disprove their uniformitarian views.

In Genesis 9:11, 15, God promised to never again destroy the earth by means of a universal flood. But that does *not* mean that He will never again enact global judgment. On the contrary, **by His word the present heavens and earth are being reserved for fire.** While the pre-Flood world system was drowned by water, the present world system will be consumed by flames (Job 21:30; Pss. 9:7; 96:13; Matt. 13:40–42; 25:32; Rom. 2:5; Heb. 9:27; 10:27). That future judgment, as with the Flood, will come **by** the power and authority of **His word.**

Scripture often associates **fire** with the final judgment. The prophet Isaiah wrote:

> For behold, the Lord will come in fire and His chariots like the whirlwind, to render His anger with fury, and His rebuke with flames of fire. For the Lord will execute judgment by fire and by His sword on all flesh, and those slain by the Lord will be many. (Isa. 66:15–16; cf. Dan. 7:9–10; Mic. 1:4; Mal. 4:1)

The New Testament also links fire with judgment. Paul told the Thessalonians:

> For after all it is only just for God to repay with affliction those who afflict you, and to give relief to you who are afflicted and to us as well when the Lord Jesus will be revealed from heaven with His mighty angels in flaming fire, dealing out retribution to those who do not know God and to those who do not obey the gospel of our Lord Jesus. (2 Thess. 1:6–8; cf. Matt. 3:10–12)

Just as the abundant presence of water facilitated the Flood, so the pervasiveness of fire makes a future inferno credible. For example, the galaxies consist of billions of burning stars. Even the earth's core contains a huge volume of molten rock that may be as hot as 12,400 degrees Fahrenheit. Only a ten-mile-thick crust separates humanity from earth's blazing interior. More significantly, the entire creation, because of its basic atomic structure, is a potential nuclear bomb. The devastating power of nuclear weapons demonstrates the destructive force God has placed within the atom. When He is ready, God will use that kind of nuclear energy in an atomic holocaust that will disintegrate the universe (see commentary on 3:10 later in this chapter and on 3:12 in the next chapter of this volume).

Peter's warning, then, is clear: God has **kept** the universe **for the day of judgment and destruction of ungodly men.** Just as in Noah's time, that final day of judgment will be for **ungodly men** and not for believers (cf. Matt. 25:41; Luke 3:17; John 5:29). The Lord will deliver His own out of the world before He unleashes His final wrath (cf. Mal. 3:16–18).

ETERNITY

But do not let this one fact escape your notice, beloved, that with the Lord one day is like a thousand years, and a thousand years like one day. (3:8)

In Psalm 90:4 Moses declared, "For a thousand years in Your sight are like yesterday when it passes by, or as a watch in the night." Peter's paraphrase from that psalm encouraged his readers to **not let this one fact escape** their **notice**—that God's perspective on time is much different from humanity's (cf. Ps. 102:12, 24–27). The amount of earthly time that passes is of no consequence from God's timeless perspective. A moment is no different from an eon, and eons pass like moments to the eternal God.

What may seem like a long time to believers, **like a thousand years,** is actually short, **like one day,** in God's sight. In context, Peter is contending that, while Christ's return may seem far off to human beings, it is imminent from God's perspective. Finite people must not confine an infinite God to their time schedule. The Lord Jesus Christ will return at the *exact* moment determined by God in eternity past. Those who foolishly demand that God operate according to their time frame ignore that He is the "High and Lofty One who inhabits eternity" (Isa. 57:15, NKJV). Similarly, those who argue that Christ will not return because He has not yet returned demonstrate the height of folly.

Beyond the general sense of **a thousand years** meaning a long time as opposed to a **day** meaning a short time, there is also here the specific indication that one thousand years actually lies between the first phase of the day of the Lord at the end of the time of tribulation (Rev. 6:17) and the last phase at the end of the millennial kingdom. At that terminus, the Lord will destroy the universe and create the new heavens and new earth (Rev. 20:1–21:1).

THE CHARACTER OF GOD

The Lord is not slow about His promise, as some count slowness, but is patient toward you, not wishing for any to perish but for all to come to repentance. (3:9)

Peter's support for the second coming culminated in an appeal to the character of God. The thrust of his argument is this: The reason Christ's return is not immediate is because God is patient with sinners. Any waiting is attributable only to God's gracious longsuffering. It is not that He is indifferent, powerless, or distracted. Instead, it is just the opposite. Because He is merciful and forbearing, He delays so that elect sinners might come to repentance (1 Peter 3:20; cf. Matt. 4:17; 9:13; Mark 6:12; Luke 15:10; Rom. 2:4; 2 Tim. 2:25; Rev. 2:5).

Despite the ridicule of the scoffers, **the Lord is not slow about His promise, as some count slowness. Slow** (*bradunō*) means "delayed," or "late," implying the idea of "loitering." None of that applies to God; His seeming slowness is not due to lack of ability, forgetfulness, or apathy. In fulfilling **His promise,** God is working everything precisely according to His perfect plan and schedule (cf. 2 Sam. 22:31; Ps. 111:5, 7–8; Isa. 25:1; Jer. 33:14; 2 Cor. 1:20). That same principle applied to Christ's first coming: "But when the fullness of the time came, God sent forth His Son, born of a woman, born under the Law" (Gal. 4:4).

Patient translates a form of the verb *makrothumeō*. It is a compound word combining "large" with "great anger." Peter used it here to show that God has a vast capacity for storing up anger and wrath before it spills over in judgment (cf. Ex. 34:6; Joel 2:13; Matt. 18:23–27; Rom. 2:4; 9:22). While that judgment is inescapable and deadly, God's merciful patience beforehand gives the chosen the opportunity for reconciliation and salvation (see 3:15). His wrath toward the individual sinner is immediately appeased whenever that person repents and believes the gospel (cf. Luke 15:7, 10; Acts 13:47–48).

You refers both to Peter's immediate readers and any who will ever come to faith in Jesus Christ (cf. John 10:16). Some have argued that **you** implies the salvation of all people. But the immediate context and comments about "the destruction of ungodly men" (v. 7) clearly limits the **you** to believers. The letter is addressed to "those who have received a faith of the same kind as ours, by the righteousness of our God and Savior, Jesus Christ.... He has granted to us His precious and magnificent promises, so that by them *you* may become partakers of the divine nature" (1:1b, 4a; emphasis added). From then on, the use of **you** is directed at believers (2:1–3; 3:2). The **you** of 3:1 are "beloved." The words of verse 8, "do not let this one fact escape *your* notice, beloved" (emphasis added), again link the **you** to the beloved. The **you** with whom the Lord is patient are therefore the same beloved ones He waits to bring to repentance.

Those who **perish**—"utterly destroyed" in eternal hell—suffer damnation because they are dead in their sins and refuse God's offer of salvation in Christ. At the same time, it is clear from Scripture that the Father takes no delight in the death of the lost: "'For I have no pleasure in the death of anyone who dies,' declares the Lord God. 'Therefore, repent and live'" (Ezek. 18:32; cf. Jer. 13:17; Matt. 23:37). In fact, God actually offers salvation to all (cf. Isa. 45:21–22; 55:1; Matt. 11:28; John 3:16; Acts 17:30; 1 Tim. 2:3–4; Rev. 22:17).

Scripture clearly states that God thoroughly hates sin (Deut. 25:16; 1 Kings 14:22; Pss. 5:4–6; 45:7; Prov. 6:16–19; 15:9; Hab. 1:13) and therefore its potential consequences for every person, including eternal punishment in hell. Yet, in order to display His own glory in wrath, God chose to save some and not to save others. As the apostle Paul explained:

> So then it does not depend on the man who wills or the man who runs, but on God who has mercy. For the Scripture says to Pharaoh, "For this very purpose I raised you up, to demonstrate My power in you, and that My name might be proclaimed throughout the whole earth." So then He has mercy on whom He desires, and He hardens whom He desires. (Rom. 9:16–18; cf. Josh. 11:20; John 1:13; 6:37, 44; Rom. 11:7)

The context indicates that **any** and **all** are limited to the elect—namely **all** those whom the Lord has chosen and will call to Himself. Put another way, Christ will not come back until every person whom God has chosen is saved. By using the term **you** (a reference to Peter's believing readers), the apostle limits **any** and **all** to the realm of elect human beings.

Of course, once all of the elect are accounted for, God's patience will run out. Having given the world as much time as He has sovereignly determined, God will pour out His wrath upon the earth. While His patience currently holds back His judgment, the time of grace that mankind now enjoys, however long it seems by human standards, will not last forever (cf. Gen. 6:3).

THE ASSURANCE OF DIVINE JUDGMENT

But the day of the Lord will come like a thief, in which the heavens will pass away with a roar and the elements will be destroyed with intense heat, and the earth and its works will be burned up. (3:10)

Based on his preceding arguments, Peter confidently asserts that the day of the Lord *will* come. No matter what the false teachers may claim, the evidence against them is overwhelming.

In Scripture **the day of the Lord** signifies the extraordinary, miraculous interventions of God in human history for the purpose of judgment, culminating in His final judgment of the wicked on earth and the destruction of the present universe. The Old Testament prophets viewed the final day of the Lord as a day of unparalleled judgment, darkness, and damnation, a day in which the Lord would completely destroy

His enemies, vindicate His name, reveal His glory, and establish His kingdom (Isa. 2:10–21; 13:6–22; Joel 1–2; Amos 5; Obad. 15; Zeph. 1:7–18; Zech. 14; Mal. 4). The New Testament writers also foresaw that day as an awesome and fearful event (2 Thess. 2:2; cf. Matt. 24:29–31). According to the book of Revelation, it will transpire in two stages: during the tribulation (Rev. 6:17) and after the millennium (Rev. 20:7–10). Afterward, God will establish the new heavens and earth (Rev. 21:1).

A deeper look into the phrase **the day of the Lord** reveals nineteen indisputable Old Testament references and four in the New Testament. The Old Testament prophets used the expression to describe both near historical judgments (Isa. 13:6–22; Ezek. 30:2–19; Joel 1:15; Amos 5:18–20; Zeph. 1:14–18) and distant eschatological judgments (Joel 2:30–32; 3:14; Zech. 14:1; Mal. 4:1, 5). Six times they call it "the day of doom" and four times "the day of vengeance." The New Testament writers name it a day of "wrath," "visitation," and "the great day of God, the Almighty" (Rev. 16:14). These are horrifying judgments from God (cf. Joel 2:30–31; 2 Thess. 1:7–10) rendered because of the world's overwhelming sinfulness.

Peter described the day of the Lord as arriving **like a thief,** meaning that it will be unexpected, without warning, and disastrous for the unprepared. The apostle Paul used the same comparison when he wrote to the Thessalonians: "For you yourselves know full well that the day of the Lord will come just like a thief in the night" (1 Thess. 5:2).

With the culmination of the final phase of the day of the Lord, **the heavens will pass away with a roar**—a universal upheaval that Jesus Himself predicted in the Olivet Discourse: "Heaven and earth will pass away" (Matt. 24:35). **Heavens** refers to the visible, physical universe of interstellar and intergalactic space. Like Christ, Peter foresaw the disintegration of the entire universe in an instant "uncreation," not by any naturalistic scenario, but solely by God's omnipotent intervention.

The term **roar** (*rhoizēdon*) is an onomatopoeia—a word that sounds like what it means. It speaks of "a rushing sound," or "a loud noise," and also connotes the whizzing, crackling sounds that objects emit as fire consumes them. On that future day, the noise from the disintegrating atoms of the universe will be deafening, unlike anything mortals have ever heard before.

As Peter continues, he expands his earlier statement from verse 7: **the elements will be destroyed with intense heat, and the earth and its works will be burned up.** The word **elements** (*stoicheia*) literally means "ones in a row," as in letters of the alphabet or numbers. When used in reference to the physical world, it describes the basic atomic components that make up the universe.

The **intense heat** will be so powerful that **the earth and its**

works will be burned up. God's power will consume everything in the material realm—the entire physical earth—with its civilizations, ecosystems, and natural resources—and the surrounding celestial universe. Yet even in the midst of that mind-boggling destruction, the Lord will protect His sheep.

At the moment, mockers may ridicule and false teachers may scoff. But their disparaging comments and outright insults are only short-lived. One day, Christ will return and God's judgment will be displayed—a fact that is guaranteed by His promise and undergirded by His power. After He returns, the entire present universe will cease to exist. It will be replaced by a completely new heaven and earth where the righteous will live with God forever (Rev. 22:5). The unrighteous, on the other hand, will face the eternal consequences of their sin (Rev. 20:10–15).

In light of all this, believers are to wait with eager expectation. After all, Jesus Christ is coming again, and His return is right on schedule.

Living in Anticipation of Christ's Return
(2 Peter 3:11–18)

9

Since all these things are to be destroyed in this way, what sort of people ought you to be in holy conduct and godliness, looking for and hastening the coming of the day of God, because of which the heavens will be destroyed by burning, and the elements will melt with intense heat! But according to His promise we are looking for new heavens and a new earth, in which righteousness dwells. Therefore, beloved, since you look for these things, be diligent to be found by Him in peace, spotless and blameless, and regard the patience of our Lord as salvation; just as also our beloved brother Paul, according to the wisdom given him, wrote to you, as also in all his letters, speaking in them of these things, in which are some things hard to understand, which the untaught and unstable distort, as they do also the rest of the Scriptures, to their own destruction. You therefore, beloved, knowing this beforehand, be on your guard so that you are not carried away by the error of unprincipled men and fall from your own steadfastness, but grow in the grace and knowledge of our Lord and Savior Jesus Christ. To Him be the glory, both now and to the day of eternity. Amen. (3:11–18)

One day—in the relatively near future—this universe will be utterly destroyed. Under the weight of God's consuming wrath, in final retribution, it will melt away in a final holocaust of unimaginable intensity.

For God's enemies, that future judgment will be an inescapable nightmare. But for God's children, it will mean the fulfillment of the Christian's hope, a dream come true, ushering in the dawn of Christ's rule on earth, followed by the creation of a new heavens and a new earth. And for God Himself, it will mark His total triumph over all who oppose Him, including the final destruction of death and the complete eradication of sin (1 Cor. 15:24–28).

This final section is Peter's exhortation to his readers to respond rightly to the Lord's return and final judgment. After all, their daily conduct needed to be consistent with their hope (cf. Rom. 15:13; Col. 1:23; Heb. 6:11; 1 John 3:3) as they considered the reality of divine recompense and the promise of eternal glory.

The phrase **since all these things are to be destroyed in this way** refers back to the previous passage (3:7–10), in which this universe's obliteration is predicted. Until everything is ultimately replaced by a glorious eternal state, Peter defines **what sort of people ought** his readers were **to be.** In English this assertion sounds like a question, but it is actually an exclamation of astonishment—a rhetorical device that does not expect a response. The phrase **what sort of people** translates the unique Greek term *potapous,* which could also be rendered "how astonishingly excellent you ought to be." In light of God's promised judgment, Peter challenged his readers to live in keeping with their Christian hope—allowing their anticipation of Christ's return to impact their daily behavior.

As aliens and pilgrims, believers are not part of the world's system (Phil. 3:20; Heb. 11:10–11, 16; 1 Peter 1:1; 1 John 2:15–17). Therefore they are to live in view of the eternal blessings they will receive when Jesus Christ is finally revealed in all His glory (cf. Matt. 5:48; Col. 3:2; 1 Peter 1:13–15). The apostle Paul, for example, exhibited that kind of attitude.

> Therefore we also have as our ambition, whether at home or absent, to be pleasing to Him. For we must all appear before the judgment seat of Christ, so that each one may be recompensed for his deeds in the body, according to what he has done, whether good or bad. (2 Cor. 5:9–10; cf. 1 Cor. 4:5*b*)

Clearly, the thought of future reward and divine accountability transformed Paul's perspective on how he lived this life. Knowing that he would one day stand before Christ, his King, powerfully motivated him to "walk in a manner worthy" (Eph. 4:1).

As Peter drew the practical implications of eschatological truth, he exhorted his readers to also live worthy lives, characterized by both **holy conduct** (external actions and behavior) and **godliness** (internal heart attitudes and reverence). The tapestry of his mandate to them—to live in light of the second coming—is woven of seven distinct threads: eternal perspective, internal peace, practical purity, faithful proclamation, doctrinal perceptiveness, spiritual progress, and continual praise.

ETERNAL PERSPECTIVE

looking for and hastening the coming of the day of God, because of which the heavens will be destroyed by burning, and the elements will melt with intense heat! But according to His promise we are looking for new heavens and a new earth, in which righteousness dwells. (3:12–13)

If believers are **looking for and hastening the coming of the day of God,** such eager anticipation precludes being worried about it or afraid of it. Instead, as Paul wrote to Titus, they will be joyfully "looking for the blessed hope and the appearing of the glory of our great God and Savior, Christ Jesus" (Titus 2:13; cf. 2 Tim. 4:8; Rev. 22:20).

Looking for expresses an attitude of expectancy, an outlook on life that watchfully waits for the Lord's arrival. Peter's use of **hastening** only strengthens that concept. Rather than fearing the world's impending demise, Christians long for it, knowing they have everything to hope for and nothing to fear from the Father who loves them (1 John 4:18). Thus, like Paul, they can readily say *maranatha,* "Lord, come!" (1 Cor. 16:22; cf. 1 John 2:28; Rev. 22:20).

The coming translates the familiar term *parousia,* which literally means "the presence." In the New Testament it does not primarily describe a place or event. Instead, the term emphasizes the personal, bodily arrival of Jesus Christ.

Some commentators equate the **day of God** with the "day of the Lord," but they are not synonymous expressions. The **day of God** refers to the eternal state when God will have permanently subdued all of His enemies (cf. Ps. 110:1; Acts 2:33–35; 1 Cor. 15:28; Phil. 2:10–11; 3:21; Heb. 10:13). However, the "day of the Lord," as discussed in the previous chapter of this volume, refers to the final, tumultuous events accompanying the last judgment of unbelievers. While Christians are certainly eager for the day of God, their attitude toward the turmoil that precedes it is more sober. The apostle John's vision experience, in which he ate the little book and found it sweet to taste but bitter to swallow (Rev. 10:9–10), dramatically illustrates those dual feelings. The little book represents the coming judgment—sweet to believers because of the **day of God,** but bitter because of the "day of the Lord."

Because of which, referring to the day of God, indicates that certain other events must first take place in order for it to occur. In preparation for that day, Peter reiterated that God will destroy the present, sin-cursed universe: **the heavens will be destroyed by burning, and the elements will melt with intense heat!** (For a discussion of Peter's similar comments in vv. 7, 10, see the commentary on those verses in the previous chapter of this volume.) There are several passages in the book of Revelation which, although describing tribulation events one thousand years earlier, offer vivid previews of the kind of power God will display at the final destruction:

> The first sounded, and there came hail and fire, mixed with blood, and they were thrown to the earth; and a third of the earth was burned up, and a third of the trees were burned up, and all the green grass was burned up. The second angel sounded, and something like a great mountain burning with fire was thrown into the sea; and a third of the sea became blood, and a third of the creatures which were in the sea and had life, died; and a third of the ships were destroyed. The third angel sounded, and a great star fell from heaven, burning like a torch, and it fell on a third of the rivers and on the springs of waters. The name of the star is called Wormwood; and a third of the waters became wormwood, and many men died from the waters, because they were made bitter. (Rev. 8:7–11)

> Then the seventh angel poured out his bowl upon the air, and a loud voice came out of the temple from the throne, saying, "It is done." And there were flashes of lightning and sounds and peals of thunder; and there was a great earthquake, such as there had not been since man came to be upon the earth, so great an earthquake was it, and so mighty. The great city was split into three parts, and the cities of the nations fell. Babylon the great was remembered before God, to give her the cup of the wine of His fierce wrath. And every island fled away, and the mountains were not found. And huge hailstones, about one hundred pounds each, came down from heaven upon men; and men blasphemed God because of the plague of the hail, because its plague was extremely severe. (16:17–21)

> For this reason in one day her plagues will come, pestilence and mourning and famine, and she will be burned up with fire; for the Lord God who judges her is strong. And the kings of the earth, who committed acts of immorality and lived sensuously with her, will weep and

lament over her when they see the smoke of her burning, standing at a distance because of the fear of her torment, saying, "Woe, woe, the great city, Babylon, the strong city! For in one hour your judgment has come." (18:8–10)

Following the final destruction of the universe, the day of God will arrive, and this corrupted world system will be forever abolished (Rom. 8:18–23; 1 John 2:16). **According to His promise,** that new day will showcase a **new heavens and a new earth,** meaning that God will create an entirely new universe (cf. Ps. 102:25–26; Isa. 65:17; 66:22).

The word rendered **new** (*kainos*) means "new in quality," "different," or "unlike anything previously known." Thus the new heavens and earth will be far more than merely new in time or chronology; they will also be new in character—a realm **in which righteousness dwells. Dwells** (*katoikeō*) means "to settle down and be at home," or "to take up permanent, comfortable residence." In God's new order, righteousness will enjoy a permanent, perfect existence. The apostle John further described the wonder of that new universe:

> Then I saw a new heaven and a new earth; for the first heaven and the first earth passed away, and there is no longer any sea. And I saw the holy city, new Jerusalem, coming down out of heaven from God, made ready as a bride adorned for her husband. And I heard a loud voice from the throne, saying, "Behold, the tabernacle of God is among men, and He will dwell among them, and they shall be His people, and God Himself will be among them, and He will wipe away every tear from their eyes; and there will no longer be any death; there will no longer be any mourning, or crying, or pain; the first things have passed away." . . . I saw no temple in it, for the Lord God the Almighty and the Lamb are its temple. And the city has no need of the sun or of the moon to shine on it, for the glory of God has illumined it, and its lamp is the Lamb. The nations will walk by its light, and the kings of the earth will bring their glory into it. In the daytime (for there will be no night there) its gates will never be closed; and they will bring the glory and the honor of the nations into it; and nothing unclean, and no one who practices abomination and lying, shall ever come into it, but only those whose names are written in the Lamb's book of life. (Rev. 21:1–4, 22–27)

On the basis of all that God has in store for them, believers ought to live in constant expectation—always looking for Christ's return and continually viewing everything in this life in light of their eternal destiny.

INTERNAL PEACE

Therefore, beloved, since you look for these things, be diligent to be found by Him in peace, (3:14*a*)

As those who **look for these things**—the day of God, the new heavens and earth, the eternal state, and the glorious everlasting kingdom—faithful believers are motivated to live in a way that reflects their eternal perspective. This requires them to **be diligent** (Ps. 34:14; 2 Cor. 13:11; 2 Tim. 2:22; James 3:18) so that when Christ returns they will **be found by Him in peace.** The phrase **to be found** is a sobering reminder that no one will be able to hide from Christ when He returns. He will overlook nothing, but "will both bring to light the things hidden in the darkness and disclose the motives of men's hearts" (1 Cor. 4:5; cf. 2 Cor. 5:9–10).

Peace (*eirēnē*) could refer to a saving relationship with God and becoming at peace with Him (cf. Rom. 5:1; Eph. 2:14). But the apostle addressed his readers as **beloved,** indicating that they were already Christians (cf. Rom. 1:7; 12:19; 1 Cor. 4:14; 15:58; Eph. 5:1; Col. 3:12; 2 Thess. 2:13; James 2:5; 1 John 3:2; Jude 1). **Peace** could also apply to unsaved but professing people in the church. Perhaps Peter was exhorting them to be diligent to pursue true salvation's peace, so that when Christ appears, He will find them genuinely saved. But that is probably just a secondary understanding of the expression, as is the idea of being at peace with other believers.

In this context, **peace** primarily refers to the true peace of mind that accompanies a confident faith in the Lord. It is an echo of Paul's admonition to the Philippians: "Be anxious for nothing, but in everything by prayer and supplication with thanksgiving let your requests be made known to God. And the peace of God, which surpasses all comprehension, will guard your hearts and your minds in Christ Jesus" (Phil. 4:6–7; cf. John 16:33; Rom. 14:17; 15:13; Col. 3:15; 1 Peter 5:14). Peter is speaking about the kind of peace that banishes both earthly worries and cosmic fears—a peace that comes from knowing for certain that one's sins are forgiven. No matter how terrible things become as human history moves toward final destruction, believers who live in hope have the settled peace sustained by what the Lord has planned for those who love Him (1 Cor. 2:9).

PRACTICAL PURITY

spotless and blameless, (3:14*b*)

In sharp contrast to the false teachers, who were "stains and blemishes" (2:13), Peter exhorted his readers to be **spotless and blameless. Spotless** can denote Christian character, the kind of people believers really are; and **blameless** denotes Christian reputation, the kind of righteous and virtuous people others perceive them to be—because they are.

Obviously, within the church there are those whose lives are neither **blameless** nor **spotless.** Such people, characterized by sinful lifestyles, may or may not be Christians (Matt. 13:20–22; Gal. 5:19–21; Eph. 5:5; 1 John 1:6, 8, 10; 2:9–11; 3:10–12; cf. John 8:34; Rom. 6:16).

There are some who are neither, and others who publicly appear **blameless,** but whose private lives are actually far from **spotless.** Like modern-day Pharisees, they work hard on looking good, but fail to truly cultivate a heart of righteousness (cf. Matt. 15:7–8; 23:25, 27). Although outwardly they maintain an honorable reputation, they do so only by hypocritically hiding their unrepented sin.

In contrast, Peter exhorted his readers to be both **spotless** *and* **blameless.** As genuine believers, he commanded them to manifest the highest levels of integrity and personal holiness (Pss. 15:1–5; 24:3–4; 37:18; 119:1; Prov. 11:3, 5; Mic. 6:8; John 14:23; Acts 24:16; Eph. 1:4; Phil. 2:15; 4:8; 1 Tim. 3:9; 1 John 2:3–6; 3:1–3; Jude 24; cf. Gen. 6:9; Num. 14:24; Ezra 7:10; Job 1:1). When the watching world observes their godly behavior, the **blameless** reputation of such Christians serves as an essential testimony to the transforming hope in the gospel.

For believers, then, the promise of Christ's return serves as a powerful incentive for holy living. After all, future accountability and heavenly reward are compelling motivations, encouraging believers to continually forsake sin and diligently practice the means of grace (such as prayer and praise—Phil. 4:6, Scripture intake—James 1:21–23; 1 Peter 2:2, worship—John 4:23–24, the Lord's Table—1 Cor. 11:23–28, and fellowship—Heb. 10:25).

FAITHFUL PROCLAMATION

and regard the patience of our Lord as salvation; (3:15*a*)

Without question, Peter wanted his audience to wait eagerly for Christ's return. At the same time, he did not want them to grow idle or detach themselves from society, being so consumed with thoughts of the future that they forgot about their compelling spiritual responsibilities in the present. God's judgment had not yet come; His wrath had not yet been poured out. There was still time to proclaim the good news to the

lost. Thus, Peter reminded his readers to continue in the ministry of reconciliation (2 Cor. 5:18–20), seeking to reach others with the life-giving
truth of the gospel.

As noted in 3:8–9 (see the discussion of those verses in the previous chapter of this volume), the **Lord** delays His return in order to save
the remainder of His elect. Thus, Christians should **regard** God's
patience with joy, knowing that He is daily adding to His family until it is
complete.

In the parable of the prodigal son (Luke 15:11–32), Jesus effectively illustrated the reality of God's merciful patience toward sinners.
The story tells of a rebellious son who abandoned his family for a life of
immorality and dissipation. For a long time he wasted his opportunity,
passing up the privilege to serve his father. But one day he came to his
senses, repented of his sinful lifestyle, and returned home. Instead of
being rejected or disowned by his father—or received reluctantly—the
father embraced the son with love and compassion. That father pictures
God who responds to penitent sinners with mercy and grace—lavishly,
joyously, and generously poured out on those who repent and come to
Him in faith. And all heaven rejoices, as described by the feast the father
had in honor of his son.

When Christians anticipate the day of God, which for them will
mean eternal blessing, they should also remember the day of the Lord,
which for the lost will mean eternal punishment. With that in mind, the
opportunity of God's current patience should only heighten the church's
evangelistic zeal (cf. Phil. 2:15; Col. 4:6; 2 Tim. 4:5).

DOCTRINAL PERCEPTIVENESS

**just as also our beloved brother Paul, according to the wisdom
given him, wrote to you, as also in all his letters, speaking in them
of these things, in which are some things hard to understand,
which the untaught and unstable distort, as they do also the rest
of the Scriptures, to their own destruction. You therefore,
beloved, knowing this beforehand, be on your guard so that you
are not carried away by the error of unprincipled men and fall
from your own steadfastness,** (3:15b–17)

With the phrase **just as also,** Peter referenced similar warnings
that the apostle Paul had given about false teaching.

Peter graciously spoke of his fellow apostle as **our beloved
brother Paul,** underscoring their common life and mission. As the two
foremost leaders of the early church, Peter and Paul were certainly well-

aware of each other's ministry. In fact, both had been present at the pivotal Jerusalem Council (Acts 15:6–21), and both had ministered with Silas (cf. Acts 15:40 with 1 Peter 5:12). More than twenty years earlier, Peter had even been confronted by Paul when he wrongly refused to eat with Gentile Christians (Gal. 2:11–21; cf. vv. 8–9; 1 Cor. 1:12; 3:22). As a primary spokesman for the early church, Peter was undoubtedly embarrassed by Paul's public admonition. Nevertheless, he graciously accepted the rebuke and responded with repentance. His respect for Paul was undiminished.

Here he appeals to Paul's inspired letters for support—reminding his readers to reject the false teachers and remember what Paul **wrote to** them, **according to the wisdom given him.** Interestingly, Peter does not specify a particular Pauline letter or letters. Instead, he gives a general endorsement for Paul's inspired writings, demonstrating the divine origin of the revelation given to Paul.

It is safe to assume that Peter sent this letter to the same regions of Asia Minor as his first epistle (cf. 1 Peter 1:1; 2 Peter 3:1). If so, his readers were most likely familiar with several of Paul's letters—since Paul wrote many of his letters to that same area (e.g., Galatians, Ephesians, Colossians). So Peter's reference to **all** of Paul's **letters** suggests Peter's audience was familiar with much of Paul's correspondence. Because Paul was **speaking in** his letters **of these** same **things** (namely, eschatological events), it makes sense that Peter would cite Paul's works here.

However, in Paul's writings about the day of the Lord, the return of Christ, and the glories of eternity, Peter acknowledged there **are some things hard to understand,** such as the rapture of the church (1 Thess. 4:15–17), the coming man of sin (2 Thess. 2:1–4), the return of Christ in judgment (1 Thess. 5:1–11; 2 Thess. 1:3–10), and the glories of heaven (2 Cor. 5:1; 12:2–4). The word rendered **hard to understand** (*dusnoētos*) carries the additional connotation of "difficult to interpret." In using this term, Peter was not implying that Paul's teachings are impossible to understand. He is simply recognizing that some are more complex than others, especially prophetic revelation (cf. 1 Peter 1:1–12).

Those complexities opened the door for **the untaught and unstable**—namely, the false teachers—to **distort** what Paul taught about the future. **Untaught** denotes a lack of information, and **unstable** a vacillating spiritual character. **Distort** speaks of wrenching someone's body on a torture rack. The term vividly pictures how the false teachers manipulated certain prophetic issues, twisting them to confuse and deceive the undiscerning. Such distortion often continues today regarding prophetic revelation.

Not surprisingly, the false teachers did not stop with prophecy, but also distorted **the rest of the Scriptures,** including the biblical teaching on God's law, repentance, justification by faith, and sanctification. The fact that Peter placed Paul's writings on a par with the **rest of the Scriptures** clearly affirms that Paul wrote divinely inspired truth (cf. 1:20–21; 1 Thess. 2:13; 2 Tim. 3:16–17). The New Testament writers were aware that they were writing the Word of God, as surely as the Old Testament prophets were. The word translated **Scriptures** is *graphas,* from the verb *graphō* ("to write") that occurs about one hundred eighty times in the New Testament, of which half refer to the Bible, "the written word." The noun *graphē* is used about fifty times, exclusively of Scripture and inclusive of the Old Testament (e.g., Mark 12:10) and the New Testament, as this reference makes clear (cf. 1 Cor. 15:3).

By distorting **the Scriptures,** the false teachers were simultaneously securing **their own destruction** (cf. 2:1, 3–12; 3:7; Jude 10, 13; Rev. 22:18–19), as well as the spiritual demise of their followers. That's why Peter warns his **beloved** readers **beforehand,** so that they might **be on** their **guard** against **the error of** such **unprincipled men** (Phil. 3:2; 1 Tim. 4:1–7; 6:20–21; 2 Tim. 2:15–19; Titus 1:10–16; 3:10). **Unprincipled** (*athesmōn*) is literally "without law or custom," and came to mean "morally corrupt"—the essential character trait of spiritual deceivers.

In keeping with Peter's warning, believers must **not** allow themselves to be **carried away** by the unscriptural lies of false teachers (cf. 1 Tim. 1:18–19). Rather, they must be alert and discerning lest they **fall from** their **own steadfastness. Steadfastness** (*stērigmos*) indicates firmness, or firm footing; it is the very opposite of being unstable. Peter's concern was not that his readers would fall from salvation, but that they might slip from doctrinal stability and lose their confidence in the truth (cf. 1 Cor. 16:13; Eph. 4:14; 1 Thess. 5:21). For this reason, the apostle urged them to be spiritually perceptive, or discerning, so that their eternal reward would not be diminished (2 John 8).

SPIRITUAL PROGRESS

but grow in the grace and knowledge of our Lord and Savior Jesus Christ. (3:18*a*)

Instead of falling prey to the schemes of false teachers, Peter encouraged his readers to pursue Christlikeness and spiritual growth—a goal that every believer should have. The apostle Paul gave similar instruction to the Ephesians.

> We are no longer to be children, tossed here and there by waves and carried about by every wind of doctrine, by the trickery of men, by craftiness in deceitful scheming; but speaking the truth in love, we are

to grow up in all aspects into Him who is the head, even Christ, from whom the whole body, being fitted and held together by what every joint supplies, according to the proper working of each individual part, causes the growth of the body for the building up of itself in love. (Eph. 4:14–16)

Grow (*auxanō*) means "to advance, or increase in the sphere of." We are to grow in **grace** through the **knowledge of** the **Lord and Savior Jesus Christ.** Because of His **grace,** God forgives the sins of His children (Rom. 3:25; Eph. 1:7; 2:5, 8; cf. Acts 15:11). They in turn feed on Scripture (Acts 17:11; 2 Tim. 2:15) and commune with Christ (John 15:1–11), thereby increasing in their **knowledge of** Him (Eph. 4:13; Col. 1:9–10; 3:10). In his earlier letter, Peter had commented on this very process, exhorting his readers: "Like newborn babies, long for the pure milk of the word, so that by it you may grow in respect to salvation" (1 Peter 2:2). As their knowledge and maturity increase, Christians are better prepared to fend off destructive doctrines and spiritual deceptions.

It is crucial to note that Peter designated Jesus as both **Lord and Savior.** Pursuing a deeper understanding of the fullness of Christ's person, both in His saving work and His lordship (Rom. 5:1–5; Eph. 4:15–16; Phil. 2:12–14; 3:10, 12–14), will provide believers with the doctrinal stability they need to avoid being misled.

CONTINUAL PRAISE

To Him be the glory, both now and to the day of eternity. Amen. (3:18*b*)

Peter closed the letter with a doxology, calling believers to worship and adore God (cf. Pss. 95:1–6; 105:1–5; 113:1–6; 148; 150; Rom. 11:36; 1 Cor. 10:31; 2 Cor. 1:20; Eph. 1:12; 3:20–21; 1 Tim. 1:17; Jude 25). They are to give **Him** all **the glory, both now,** in the present, and in **eternity.**

Clearly the pronoun **Him** refers back to Christ and is a sure affirmation of His deity and equality with God. After all, the Old Testament declares that divine **glory** belongs to God alone: "I am the Lord, that is My name; I will not give My glory to another, nor My praise to graven images" (Isa. 42:8; cf. 48:11; Deut. 5:24; 28:58; Neh. 9:5; Pss. 93:1–2; 104:31; 138:5; Ezek. 11:23). Yet various places in the Gospels attribute that same glory to Jesus Christ: "And the Word became flesh, and dwelt among us, and we saw His glory, glory as of the only begotten from the Father, full of grace and truth" (John 1:14; cf. Matt. 16:27; 25:31; John 17:24). The only possible conclusion, then, is that Christ is worthy of the Father's glory *because* He Himself is God (cf. John 5:23; Rev. 1:5–6). Peter began this epistle with an affirmation of Christ's deity in 1:1, and he now ends with the same.

Having reassured his readers of the certainty of Christ's return (in 3:1–10), Peter concluded with an exhortation to live this life in light of that reality (in vv. 11–18). Accordingly, he echoed one of the New Testament's foremost themes. In the words of the apostle Paul:

> Therefore if you have been raised up with Christ, keep seeking the things above, where Christ is, seated at the right hand of God. Set your mind on the things above, not on the things that are on earth. For you have died and your life is hidden with Christ in God. When Christ, who is our life, is revealed, then you also will be revealed with Him in glory. (Col. 3:1–4)

Introduction to Jude

Solomon's admonition "Buy truth, and do not sell it" (Prov. 23:23) reflects the fact that truth is a precious commodity in Scripture. After all, God is the "God of truth" (Ps. 31:5; Isa. 65:16), having magnified His word which is truth (Ps. 119:160; 138:2; John 17:17). The Lord Jesus Christ, God in human flesh, is "full of grace and truth" (John 1:14; cf. v. 17), being Himself "the way, and the truth, and the life" (John 14:6; cf. Eph. 4:21). The Holy Spirit is the "Spirit of truth" (John 14:17; 15:26; 16:13; 1 John 5:6), sealing the salvation of those who embrace "the message of truth" (Eph. 1:13). And the church is the "pillar and support of the truth" (1 Tim. 3:15), protecting and proclaiming the truth of the gospel (cf. Col. 1:5). In fact, it is by believing the truth that people are set free from sin and death (John 8:32).

Although God's people sometimes forget the importance of the truth, Satan never does. Ever since the fall, the father of lies (cf. John 8:44) has done everything in his power to destroy, hide, and twist the truth—constantly attempting to replace it with falsehood and deception. Ironically, his deadliest attacks do not come from those who openly reject the truth, but rather from those who profess to know and believe it, but lie. Satan's most effective agents, like spiritual terrorists, secretly infiltrate the church where they pass themselves off as genuine shepherds and leaders. In reality, however, they are imposters and defectors, apostates who claim to know Christ, but in fact reject Him. They verbally affirm their knowledge of His Word, but their actions indicate that they are actually enemies of the truth.

Like Simon Magus (Acts 8:9–24), Hymenaeus (1 Tim. 1:20; 2 Tim. 2:17), Alexander (1 Tim. 1:20; cf. 2 Tim. 4:14), and Diotrephes (3 John 9), these spiritual Benedict Arnolds "are slaves, not of our Lord Christ but of their own appetites; and by their smooth and flattering speech they deceive the hearts of the unsuspecting" (Rom. 16:18). "Such men are false apostles, deceitful workers, disguising themselves as apostles of Christ" (2 Cor. 11:13), "men of depraved mind and deprived of the truth" (1 Tim. 6:5). They must be vigorously opposed and rooted out, lest they entice unstable souls and lead them to destruction (cf. 2 Peter 2:14).

The New Testament repeatedly warns of the danger that apostate false teachers pose to the church. Both Jesus (Matt. 7:15) and Paul (Acts 20:29) likened their deceptive savagery to the attacks of vicious wolves. "Many false prophets will arise," Jesus warned, "and will mislead many" (Matt. 24:11). Paul cautioned Timothy, "But the Spirit explicitly says that in later times some will fall away from the faith, paying attention to deceitful spirits and doctrines of demons" (1 Tim. 4:1). Peter and John also warned of these spiritual pretenders (2 Peter 2, 3; 1 John 4:1–3; 2 John 7; Rev. 2:14–15, 20–24), as did Jude in his brief one-chapter epistle.

Jude's concise letter is a forceful condemnation of the false teachers who were infiltrating the church in his day, and, by extension, all who were yet to come. In our postmodern culture, in which truth is considered relative and tolerance is prized above all else, Jude's eloquent plea for doctrinal purity is particularly applicable. As Thomas R. Schreiner notes:

> [Jude's] message of judgment is especially relevant to people today, for our churches are prone to sentimentality, suffer from moral breakdown, and too often fail to pronounce a definitive word of judgment because of an inadequate definition of love. Jude's letter reminds us that errant teaching and dissolute living have dire consequences. (*1, 2 Peter, Jude,* The New American Commentary [Nashville: Broadman & Holman, 2003], 403–4)

In the end, failure to heed Jude's message results in compromising the very "faith which was once for all handed down to the saints" (v. 3).

EXTERNAL ATTESTATION

The external evidence for the existence and authenticity of Jude is more complete than it is for 2 Peter. There are even possible allusions to it in the Apostolic Fathers (*The Didache,* Clement's *Epistle to the Corinthians, The Epistle of Barnabas, The Shepherd of Hermas,* and Polycarp's *Epistle to the Philippians*), but they are too vague to be conclusive. By the late second century, however, the evidence is undeniable. For example, the Muratorian Canon (a late second-century list of New Testament books) includes Jude as canonical. At about that same time, the Christian philosopher Athenagoras reflected an awareness of Jude's epistle in his defense of Christianity (which he addressed to Emperor Marcus Aurelius). Theophilus of Antioch, a contemporary of Athenagoras, was also familiar with the letter.

Later in the second century or early in the third, Tertullian referred to the epistle as Scripture and Jude as its author. At about that same time, Clement of Alexandria wrote a commentary on the Scriptures, including Jude (cf. the discussion in the Introduction to 2 Peter in this volume). Clement's student, Origen, acknowledged that some in his day had doubts about Jude's authenticity. Origen, however, did not share those doubts. Instead, he quoted Jude frequently. The third-century Bodmer papyrus P[72] also contains Jude, indicating that the third-century church affirmed it to be part of the canon.

In the fourth century, Eusebius included Jude among the books whose authenticity was questioned by some (he did the same with 2 Peter). He did not, however, list it as one of the spurious books. Eusebius also acknowledged that Jude was accepted by many in the church. Later in the fourth century, Didymus the Blind (who headed the Christian training school at Alexandria) defended Jude's authenticity against its detractors. Those who questioned the epistle primarily did so because it quotes from the Jewish apocrypha. Nonetheless, the book was commonly accepted by the fourth-century church—as evidenced by the testimonies of Athanasius, the Council of Laodicea, Cyril of Jerusalem, Gregory of Nazianzus, Epiphanius, and Jerome (each of whom regarded Jude as canonical).

AUTHOR

The New Testament lists eight men named Judas ("Jude" is an English form of the Greek word "Judas," which translates the Hebrew name "Judah"). The name was extremely popular, both because of Judah, the founder of the tribe of Judah, and because of Judas, the hero of the Maccabean revolt against the Greek ruler Antiochus Epiphanes in the second century B.C. Of the eight mentioned in the New Testament, only two are associated with a man named James (v. 1) and hence plausible candidates to have written this epistle: the apostle Jude, and Jude the half brother of the Lord. The apostle Jude can be ruled out, since he was the *son,* not the *brother* of a man named James (Luke 6:16; Acts 1:13; the KJV translation "Judas the brother of James" in those two verses is incorrect [the NASB correctly renders the same Greek construction "James the son of Alphaeus" in keeping with normal Greek usage]). Further, if Judas the son of James were the author, he would have identified himself as an apostle, since he was one. The writer of Jude, however, distinguished himself *from* the apostles (v. 17).

The James with whom Jude identified himself was the Lord's brother (Gal. 1:19), the head of the Jerusalem church and author of the epistle of James. After the martyrdom of the apostle James (Acts 12:2) there was no other James in the early church who could be referred to simply by name without further qualification. Thus Jude, like James, was one of the half brothers of Jesus (Matt. 13:55). Jude is the only New Testament writer who identifies himself by family relationship.

Ironically, the man who penned the sharpest condemnation of apostates in Scripture shares the same name as the most notorious of all apostates, Judas Iscariot. That may help explain why nearly all modern English translations use "Jude" instead of "Judas" in this epistle.

Jude's deep humility is reflected in the fact that he, like his brother James (James 1:1), referred to himself as a "bond-servant of Jesus Christ" (v. 1) rather than "the brother of Jesus." Like his other brothers (including James), Jude did not believe in the deity and messiahship of Jesus until after the Resurrection (John 7:5; Acts 1:14; cf. 1 Cor. 15:7, where "James" may be the Lord's half brother). After the resurrection, Jesus' relationships with His siblings changed from brother to Lord and Messiah (cf. Mark 3:32–35; John 2:4).

Little is known about Jude apart from this epistle. According to 1 Corinthians 9:5 he was married and had an itinerant ministry as an evangelist. Church history relates the story (possibly legendary) of how Jude's grandsons were brought before the Roman emperor Domitian. The emperor questioned their loyalty because they were descendants of the Davidic royal line. But upon learning that they were simple farmers, the emperor contemptuously dismissed them (Eusebius *Ecclesiastical History,* 3.19–20). Apart from that account, tradition is silent regarding Jude.

Some critics deny that Jude the brother of James wrote this epistle, claiming there is internal evidence that the book dates from after his lifetime. But that is not the case (see the discussion under "Date and Place of Writing" below). It is highly unlikely that a forger would write a book impersonating a relatively unknown figure such as Jude; pseudepigraphic works were attributed to well-known apostles, such as Peter or Paul. Nor would a forger pretending to be Jude have failed to identify himself as the Lord's brother.

Other unbelieving critics insist that the Greek of the epistle is too good for a simple Galilean peasant to have composed it. But as noted in the Introduction to 2 Peter, Galilee was near the predominantly Gentile region known as the Decapolis, which was east and south of the Sea of Galilee. There is also evidence that Greek was commonly spoken throughout Palestine in the first century (cf. Robert L. Thomas and Stanley N. Gundry, "The Languages Jesus Spoke," in *A Harmony of the Gospels* [Chicago: Moody, 1978], 309–12). Thus, dogmatic presumptions regarding Jude's competency in Greek (or lack thereof) are simply unwarranted. It is also possible that Jude worked with an amanuensis, as Peter did when he wrote 1 Peter (1 Peter 5:12).

Still others, especially in the early church, questioned Jude's use of apocryphal material (*1 Enoch* and possibly the *Assumption of Moses*). But the mere fact that Jude cited those works does not imply that he endorsed everything in them. Paul quoted Greek poets (Acts 17:28; 1 Cor. 15:33; Titus 1:12) and alluded to extrabiblical Jewish tradition (1 Cor. 10:4; 2 Tim. 3:8). Yet he obviously did not endorse everything in those works; neither did he consider them to be inspired Scripture. Jude, like Paul, cited the familiar apocryphal works by way of illustration. There is no indication that he regarded them as divinely inspired.

DATE AND PLACE OF WRITING

There is nothing in the epistle itself that indicates when it was written. Those who deny that Jude wrote it usually date it in the second century. In support of that late date, they argue that Jude 17 speaks of the apostolic age as long past. They also argue that the false teachers described in the epistle were second-century Gnostics. But Jude 17 merely suggests that most of the apostles (perhaps all except John) were dead; it says nothing about how long ago they had died. In fact, verse 18 implies that Jude's readers had heard some of the apostles preach, so they could not have been dead very long. Nor were the false teachers of Jude's day second-century Gnostics (see the discussion under "Occasion" below). A second-century date is also difficult to harmonize with the early attestation to Jude in the writings of the church fathers (see "External Attestation" above).

Others place Jude in the apostolic age (i.e., before the deaths of Peter and Paul), possibly as early as the midfifties of the first century. But since Jude was probably written after 2 Peter (see "The Relation of Jude to 2 Peter" below), it was not likely to have been written before Peter's death (see "Date, Place of Writing, and Destination" in the Introduction to 2 Peter in this volume). Since Jude does not use the destruction of

Jerusalem (A.D. 70) as an illustration of God's judgment of the ungodly, he probably wrote his epistle before that event. The most likely date for Jude, then, is the period between Peter's death and the destruction of Jerusalem (c. A.D. 68–70).

It is not known where Jude was when he penned this epistle. Since his brother James headed the Jerusalem church, it is possible that though Jude traveled in his ministry, Jerusalem was his home base. If that were the case, he may have written his epistle from there.

RECIPIENTS

The specific church or churches to which Jude addressed his epistle are not known. In light of his choice of illustrations from the Old Testament and the Jewish apocrypha, his readers likely were predominantly Jewish believers.

OCCASION

Jude had originally planned to write a positive letter, celebrating the great truths of the "common salvation" that he shared with his readers (v. 3). But the alarming news that false teachers had invaded the congregations to which he wrote, threatening that salvation truth (v. 4), compelled him to change his plans. Thus he wrote a strong denunciation of the false teachers and their godless lifestyle—warning his readers and calling them to "contend earnestly for the faith" so as to protect the one common gospel (v. 3). The magnificent doxology with which the letter concludes (vv. 24–25) reveals Jude's confidence that his readers would stand firm by God's grace.

The exact identity of the false teachers is unknown. That they were not second-century Gnostics is clear, since there is no evidence of the distinctive teachings of Gnosticism (such as a cosmological dualism with the transcendent good God opposed to the evil emanation who created the material world; the evil of the material world; salvation through a secret or hidden knowledge, etc.) in Jude's description of them.

In fact, Jude did not focus on the nuances of their false doctrine. Instead he denounced their godless lifestyle—condemning them as "ungodly" a total of six times (vv. 4, 15, 18). That alone marked them as false teachers, since as Jesus said, "You will know them by their fruits" (Matt. 7:16, 20). Having exposed their corrupt lives, there was no need for Jude to refute their specific heretical teachings, since "by revealing their character Jude stripped them of any authority in the congregation. No thinking Christian would follow people who are fundamentally selfish. Jude did not merely revile them. He unveiled who they truly were, removing any grounds for their influence in the church" (Schreiner, *1, 2 Peter, Jude,* 415).

The picture Jude paints of the false teachers reveals the shocking depths of their depravity. Like stealthy beasts of prey, they "crept in unnoticed" (v. 4) among God's people. They perverted "the grace of our God into licentiousness" (v. 4), turning the very grace that instructs believers "to deny ungodliness and worldly desires and to live sensibly, righteously and godly" lives (Titus 2:11–12) into a license to sin. They were so corrupt that Jude compared them to such notorious sinners as the fallen angels, the men of Sodom and Gomorrah, Cain, Balaam, and the rebels under Korah (vv. 6, 7, 11). Put simply, they were like "unreasoning animals" (v. 10). In their brazen audacity, they "reject[ed] authority, and revile[d] angelic majesties" (v. 8)—something even the powerful archangel Michael did not do (v. 9). Because of their arrogant pride "these men revile[d] the things which they [did] not understand" (v. 10).

Jude described their deceitful hypocrisy using vivid metaphors:

> These are the men who are hidden reefs in your love feasts when they feast with you without fear, caring for themselves; clouds without water, carried along by winds; autumn trees without fruit, doubly dead, uprooted; wild waves of the sea, casting up their own shame like foam; wandering stars, for whom the black darkness has been reserved forever. (vv. 12–13)

In short, although they were in the church, they were not part of it; they were "devoid of the Spirit" (v. 19) and hence unredeemed (Rom. 8:9). The reality of their wicked hypocrisy and the consequent danger they posed for the church summoned Jude's strongest possible condemnation and warning.

THE RELATIONSHIP OF JUDE TO 2 PETER

Even a cursory reading of Jude and 2 Peter reveals the striking parallels between them. In fact, nineteen of Jude's twenty-five verses find parallels in 2 Peter. Scholars are divided about which author used the other as a source. (There is a third possibility, that both Peter and Jude drew from a common source. However, there is no evidence that such a source existed.) Many of the arguments for the priority of either epistle are subjective and tend to cancel each other out. There are two objective arguments, however, that favor the chronological priority of 2 Peter. First,

Peter predicts that the false teachers will come in the future (e.g., 2:1, 2; 3:3), while Jude describes them as already present (e.g., vv. 4, 10, 11, 12, 16). That strongly implies that 2 Peter was written before Jude. That Peter refers a few times to the false teachers using the present tense does not nullify the force of that argument, since "the present tense is used consistently [by Peter] to describe the *character* of the false teachers, while the future tense is used to describe their *coming*" (Daniel B. Wallace, "Jude: Introduction, Argument, and Outline" [Biblical Studies Press: www.bible. org, 2000], emphasis in original). If Peter was familiar with Jude's epistle, which describes the false teachers as already present in the church, his use of the future tense would not make sense.

Second, the wording of verses 17–18 is almost identical to 2 Peter 3:3. It appears that Jude is citing Peter's prophecy (that false teachers would come) and noting its fulfillment in his day. There is no other similarly-worded prophecy in Scripture to which Jude could be referring. Further, the word translated "mockers" (*empaiktēs*) appears in the New Testament only in Jude 18 and 2 Peter 3:3. Jude used the plural "apostles" in verse 17, even though he quoted only Peter, because the other apostles had made similar predictions (cf. 1 Tim. 4:1; 2 Tim. 3:1–5; 4:3).

OUTLINE

The Salutation (1–2)
I. The Danger of Apostates (3–4)
II. The Doom of Apostates (5–7)
III. The Description of Apostates (8–16)
IV. The Defense Against Apostates (17–23)
The Concluding Doxology (24–25)

Compelled to Contend (Jude 1–3)

10

Jude, a bond-servant of Jesus Christ, and brother of James, To those who are the called, beloved in God the Father, and kept for Jesus Christ: May mercy and peace and love be multiplied to you. Beloved, while I was making every effort to write you about our common salvation, I felt the necessity to write to you appealing that you contend earnestly for the faith which was once for all handed down to the saints. (1–3)

Without question, the greatest threat to the church has always been false teaching. Its subtlety and severity make it a spiritual poison unlike any other. While external threats—such as religious persecution and the world's animosity—are certainly unpleasant, the wounds they inflict are only physical and the injuries they cause only temporary. The deadliest false teaching, on the other hand, comes not from deceptive, non-Christian religions outside the church, but from spiritual pretenders *inside* the church. And the resulting damage is far greater than that caused by any external assault; the casualties are spiritual and the consequences are eternal. It's no wonder, then, that Jesus warned His followers about the deadly dangers of apostasy:

> Beware of the false prophets, who come to you in sheep's clothing, but inwardly are ravenous wolves. You will know them by their fruits. Grapes are not gathered from thorn bushes nor figs from thistles, are they? So every good tree bears good fruit, but the bad tree bears bad fruit. A good tree cannot produce bad fruit, nor can a bad tree produce good fruit. Every tree that does not bear good fruit is cut down and thrown into the fire. So then, you will know them by their fruits. (Matt. 7:15–20)

In his exhortation to the Ephesian elders, the apostle Paul echoed the Lord's admonition:

> I know that after my departure savage wolves will come in among you, not sparing the flock; and from among your own selves men will arise, speaking perverse things, to draw away the disciples after them. Therefore be on the alert, remembering that night and day for a period of three years I did not cease to admonish each one with tears. (Acts 20:29–31)

The rest of the New Testament records similar warnings, instructing believers to guard themselves against the deceptive nature of false teaching masquerading as Christian truth (Matt. 24:10–14; 2 Thess. 2:3–12; 1 Tim. 4:1–3; 2 Tim. 3:1–9; 2 Peter 2:1–3:7; 1 John 2:18–19; 4:1–3; 2 John 7–10; Rev. 2:6, 14–16, 20–23; 3:1–3, 14–18; cf. James 5:1–6).

And those warnings were well-founded. By the end of the first century, when the apostle John wrote the book of Revelation, only two of the seven churches he addressed (Smyrna and Philadelphia) remained completely faithful. The other five churches, to one degree or another, had fallen prey to infiltrating doctrinal error and its moral consequences. Thus, Christ commanded them to repent, stand firm, and combat the falsehood they encountered; they were to wage war against apostasy and overcome it.

Although Jude's letter was written some twenty-five years earlier, he also recognized that the battle for the truth in the church had already begun, as Peter a few years earlier had prophesied in 2 Peter 1:1–3 and 3:1–3. That's why Jude devoted his entire letter to the presence of apostate false teachers. He wanted his readers to stand strong against the spiritual deceptions that threatened to wreak havoc in their fellowship. And he also wanted all who propagated such errors in the church to be exposed and expelled.

As the last of the New Testament epistles, the book of Jude serves as a literary vestibule to the book of Revelation. In Jude, false teachers are examined, their motives uncovered, and their doom predicted. In

Revelation, that inevitable destruction is developed in detail, as Christ's future triumph ultimately eliminates error and establishes truth forever.

Jude wrote this letter in A.D. 68–70, shortly after Peter finished his second epistle. The two letters are closely related, containing several nearly identical descriptions of false teachers and apostasy. In fact, Jude is likely a sequel to 2 Peter, perhaps written to the same group of Christians to tell them that what Peter had said was coming was now present. Second Peter 2–3 uses future tenses in its references to false teachers. Jude wrote in the present tense. As he began his letter, setting the stage in the first three verses, he revealed his background, his audience, and his exhortation.

JUDE'S BACKGROUND

Jude, a bond-servant of Jesus Christ, and brother of James, (1*a*)

Jude (Heb. "Judah") or "Judas" was a common New Testament name. Two of the disciples, for example, were named Judas—Judas Iscariot and Judas, son of James (Luke 6:16; John 6:71; 14:22; Acts 1:13). The apostle Paul, shortly after his conversion, met Ananias at the house of a Judas of Damascus (Acts 9:11). And Judas Barsabbas, a leader in the early church, joined Paul, Barnabas, and Silas in carrying a letter from the Jerusalem Council to the believers in Antioch (Acts 15:22–33). There was even a Judas of Galilee, who founded the Zealots and led an uprising in early first-century Palestine (Acts 5:37).

But the **Jude** who penned this letter was not any of those men. Instead, he was the **brother of James** who was the half brother of Jesus (Matt. 13:55; Mark 6:3; cf. Gal. 1:19) and the leader of the Jerusalem Council (Acts 15:13). Jude's salutation here is similar to that of his brother's (cf. James 1:1), although, unlike James (cf. Gal. 1:19), he did not consider himself an apostle (cf. v. 17). Nonetheless, his close relation to both Jesus (as a half brother) and James certainly gave Jude a position of prominence and authority in the early church—a platform from which he could address the dangers of false teaching. It is ironic that in God's providence the Holy Spirit chose a man with the same first name as Judas Iscariot, the most infamous apostate of all time (Acts 1:16–20, 25), to write the New Testament epistle on apostasy. (For a discussion of the authorship of this epistle, see the Introduction to Jude earlier in this volume.)

Jude introduced himself as **a bond-servant of Jesus Christ,** indicating that the death, resurrection, and ascension of Christ had transformed his heart. He went from being an unbeliever (cf. John 7:5) to being **a bond-servant** (*doulos,* "slave"), one who trusted Christ as his Lord and

Master (cf. Matt. 24:46; Luke 2:29; Acts 4:29; Gal. 1:10; Col. 1:7; 2 Tim. 2:24; Rev. 19:5). Accordingly, his saving relationship to Christ became more important than family ties (cf. Mark 3:31–35). Thus Jude chose to humbly call himself Jesus' **bond-servant** rather than note the more impressive fact that he was Jesus' half brother.

In the Greco-Roman world slavery was widespread, making the familiar New Testament designation **bond-servant** (cf. Rom. 1:1; Phil. 1:1; 2 Peter 1:1) very significant. It denoted being owned and rendering absolute, selfless submission to someone, in this case to Jesus as Lord. In this letter such identification is especially fitting because it sets Jude in sharp contrast to the apostates. He was a grateful, willing slave of the Lord Jesus Christ, whereas the apostates denied Christ's lordship through their overtly sinful lifestyles (v. 4; cf. 2 Peter 2:1).

JUDE'S AUDIENCE

To those who are the called, beloved in God the Father, and kept for Jesus Christ: May mercy and peace and love be multiplied to you. (1b–2)

Jude's salutation clearly outlines that he was writing to genuine believers. His greeting emphasizes the reassuring truth that as believers contend with growing apostasy, they remain safe and secure in the sovereign purpose of God. Like Peter, who comforted his readers with two Old Testament examples of God's protection and deliverance (Noah and Lot), Jude encouraged his audience to trust God even in the midst of intense spiritual battle. In fact, he listed four reasons for believers to rest in God and not fear—namely, because they are called, loved, kept, and blessed by Him.

CALLED

To those who are the called, (1b)

Called translates the adjectival pronoun *klētos*, which is related to the familiar verb *kaleō*, "to call." It is the main word in the sentence, with two perfect passive participles (describing believers) in apposition to it. Even as the English translation suggests, the word conveys the idea of being personally chosen or selected. God has called believers to Himself; He has set them apart and chosen them as His children.

Jude here is not speaking about God's general invitation to sinners (Isa. 45:22; 55:6; Ezek. 33:11; Matt. 11:28; 22:14; 23:37; Luke 14:16–24; John 7:37; Rev. 22:17)—a call which often goes unheeded and rejected (cf. Matt. 12:14; Luke 4:16–19, 28–30; Acts 4:13–18; 5:17–18, 26–28, 33–40; 7:54–58; 2 Cor. 2:15–16). Rather, he is speaking of God's special, internal call through which He awakens the human will and imparts spiritual life—enabling once-dead sinners to embrace the gospel by faith (cf. John 5:21; Acts 16:14; Eph. 2:5). It is what Christ referred to when He said, "No one can come to Me unless the Father who sent Me draws him" (John 6:44; cf. v. 65). Paul also referred to the effectual call of believers when he wrote Timothy,

> Therefore do not be ashamed of the testimony of our Lord or of me His prisoner, but join with me in suffering for the gospel according to the power of God, who has saved us and called us with a holy calling, not according to our works, but according to His own purpose and grace which was granted us in Christ Jesus from all eternity. (2 Tim. 1:8–9; cf. Rom. 1:6–7; 8:30; 1 Cor. 1:1–2, 9, 24; 1 Tim. 6:12; 1 Peter 3:9; Rev. 17:14)

In His sovereign wisdom, God chose believers based solely on His gracious purpose in Christ from before time began. His call was not rooted in anything He saw in them—not even their foreseen faith (see the discussion of divine foreknowledge in John MacArthur, *1 Peter*, MacArthur New Testament Commentary [Chicago: Moody, 2004], 19–21). Rather, His call was motivated by His own glory and good pleasure, that His mercy might be eternally put on display (Rom. 9:23–24). Believers, then, are **those who are** divinely elected to salvation. They did not earn God's choice; nor can they lose it or have it taken away (cf. John 6:37–40; 10:27–30; Rom. 8:28–30, 38–39). Thus, they can rest in the security of God's gracious call, even in the most dangerous conflict with false teaching.

LOVED

beloved in God the Father, (1c)

God chose to save believers because He loved them. Based totally on His sovereign pleasure and for reasons beyond human comprehension (cf. Rom. 9:11–13; 10:20; 1 Cor. 1:26–29; James 2:5), **the Father** purposed to set His love on certain sinners and redeem them (Matt. 11:27; Rom. 8:28–30; Eph. 1:4). Even when they were rebels, He chose them to be His children and the beneficiaries of Christ's death. As Paul told the Romans, "But God demonstrates His own love toward us, in that while we were yet sinners, Christ died for us" (Rom. 5:8; cf. John 3:16; 13:1; 1 John 4:10,19).

Beloved translates a perfect passive participle derived from the familiar verb *agapaō*. The perfect tense indicates that God placed His love on believers in eternity past (Eph. 1:4–5), with results that continue in the present and into the future. Out of His uninfluenced and selective love, the Father determined who would believe from before the foundation of the world (cf. Acts 13:48; 2 Thess. 2:13; 2 Tim. 1:9). That love required that He also give His Son to die on the cross in their stead, paying the penalty for their sin (Isa. 53:5–6; Mark 10:45; John 3:16; 1 Peter 2:24). Out of His love, He sent the Holy Spirit to convict them of sin, draw them to saving faith, and regenerate their sinful hearts (John 3:3–8; 6:37, 44; Rom. 3:25–26; 8:1; 1 Cor. 6:11; Titus 3:5, 7). And it is out of His love that God continues to secure and protect His children—promising them a relationship with Him that will last for all eternity (cf. John 14:1–4; Eph. 1:13–14; 5:27; 1 Peter 1:3–4).

The apostle John wrote this about God's love for believers: "See how great a love the Father has bestowed on us, that we would be called children of God; and such we are" (1 John 3:1). The expression rendered "how great" is from *potapos,* which originally meant, "From what country?" It describes divine love as something that is alien to human beings and outside their natural realm of understanding—an other worldly kind of love—as if it were a concept from a foreign culture or unknown race. People do not usually love strangers; and they especially do not love their enemies (cf. Matt. 5:43–48). Yet, God chose to love elect sinners even when they were *defiant* sinners (Eph. 2:1–10; cf. John 15:13, 16; Rom. 5:8; 1 Tim. 1:12–16; 1 John 4:19).

In His High Priestly Prayer, Jesus further described the kind of love that His Father has for His children:

> The glory which You have given Me I have given to them, that they may be one, just as We are one; I in them and You in Me, that they may be perfected in unity, so that the world may know that You sent Me, and loved them, even as You have loved Me. Father, I desire that they also, whom You have given Me, be with Me where I am, so that they may see My glory which You have given Me, for You loved Me before the foundation of the world. O righteous Father, although the world has not known You, yet I have known You; and these have known that You sent Me; and I have made Your name known to them, and will make it known, so that the love with which You loved Me may be in them, and I in them. (John 17:22–26)

Although believers did nothing to gain His affection (and, in fact, did everything to invite His wrath), the Father loves redeemed sinners with the same love that He has for His Son. It is a love that is infinite, eternal, and completely secure. John wrote in his Gospel that He "loved His own . . . He loved them to the end" (13:1), meaning to perfection as well as forever. In fact, nothing will ever separate believers from it, as Paul declares in Romans 8:38–39:

> For I am convinced that neither death, nor life, nor angels, nor principalities, nor things present, nor things to come, nor powers, nor height, nor depth, nor any other created thing, will be able to separate us from the love of God, which is in Christ Jesus our Lord.

KEPT

and kept for Jesus Christ: (1*d*)

Kept for translates a perfect passive participle (*tetērēmenois*), from the verb *tēreō*, "to observe, pay attention to, keep under guard, maintain." Although the *New American Standard* translators rendered Jude's wording **kept for,** the dative case of the participle suggests that "kept by" might be a preferable translation. Thus Jude's phrase echoes Jesus' own teaching on the preservation of believers:

> My sheep hear My voice, and I know them, and they follow Me; and I give eternal life to them, and they will never perish; and no one will snatch them out of My hand. My Father, who has given them to Me, is greater than all; and no one is able to snatch them out of the Father's hand. (John 10:27–28; cf. 6:37–44; 17:11, 15; Rom. 8:31–39)

Jesus Christ has promised to keep believers secure for all eternity (John 6:35–40; 10:27–30; Rom. 8:35–39), a guarantee that is made possible by His death on the cross. Through His once-for-all sacrifice (1 Peter 3:18), Christ extends the forgiveness of sins, the reality of eternal life, and the hope of glorification to His followers.

Furthermore, what Christ secured at the cross, the Father protects through His power (1 Peter 1:5). There is no person or power in the universe that is greater than God. Nor is there any force that could ever break the loving grip He has on His own. As a result, believers can rest in Him, knowing that their eternal safekeeping is in His omnipotent hands. This is an important ground on which believers may fearlessly fight against false teachers. Those who believe salvation can be lost should be consistent and be reluctant to engage deadly error at close quarters. Jude began his letter by removing that needless fear—believers are **kept!**

BLESSED

May mercy and peace and love be multiplied to you. (2)

The salvation God provides for His children is one that is rich with blessings (Pss. 37:6, 17, 24, 39; 84:5, 11; 92:12–14; Matt. 6:31–33; John 10:10; Acts 20:32; Rom. 9:23; 2 Cor. 9:8–10; Phil. 4:19), three of which Jude lists in his greeting. Jude takes the phrase **mercy and peace,** a common Jewish greeting (cf. 1 Tim. 1:2; 2 Tim. 1:2; 2 John 3), and adds **love** to remind his readers of Christ's love for them (cf. Eph. 3:19; Rev. 1:5). This threefold expression occurs only here in the New Testament.

Be multiplied (a form of the verb *plēthunō*) means "to be increased," implicitly to the fullest measure. Jude's prayer is that his audience would continually enjoy the Lord's blessing, no matter how difficult the spiritual battle might become (cf. 1 Peter 1:2; 2 Peter 1:2).

First, God's blessing includes a generous supply of His **mercy** (Mark 5:19; Luke 1:50; Rom. 9:15; Gal. 6:16; Eph. 2:4; Titus 3:5; 1 Peter 2:10; cf. Isa. 63:9; Jer. 31:20). Whenever believers commit sin, they will always find an ample supply of mercy at God's throne of grace (Heb. 4:16). Paul told the Romans that God manifested "the riches of His glory upon vessels of mercy, which He prepared beforehand for glory" (Rom. 9:23). The "vessels of mercy," those sinners whom God has chosen for salvation, continually receive outpourings of His mercy, like cups or bowls that are constantly refilled with water.

To meet the needs of every circumstance, God also multiplies His **peace** to believers—a peace that stems from knowing that their sins are forgiven. Jesus comforted the apostles with these words, "Peace I leave with you; My peace I give to you; not as the world gives do I give to you. Do not let your heart be troubled, nor let it be fearful" (John 14:27; cf. 16:33; Pss. 29:11; 85:8; 119:165; Isa. 9:7; 26:3; Jer. 33:6; Luke 2:14; Rom. 5:1; 15:13; 1 Cor. 14:33; Gal. 5:22; Phil. 4:7; Col. 3:15; 1 Thess. 5:23).

God further blesses believers with constant outpourings of His **love.** Paul said, "The love of God has been poured out within our hearts through the Holy Spirit who was given to us" (Rom. 5:5; cf. 8:39; John 16:27; 17:23; Eph. 2:4; 2 Thess. 2:16; 1 John 4:7–10). (For more on God's love for believers, see John MacArthur, *The God Who Loves* [Nashville: Word Publishing, 2001].)

Clearly, God pours out His abundant blessings on those whom He calls, loves, and keeps. Being His child includes infinite privilege and spiritual blessing (Eph. 1:3). But with those blessings comes great responsibility, a sobering subject to which Jude now turns.

JUDE'S EXHORTATION

Beloved, while I was making every effort to write you about our common salvation, I felt the necessity to write to you appealing that you contend earnestly for the faith which was once for all handed down to the saints. (3)

By his use of the term **beloved,** Jude displayed his sincere pastoral concern for his readers (cf. Rom. 1:7; 12:19; 1 Cor. 4:14; 15:58; Eph. 5:1; Phil. 2:12; James 1:16, 19; 2:5; 1 Peter 4:12; 1 John 2:7; 3:2, 21). That concern was not a shallow form of sentimentalism, but a heartfelt expression of affection for God's people. It also embodied a concern born out of a deeply held conviction for the crucial importance of God's truth.

Jude initially made **every effort to write** regarding the **common salvation** he shared with his readers. **Effort** (*spoudē*) connotes hastening or speed, and could mean Jude hurried in vain **to write,** or that he tried hard but could not complete what he originally planned to say. Whatever the case, the presence of false teaching restrained him, impressing him with the urgent need to call the church to battle. His initial notion was to speak positively of the shared blessings of **salvation.** But that very salvation was under assault by apostates, hence his change of subjects.

Like Paul, who wrote to the Corinthians, "For necessity is laid upon me; yes, woe is me if I do not preach the gospel" (1 Cor. 9:16, NKJV), Jude felt **the necessity**—a heavy burden or mandate—**to write.** *Agchō,* the root of the noun rendered **necessity,** means literally "compress." Jude recognized that he was a watchman for the truth (cf. Ezek. 3:16–21) who could not simply watch in silence as his readers slipped into error. His fervent passion for sound doctrine, especially regarding the gospel, made even the thought of false teaching a heavy burden on his heart (cf. 2 Cor. 11:28). And he and his readers would not be able to share a **common salvation** if they lost the gospel.

Jude also had a deep love for his readers—meaning that he was dedicated to their spiritual well-being. Accordingly his tone conveyed a genuine care similar to that of Paul, who wrote to the Ephesian elders: "Therefore be on the alert, remembering that night and day for a period of three years I did not cease to admonish each one with tears" (Acts 20:31; cf. Col. 1:29).

Jude could not resist **appealing** (*parakaleō,* "exhorting, encouraging") to his readers that they **contend earnestly for the faith.** The powerful expression **contend earnestly** translates a present infinitive (*epagōnizomai*) and stresses the need to defend the truth continually and vigorously (cf. 1 Tim. 1:18; 6:12; 2 Tim. 4:7). It is a compound verb from which the English *agonize* is transliterated. From Jude's day until now, true believers have always had to battle for the purity of the salvation gospel.

In referring to **the faith,** Jude is not speaking of a nebulous body of religious doctrines. Rather, **the faith** constitutes the Christian faith, the faith of the gospel, God's objective truth (i.e., everything pertaining to **our common salvation**). It is what Luke wrote about in Acts 2:42, noting that the early believers "were continually devoting themselves to the apostles' teaching" (cf. 1 Cor. 15:1–4; 2 Thess. 3:6). Paul admonished Timothy to protect that faith: "Retain the standard of sound words which you have heard from me, in the faith and love which are in Christ Jesus. Guard, through the Holy Spirit who dwells in us, the treasure which has been entrusted to you" (2 Tim. 1:13–14; cf. 1 Tim. 6:19–20).

In life and ministry, God's truth is paramount (cf. Pss. 25:5, 10; 71:22; 119:142, 160; Prov. 23:23; John 4:24; 8:32; 2 Cor. 13:8; 1 Tim. 2:4; 2 Tim. 2:15). To manipulate and distort that truth, or to mix it with error, is to invite God's eternal wrath. That's why Paul told the Galatians, "If any man is preaching to you a gospel contrary to what you received, he is to be accursed!" (Gal. 1:9). And the apostle John told his readers,

> Anyone who goes too far and does not abide in the teaching of Christ, does not have God; the one who abides in the teaching, he has both the Father and the Son. If anyone comes to you and does not bring this teaching, do not receive him into your house, and do not give him a greeting; for the one who gives him a greeting participates in his evil deeds. (2 John 9–11)

Jude further defines **the faith** in succinct, specific terms as that **which was once for all handed down to the saints.** *Hapax* (**once for all**) refers to something that is accomplished or completed one time, with lasting results and no need of repetition. Through the Holy Spirit, God revealed the Christian faith (cf. Rom. 16:26; 2 Tim. 3:16) to the apostles and their associates in the first century. Their New Testament writings, in conjunction with the Old Testament Scriptures, make up the "true knowledge" of Jesus Christ, and are all that believers need for life and godliness (2 Peter 1:3; cf. 2 Tim. 3:16–17).

The authors of the New Testament did not discover the truths of the Christian faith through mystical religious experiences. Rather God, with finality and certainty, delivered His complete body of revelation in Scripture. Any system that claims new revelation or new doctrine must be disregarded as false (Rev. 22:18–19). God's Word is all-sufficient; it is all that believers need as they contend for the faith and oppose apostasy within the church.

Apostates Be Warned
(Jude 4–7)

11

For certain persons have crept in unnoticed, those who were long beforehand marked out for this condemnation, ungodly persons who turn the grace of our God into licentiousness and deny our only Master and Lord, Jesus Christ. Now I desire to remind you, though you know all things once for all, that the Lord, after saving a people out of the land of Egypt, subsequently destroyed those who did not believe. And angels who did not keep their own domain, but abandoned their proper abode, He has kept in eternal bonds under darkness for the judgment of the great day, just as Sodom and Gomorrah and the cities around them, since they in the same way as these indulged in gross immorality and went after strange flesh, are exhibited as an example in undergoing the punishment of eternal fire. (4–7)

Sound doctrine is under siege. In fact, it always has been.

The attack on truth is as old as human history. It began in the Garden of Eden, when Satan twisted God's Word and convinced Eve to disobey her Creator (Gen. 3:1–6). Ever since, the father of lies (John 8:44) has tirelessly continued his bitter offensive against divine truth (cf. Acts 20:29–30; Eph. 6:10–18). His goal is simple, to resist the advancement of

God's kingdom at any cost. His tactics are stealthy, as he baits his victims through deception and distortion. And his strategy is successful among unbelievers (within God's sovereign limits), as the muddled quagmire of modern religion makes abundantly clear.

Yet, despite his apparent victories, Satan's days are numbered. God Himself promises that the truth will ultimately prevail (cf. 2 Thess. 2:5–17); Christ's eternal kingdom—in which error has no part—will one day be established (2 Peter 3:13). As for the Evil One and his guerrilla tactics, they will be vanquished forever (Rev. 20:10).

In the meantime, recognizing that Satan is still on the prowl (1 Peter 5:8), Christians must be earnest and steadfast in contending for the faith (see v. 3). They must be proactive in pursuing the truth, and also in confronting and resisting everything false. Such requires much wisdom, discernment, fortitude, and endurance. The apostle Paul exhorted Timothy, "Retain the standard of sound words which you have heard from me, in the faith and love which are in Christ Jesus. Guard, through the Holy Spirit who dwells in us, the treasure which has been entrusted to you" (2 Tim. 1:13–14; cf. 1 Tim. 6:20–21). Like Timothy, present-day believers have a mandate to take the truth of the gospel seriously, doing all they can to protect and preserve its purity. This is especially crucial for pastors and elders. As those who are responsible for "the flock of God" (1 Peter 5:2) they must be faithful to hold "fast the faithful word which is in accordance with the teaching, so that [they] will be able both to exhort in sound doctrine and to refute those who contradict" (Titus 1:9). They are responsible to interpret Scripture accurately or be brought to shame (cf. 2 Tim. 2:15).

Jude certainly understood what was at stake; he knew that the church was being infiltrated by its enemies. He recognized that a battle was brewing—a conflict that marked Satan's newest campaign in his long war against the truth. And that is why Jude wrote this letter: to alert his readers to the doctrinal dangers they faced from Satan's covert agents. Like a general briefing his troops about the enemy, Jude profiles these apostate foes for his audience. Thus, in this section, he dealt with their presence, prediction, portrayal, and perishing so that his readers might be well-equipped to expose and disarm any such spiritual terrorists.

THE PRESENCE OF THE APOSTATES

For certain persons have crept in unnoticed, (4a)

Jude's warning was not merely hypothetical; the false teachers were already present. The word translated **crept in unnoticed** (*pareis-*

duō) appears only here in the New Testament. It has the connotation of slipping in secretly with an evil intention. In extrabiblical Greek it described the cunning craftiness of a lawyer who, through clever argumentation, infiltrated the minds of courtroom officials and corrupted their thinking. Having already permeated the church, the apostates were in position to "secretly introduce destructive heresies" (2 Peter 2:1).

To be sure, there are many false teachers outside the church who propagate lies and deceptions and openly proclaim their opposition to Christianity. Jesus warned the apostles, "But be on your guard; for they will deliver you to the courts, and you will be flogged in the synagogues, and you will stand before governors and kings for My sake, as a testimony to them" (Mark 13:9; cf. Acts 4:1–3, 13–18; 5:17–18, 26–40; 6:12–14; 7:54, 57–59; 8:1–3; 12:1–4; 14:19; 16:19–24; 17:5–9; 21:26–36; 23:12–24:9). However, the counterfeit pastors, elders, deacons, and teachers within the church are usually far more dangerous. Attacks from outside the church often unite God's people, but attacks from inside—coming from false teachers—usually divide and confuse the flock.

Such false teachers creep in **unnoticed,** infiltrating the fabric of the church, and orchestrating as much harm as possible. As a result, genuine fellowship, worship, ministry, and evangelism fade away as the church succumbs to devastating errors in both doctrine and practice. The New Testament repeatedly warns of the danger posed by apostasy within the church (cf. Acts 20:28–31; 2 Cor. 11:12–15; Gal. 1:6–9; 3:1–3; Col. 2:8, 18–19; 2 Peter 2; 1 John 2:9–11, 18–22; 4:1–6; 2 John 7–11). In today's church, such apostasy takes many forms. False teachers write books and edit publications, speak on radio and television, teach in colleges and seminaries, preach from pulpits, and have Web sites on the Internet. Satan always sows his tares among the wheat (Matt. 13:24–30), raising up false brethren whom he disguises as messengers of truth (cf. 2 Cor. 11:14).

Although Jude's description of the apostates as **certain persons** is vague, their specific historical identity is not essential to his main point—namely, that any and all spiritual pretenders pose a clear and present danger to the church, whatever their error. Nor did Jude consider it necessary to detail the nuances of their particular false theology. It might have been an incipient form of Gnosticism or an early version of Nicolaitanism (a heresy that perverted grace and promoted wicked and immoral behavior; see Rev. 2:6, 15). Whatever the case, Jude's readers knew who the apostates were and what they taught. Thus, he warned them to be on their guard. In the same way, contemporary Christians must also be aware that similar heretics still threaten the church today (Matt. 7:15; 24:11; Acts 20:29).

THE PREDICTION CONCERNING THE APOSTATES

those who were long beforehand marked out for this condemnation, (4*b*)

From the earliest times of redemptive history, God has promised to judge apostates with the utmost severity. The perfect tense of the participle *progegrammenoi* (**beforehand marked out**) suggests that long ago God pronounced damnation against all apostates. They are sons of wrath whom He has ordained **for this** prophesied **condemnation.** Jude would also refer to their condemnation in verses 14–15 of this letter,

> It was also about these men that Enoch, in the seventh generation from Adam, prophesied, saying, "Behold, the Lord came with many thousands of His holy ones, to execute judgment upon all, and to convict all the ungodly of all their ungodly deeds which they have done in an ungodly way, and of all the harsh things which ungodly sinners have spoken against Him." (See the discussion of this passage in chapter 13 of this volume; cf. Isa. 47:12–15; Zeph. 1:4–6; 2 Peter 2:17, 20–22.)

The Old Testament prophets also made many predictions concerning the judgment of apostates (Isa. 8:20–22; Jer. 5:13–14; 8:12–13; Hos. 9:7–9; Zeph. 3:1–8), as did the apostle Peter:

> In their greed they will exploit you with false words; their judgment from long ago is not idle, and their destruction is not asleep. For if God did not spare angels when they sinned, but cast them into hell and committed them to pits of darkness, reserved for judgment; and did not spare the ancient world, but preserved Noah, a preacher of righteousness, with seven others, when He brought a flood upon the world of the ungodly; and if He condemned the cities of Sodom and Gomorrah to destruction by reducing them to ashes, having made them an example to those who would live ungodly lives thereafter. (2 Peter 2:3–6)

(See also the discussion of those verses in chapter 6 of this volume.) The verdict against these apostates was pronounced long ago, meaning that their inevitable, final judgment is unalterable.

THE PORTRAYAL OF THE APOSTATES

ungodly persons who turn the grace of our God into licentiousness and deny our only Master and Lord, Jesus Christ. (4*c*)

Without question, the apostates of Jude's day (as with false teachers of any time period) were primarily characterized by ungodliness (cf. v. 15). They claimed to belong to God and speak for Him; however, their hearts were far from Him (cf. Matt. 7:15–23). In light of this, Jude portrayed their character, their conduct, and their creed as corrupt.

THEIR CHARACTER

ungodly persons (4c)

As **ungodly persons** (*asebēs*), the false teachers could not worship God properly. In fact, they were and are devoid of any and all reverence for Him. The early church fathers used the term *asebēs* in reference to atheists and heretics. Such people only play at religion, while possessing no genuine fear of God or love for Him (cf. Matt. 23:25; 1 Tim. 6:5; 2 Tim. 3:5; Titus 1:16). Although they purport to be spiritual leaders, in reality they egregiously betray their constituents' trust in shockingly immoral and unethical ways. They all claim to know and speak truthfully of God, Jesus, and Scripture, but their sinful character undermines that claim.

THEIR CONDUCT

who turn the grace of our God into licentiousness (4c)

The false spirituality of the apostates could not restrain their fleshly lusts. They perverted God's **grace** and changed it to **licentiousness** (*aselgeia,* "sensuality, indecency, unrestrained vice") or "sensuality" (which is the *New American Standard* translation of *aselgeia* in Gal. 5:19). Under the tyranny of their unredeemed passions (cf. Rom. 8:3–6; 2 Cor. 7:1; Gal. 5:16–17, 24; 6:8; Phil. 3:3), the false teachers secretly indulged their fleshly desires. Then, to make matters worse, they excused their behavior by perverting the biblical concept of grace. In so doing, they demonstrated that they had never actually embraced Christ's salvation at all; if they had truly tasted divine forgiveness, they would not have used grace as a license for sin (cf. Rom. 6:1–2; Gal. 5:13; 1 Peter 2:16; 2 Peter 2:19).

THEIR CREED

and deny our only Master and Lord, Jesus Christ. (4c)

Apostate false teachers view themselves as their own masters. Therefore, they refuse to honestly acknowledge the sovereign lordship of **Jesus Christ** (Ps. 89:27; Acts 7:55–56; 10:36; Rom. 5:1; 6:23; 10:9, 12; Eph. 1:21–22; 4:15; Phil. 2:11; Col. 1:18; 2:10; 1 Tim. 6:15; Rev. 5:12; 19:16). They will not submit to Jesus as divine **Master** (*despotēs,* "sovereign ruler") and **Lord** (*kurios,* "sir," "owner," used as titles of deference and honor); nor will they give Him the honor He singularly requires as God the Son and the Savior of sinners. Thus they **deny** Christ His rightful position as God (John 5:23), as King (Matt. 25:34; John 1:49–51; 12:13; 18:37), and as Messiah (Matt. 2:4–6; Mark 8:27–29; Luke 2:25–35; John 4:25–26). In so doing, they confirm that they are counterfeit; "they profess to know God, but by their deeds they deny Him, being detestable and disobedient and worthless for any good deed" (Titus 1:16).

THE PERISHING OF THE APOSTATES

Now I desire to remind you, though you know all things once for all, that the Lord, after saving a people out of the land of Egypt, subsequently destroyed those who did not believe. And angels who did not keep their own domain, but abandoned their proper abode, He has kept in eternal bonds under darkness for the judgment of the great day, just as Sodom and Gomorrah and the cities around them, since they in the same way as these indulged in gross immorality and went after strange flesh, are exhibited as an example in undergoing the punishment of eternal fire. (5–7)

In this passage, Jude provided further insight into the deceivers' condemnation (v. 4b) by citing three of God's past judgments against other apostates—namely, apostate Israelites, apostate angels, and apostate Gentiles. This section closely parallels 2 Peter 2:3–10. There Peter wrote about God's judgment on fallen angels, on unbelievers through the Flood, and on the grossly wicked people of Sodom and Gomorrah. (See the discussion of 2 Peter 2:3b–10a in chapter 6 of this volume.) Jude likewise focused on fallen angels and the people of Sodom and Gomorrah, but he referenced the unbelieving Israelites instead of the people of Noah's time. In both Peter's and Jude's letters, the references are brief and general because they were already familiar to their readers.

THE APOSTATE ISRAELITES

Now I desire to remind you, though you know all things once for

all, that the Lord, after saving a people out of the land of Egypt, subsequently destroyed those who did not believe. (5)

Jude's use of familiar Old Testament examples stemmed from a **desire to remind** his readers (cf. 2 Peter 1:12) that defectors from the truth will always meet divine judgment.

His first such example centered on God's **saving a people** (Israel) **out of the land of Egypt** and then leading them through the wilderness. As a vivid picture of redemption, the story of the Exodus was a powerful illustration of God's love for His people, symbolized and memorialized in the Passover (Ex. 12; cf. Luke 22:20; 1 Cor. 5:7). But it was also a stern reminder of divine judgment—not only on the Egyptians, but also on those Israelites who faithlessly turned away from God (1 Cor. 10:1–18). Although Jude knew that his readers were fully aware of the story—that they knew **all things once for all**—he used it to reveal God's unchanging attitude toward anyone in any time or place who corrupts His Word. In fact, God's judgment against apostates is detailed throughout the entire Old Testament (Judg. 11:14–21; Neh. 9:21; Pss. 78; 95; 105; 106; cf. Deut. 4:27; 28:64; Hos. 9:17; Zech. 7:14).

Once God delivered the Israelites from Egypt, He **subsequently destroyed those who did not believe** (Ex. 7:14–17:7; Num. 11:1–14:38). Numbers 14:26–38 summarizes Israel's rebellion and God's response:

> The Lord spoke to Moses and Aaron, saying, "How long shall I bear with this evil congregation who are grumbling against Me? I have heard the complaints of the sons of Israel, which they are making against Me. Say to them, 'As I live,' says the Lord, 'just as you have spoken in My hearing, so I will surely do to you; your corpses will fall in this wilderness, even all your numbered men, according to your complete number from twenty years old and upward, who have grumbled against Me. Surely you shall not come into the land in which I swore to settle you, except Caleb the son of Jephunneh and Joshua the son of Nun. Your children, however, whom you said would become a prey—I will bring them in, and they will know the land which you have rejected. But as for you, your corpses will fall in this wilderness. Your sons shall be shepherds for forty years in the wilderness, and they will suffer for your unfaithfulness, until your corpses lie in the wilderness. According to the number of days which you spied out the land, forty days, for every day you shall bear your guilt a year, even forty years, and you will know My opposition. I, the Lord, have spoken, surely this I will do to all this evil congregation who are gathered together against Me. In this wilderness they shall be destroyed, and there they will die.'" As for the men whom Moses sent to spy out the land and who returned and made all the congregation grumble against him by bringing out a bad report concerning the land, even those men who brought out the very bad report of

the land died by a plague before the Lord. But Joshua the son of Nun and Caleb the son of Jephunneh remained alive out of those men who went to spy out the land.

For Jude's readers, Israel's judgment was a vivid reminder of what happens to those who (whether or not they become teachers of His), having heard what God expects and witnessed what He can do, still fail to believe (cf. Matt. 13:54–58; Mark 3:1–6, 20–30; 6:1–6; John 6:60–71; 8:31–59). The Lord will condemn and destroy all such renegades (cf. Matt. 11:20–24; Heb. 3:7–12; 10:26–31).

THE APOSTATE ANGELS

And angels who did not keep their own domain, but abandoned their proper abode, He has kept in eternal bonds under darkness for the judgment of the great day, (6)

The second example that Jude gave was that of apostate **angels.** The fact that these angels are not specifically identified indicates that Jude assumed his audience was already familiar with the details of their extraordinary defection.

Commentators have offered three main views as to the identity of these angels. Some argue that Jude's reference is to an episode his readers knew nothing about. But that does not fit the larger context in which, as noted above, Jude reminded his readers of things they already knew (cf. v. 5). Thus one has to assume that Jude wrote of an Old Testament account that was generally familiar to his audience.

Others assert that Jude referred to the original fall of Satan (Isa. 14:12–15; Ezek. 28:12–17; cf. Luke 10:18; Rev. 12:7–10). That is a possible interpretation, but it fails to explain Jude's mention of **eternal bonds,** which does not apply to the current status of Satan and demons. The apostle Peter correctly wrote that the devil "prowls around like a roaring lion, seeking someone to devour" (1 Peter 5:8; cf. Job 1:6–7). Therefore it is unlikely that Jude is referring to Satan's fall.

A third and most plausible viewpoint is that Jude referred to an extraordinarily heinous infraction by some of the fallen angels. That sin, recorded in the Old Testament (Gen. 6:1–4), was so severe that God placed the offending demons in chains to prevent them from committing such perversity ever again. (For more discussion of the sin committed by those angels, see the comments on 2 Peter 2:4 in chapter 6 of this volume and the lengthier section in John MacArthur, *1 Peter,* MacArthur New Testament Commentary [Chicago: Moody, 2004], 209–16.)

Peter said they sinned, whereas Jude described two closely related aspects of the fallen angels' sin. First, they **did not keep their own domain.** Instead of staying in their own realm of authority given by God, they went outside it. Second, they **abandoned their proper abode.** With Lucifer they rebelled against their created role and place in heaven (cf. Isa. 14:12, NKJV). When God expelled them from heaven for that rebellion (cf. Rev. 12:4, 9), some continued their downward fall to the point of taking masculine human form and cohabitating with human women to produce a generation of demon-influenced, thoroughly corrupt children (cf. Gen. 6:11–13). God sent those particular apostate angels (demons) to a place under darkness for the judgment of the great day. Peter wrote that God "committed them to pits of darkness, reserved for judgment" (2 Peter 2:4).

THE APOSTATE GENTILES

just as Sodom and Gomorrah and the cities around them, since they in the same way as these indulged in gross immorality and went after strange flesh, are exhibited as an example in undergoing the punishment of eternal fire. (7)

For his third illustration of past divine judgment on apostates, Jude reminded his readers about **Sodom and Gomorrah.** The wicked people who lived in those cities, **and the cities around them,** engaged in sins equally as shocking and horrific as those of the angels. Genesis 18:16–19:29 recounts the sordid details, with 19:1–11 giving particular focus to the debauched actions of their unrepentant residents:

> Now the two angels came to Sodom in the evening as Lot was sitting in the gate of Sodom. When Lot saw them, he rose to meet them and bowed down with his face to the ground. And he said, "Now behold, my lords, please turn aside into your servant's house, and spend the night, and wash your feet; then you may rise early and go on your way." They said however, "No, but we shall spend the night in the square." Yet he urged them strongly, so they turned aside to him and entered his house; and he prepared a feast for them, and baked unleavened bread, and they ate. Before they lay down, the men of the city, the men of Sodom, surrounded the house, both young and old, all the people from every quarter; and they called to Lot and said to him, "Where are the men who came to you tonight? Bring them out to us that we may have relations with them." But Lot went out to them at the doorway, and shut the door behind him, and said, "Please, my brothers, do not act wickedly. Now behold, I have two daughters who have not had relations with man; please let me bring them out to you, and do to them whatever you

like; only do nothing to these men, inasmuch as they have come under the shelter of my roof." But they said, "Stand aside." Furthermore, they said, "This one came in as an alien, and already he is acting like a judge; now we will treat you worse than them." So they pressed hard against Lot and came near to break the door. But the men reached out their hands and brought Lot into the house with them, and shut the door. They struck the men who were at the doorway of the house with blindness, both small and great, so that they wearied themselves trying to find the doorway.

Somewhat like the perverted angels before them, the Sodomites **in the same way as these indulged in gross immorality and went after strange flesh.** They too perverted God's intended design for them by soliciting sexual favors from His holy messengers. **Gross immorality** translates a compound word (*ekporneuō*), which suggests that their homosexual behavior and attempted fornication was especially deviant from the God-ordained design for human sexuality (cf. Lev. 18:22; 20:13; Rom. 1:26–27; 1 Cor. 6:9; 1 Tim. 1:9–10). That they **went after strange flesh** indicates that, like the apostate angels, the men of Sodom pursued creatures (angels) outside of what was proper for them. (For additional discussion of Sodom and Gomorrah, see the exposition of 2 Peter 2:6–8 in chapter 6 of this volume.)

The people of Sodom and Gomorrah **are exhibited as an example** that God will certainly and severely punish apostates (Matt. 11:23; Rom. 9:29; 2 Peter 2:6; cf. Isa. 1:9–10; Amos 4:11). They will finally be sentenced to **the punishment of eternal fire,** the burning hell of horrific torment, where punishment lasts forever (Matt. 3:12; 13:42, 50; 25:41; cf. Ps. 9:17; Prov. 5:5; 9:17–18; 15:24; Isa. 33:14; Matt. 5:29; 8:12; 10:28; 25:46). It is God's final, permanent judgment on the unregenerate, especially on those who scorn His truth or defect from it (cf. Rev. 19:20). The apostle John described hell this way: "The devil who deceived them was thrown into the lake of fire and brimstone, where the beast and the false prophet are also; and they will be tormented day and night forever and ever" (Rev. 20:10; cf. Isa. 30:33).

This powerful passage, with its three dramatic illustrations of apostasy, is a sobering reminder of the ultimate fate that awaits those who defect from the faith. As such, it provides a fitting motivation for believers as they continue to contend for the truth. And it also serves as a solemn warning to anyone who knows the truth but, for whatever reason, is inclined to walk away from the gospel (Heb. 6:4–8). After all, if Jude's admonition is ignored, the consequences are terrifying:

How much severer punishment do you think he will deserve who has trampled under foot the Son of God, and has regarded as unclean the blood of the covenant by which he was sanctified, and has insulted the

Spirit of grace? For we know Him who said, "Vengeance is Mine, I will repay." And again, "The Lord will judge His people." It is a terrifying thing to fall into the hands of the living God. (Heb. 10:29–31)

Thus the severest eternal suffering will belong to those who know and reject the truth. Even more terrible will judgment be to those who, having done that, go on to teach demonic lies as if they are true (cf. James 3:1).

Apostates Illustrated (Jude 8–13)

12

Yet in the same way these men, also by dreaming, defile the flesh, and reject authority, and revile angelic majesties. But Michael the archangel, when he disputed with the devil and argued about the body of Moses, did not dare pronounce against him a railing judgment, but said, "The Lord rebuke you!" But these men revile the things which they do not understand; and the things which they know by instinct, like unreasoning animals, by these things they are destroyed. Woe to them! For they have gone the way of Cain, and for pay they have rushed headlong into the error of Balaam, and perished in the rebellion of Korah. These are the men who are hidden reefs in your love feasts when they feast with you without fear, caring for themselves; clouds without water, carried along by winds; autumn trees without fruit, doubly dead, uprooted; wild waves of the sea, casting up their own shame like foam; wandering stars, for whom the black darkness has been reserved forever. (8–13)

Terrorism has always existed in various forms. From political assassinations to high-profile kidnappings to guerrilla warfare, history is full of men who have tried to enact change through violent means. But on the watershed date of September 11, 2001, terrorism reached a new level, when mercenaries from the Al Qaeda terrorist network hijacked four jetliners and used them as missiles. The resulting destruction of the World Trade Center in New York City and damage to the Pentagon in Washington, D.C. (along with the crash of the fourth plane in rural Pennsylvania), killed more than three thousand people and dealt a severe blow to the American economy, raising the threat of international terrorism to an unprecedented height. In response, strict security precautions were put in place, especially for airline travel, vital industries, and high-profile public events. Prior to September 11, the United States seemed blissfully immune to terrorist attack. But after the incredible collapse of the twin towers, Americans gained firsthand knowledge of terrorism's deadly tactics.

In contrast to conventional warfare, terrorism presents a uniquely serious threat for two primary reasons. First, terrorists operate clandestinely. They are relatively few in number, remain hidden, and certainly do not wear uniforms. Their plans stay secret until after they strike, making their attacks very difficult to counteract. Second, terrorists are usually willing to die for their cause (often by suicide as they carry out their objectives). They are eager to sacrifice themselves for the sake of their mission. Thus the prospect of even the severest human punishment, such as the death penalty, does not deter them. If they are to be thwarted, they must be unmasked and apprehended before they act. Otherwise it will be too late.

The same features that make political terrorists so dangerous in the world make apostate teachers even more dangerous in the church. Because they often come disguised as angels of light (2 Cor. 11:14) or wolves in sheep's clothing (Matt. 7:15), apostates are difficult to identify. And, because of their own self-deception, they willingly (albeit unwittingly) embrace their own eternal ruin for the sake of their poisonous lies. In destroying souls, they themselves commit spiritual suicide.

Since it is important for freedom-loving nations to fight ideological terrorists, it is infinitely more crucial for believers to expose and reject spiritual terrorists. Political terrorists can inflict material damage and physical death, but apostates disguised as genuine teachers can subvert God's truth and entice people to believe damning lies.

Jude realized the immense danger that apostates pose to divine truth. Therefore, he exhorted his readers to "contend earnestly for the faith" (v. 3), to keep battling for the pure doctrine of "our common salvation" against those who would undermine the gospel. But because the false teachers had "crept in unnoticed" (v. 4), the challenge came in recognizing and exposing them before they inflicted harm.

With that in view, this passage continues to depict the true face of the apostates. They were so ungodly and so spiritually dangerous that Jude used the most stinging and condemnatory language to describe them. In so doing, he presented three characteristics of the apostates' nature, three correlations to past apostates, and five comparisons to natural phenomena.

CHARACTERISTICS OF THE APOSTATE'S NATURE

Yet in the same way these men, also by dreaming, defile the flesh, and reject authority, and revile angelic majesties. But Michael the archangel, when he disputed with the devil and argued about the body of Moses, did not dare pronounce against him a railing judgment, but said, "The Lord rebuke you!" But these men revile the things which they do not understand; and the things which they know by instinct, like unreasoning animals, by these things they are destroyed. (8–10)

In the same way is an important transition, further unlocking the significance of the previous passage. Apostates typically exhibit ungodly character traits, just like the apostate Israelites, the fallen angels, and the debauched population of Sodom and Gomorrah. The wicked behavior of **these men** often derives from their **dreaming,** a term that Jude used to identify the apostates as phony visionaries. The New Testament normally uses the noun *onar* to refer to dreams (Matt. 1:20; 2:12, 13, 19, 22; 27:19), but here Jude chose a form of the verb *enupniazō*, which is used only one other place in the New Testament, Acts 2:17. In that passage, Peter (preaching on the Day of Pentecost) declared, "But this is what was spoken of through the prophet Joel: 'And it shall be in the last days,' God says, 'that I will pour forth of My Spirit on all mankind; and your sons and your daughters shall prophesy, and your young men shall see visions, and your old men shall dream dreams'" (2:16–17).

Joel's prophecy (Joel 2:28–32) and its affirmation in Peter's sermon show that the dreams in question may refer to revelatory dreams (rather than normal dreams). During the tribulation, prophecies, revelations, and visions that have now ceased will return, along with divine revelation. God will speak to people through dreams, just as He did earlier in biblical history (e.g., Joseph in Egypt, Daniel in Babylon, and others).

False teachers often claim dreams as the authoritative, divine source for their "new truths," which are really just lies and distortions. Such claims allow apostates to substitute their own counterfeit authority for God's true scriptural authority.

Dreaming surely also includes apostates' perverted, evil imaginations. Rejecting the Word of God, they base their deceptive teachings on the misguided musings of their own deluded and demonized minds. In the Old Testament, the term "dreamer" was virtually synonymous with false prophet, as in Moses' warning:

> If a prophet or a dreamer of dreams arises among you and gives you a sign or a wonder, and the sign or the wonder comes true, concerning which he spoke to you, saying, "Let us go after other gods (whom you have not known) and let us serve them," you shall not listen to the words of that prophet or that dreamer of dreams; for the Lord your God is testing you to find out if you love the Lord your God with all your heart and with all your soul. You shall follow the Lord your God and fear Him; and you shall keep His commandments, listen to His voice, serve Him, and cling to Him. But that prophet or that dreamer of dreams shall be put to death, because he has counseled rebellion against the Lord your God who brought you from the land of Egypt and redeemed you from the house of slavery, to seduce you from the way in which the Lord your God commanded you to walk. So you shall purge the evil from among you. (Deut. 13:1–5; cf. Jer. 23:25–32)

Along those lines, the apostle Paul cautioned,

> Let no one keep defrauding you of your prize by delighting in self-abasement and the worship of the angels, taking his stand on visions he has seen, inflated without cause by his fleshly mind, and not holding fast to the head, from whom the entire body, being supplied and held together by the joints and ligaments, grows with a growth which is from God. (Col. 2:18–19; cf. 1 Tim. 4:1–2)

Having identified the apostates as false dreamers, Jude went on to outline three characteristics of their nature: immorality, insubordination, and irreverence.

THEIR IMMORALITY

defile the flesh, (8b)

Flesh (*sarx*) refers here to the physical body, not the essence of depravity. Had Jude intended the latter, he would have used *sarkinos,* as Paul did in Romans 7:14. The word translated **defile** is from the verb *miainō,* which means to dye or stain something, such as clothing or glass. In addition, it can mean "to pollute," "to contaminate," "to soil," or "to corrupt." When linked with *sarx,* the reference is to moral and physical defilement, or sexual sin.

Apostate teachers are inevitably immoral, even if their immorality is not publicly known. After all, they have no ability to restrain their lusts, and they are generally characterized as those who live in the passion of lust because they do not know God (cf. 1 Thess. 4:5). Later in this letter, Jude wrote that false teachers are "devoid of the Spirit" (v. 19), as is evidenced in their abandonment of the truth (cf. 1 John 2:19–23). Thus they have no divine power to control their own sinful impulses (cf. Rom. 6:20–21; 8:7–8; Gal. 5:19), left instead to "indulge the flesh in its corrupt desires" (2 Peter 2:10; cf. 2:18; see the commentary on these verses in chapter 7 of this volume). In time, the truth about their immorality will inevitably emerge (cf. 2 Tim. 3:1–9).

THEIR INSUBORDINATION

and reject authority, (8c)

Since apostate teachers love their immorality, it follows that they **reject authority. Reject** is from the verb *atheteō,* which refers to destroying something established, such as existing authority. The word rendered **authority** (*kuriotēs*) is related to the more familiar term *kurios* ("lord"). Because they demand to rule their own lives, apostates refuse to submit to Christ's lordship over them (cf. v. 4).

The reality, however, is that they are much like the scribes and Pharisees whom Jesus confronted in Matthew 23:27–28: "You are like whitewashed tombs which on the outside appear beautiful, but inside they are full of dead men's bones and all uncleanness. So you, too, outwardly appear righteous to men, but inwardly you are full of hypocrisy and lawlessness."

THEIR IRREVERENCE

and revile angelic majesties. But Michael the archangel, when he disputed with the devil and argued about the body of Moses, did not dare pronounce against him a railing judgment, but said, "The Lord rebuke you!" But these men revile the things which they do not understand; and the things which they know by instinct, like unreasoning animals, by these things they are destroyed. (8d–10)

The unusual phrase they **revile angelic majesties** introduces Jude's third indictment of the apostates' character. **Revile** is from *blasphēmeō*, "to slander," or "to speak evil of," especially to speak profanely of sacred matters, including God Himself (cf. 2 Kings 19:22; Ps. 74:22; Isa. 65:7; Ezek. 20:27; Matt. 12:31–32). The false teachers were not just irreverent in some mild sense; they were blasphemers, and specifically of **angelic majesties.**

The *New American Standard* translates the single Greek word *doxa* ("glory") as **angelic majesties.** Although it is possible to interpret the word as a reference to God's majesty, the translation **angelic majesties** is best in light of the parallel passage in Peter's epistle (2 Peter 2:10). In his letter, Peter used the same word to identify angels as the objects of such blasphemy (see the discussion of that verse in chapter 7 of this volume; cf. Dan. 10:13,20).

Throughout redemptive history, holy angels, who are devoted to God's holy glory, have had a special role in establishing God's moral order. For instance, God gave them the ministry of helping communicate His law (Deut. 33:2; cf. Acts 7:53; Gal. 3:19; Heb. 2:1–2). The holy angels will also be involved in the ultimate judgment of the wicked: "Behold, the Lord came with many thousands of His holy ones, to execute judgment upon all, and to convict all the ungodly of all their ungodly deeds which they have done in an ungodly way, and of all the harsh things which ungodly sinners have spoken against Him" (Jude 14*b*–15). By their lawless immorality and insubordination, apostates not only blaspheme the holy angels; they also blaspheme God Himself.

Jude further demonstrated the seriousness of the apostates' irreverence by contrasting their behavior with that of **Michael the archangel.** As God's most powerful angel and the protector of God's people (cf. Dan. 10:13–21; 12:1), Michael did not demonstrate irreverence **when he disputed with the devil and argued about the body of Moses.** Michael knew that God could grant him power over Satan (cf. Rev. 12:7–9), yet he also understood that he was not to act beyond God's prescribed limits. Out of respect for Satan's status and power as the highest created being, Michael **did not dare pronounce against him** (Satan) **a railing judgment** as if he possessed sovereign dominion over him. In fact, he did nothing more than utter the words, **"The Lord rebuke you!"**

Michael's response anticipated the example of the Angel of the Lord in Zechariah 3:2: "The Lord said to Satan, 'The Lord rebuke you, Satan! Indeed, the Lord who has chosen Jerusalem rebuke you! Is this not a brand plucked from the fire?'" In the prophet Zechariah's vision, Joshua the high priest—who along with Zerubbabel led the first group of Jews back from Babylonian captivity—was standing in heaven before the

Angel of the Lord. The devil was also there, at the right hand of Joshua, accusing Joshua and the nation of Israel whom he represented.

Satan's argument, based on Israel's sinfulness, was that God should break His covenant promises (cf. Gen. 12:3, 7; 26:3–4; 28:14; Deut. 5:1–21; 2 Sam. 7:12; Ps. 89:3–4; cf. Rom. 9:4; Gal. 3:16). In response, the Angel of the Lord (the preincarnate Christ) defended Israel by deferring to God the Father and asking Him to rebuke Satan (cf. 1 John 2:1). And the Father honored the preincarnate Son. Instead of breaking His covenant with His chosen people, God reaffirmed His commitment to Israel's future justification, promising to forgive Israel's sin and clothe her with garments of righteousness (Zech. 3:3–5).

When Michael contended for **the body of Moses,** he did just what the Angel of the Lord did. His appeal to the Lord as sovereign apparently ended the dispute with Satan. Interestingly, this is the only place Scripture mentions this incident; the Old Testament provides no details about Moses' death other than to say, "So Moses the servant of the Lord died there in the land of Moab, according to the word of the Lord. And He buried him in the valley in the land of Moab, opposite Beth-peor; but no man knows his burial place to this day" (Deut. 34:5–6). Because God did not want anyone to preserve Moses' body and venerate it, He gave Michael the responsibility of burying it where no one—including Satan—could find it. False teachers exercise no such restraint but pretend to have personal power over Satan and angelic beings.

To conclude this section, Jude wrote that **these men** [the apostates] **revile the things which they do not understand.** Their behavior evidenced their incredible ignorance and presumption. (See the exposition of 2 Peter 2:10*b*–13*a* in chapter 7 of this volume for commentary on Peter's parallel statement; also cf. 1 Cor. 1:18–31; 2:11–16.)

Like the apostle Peter, Jude compared the apostates to **unreasoning animals,** who know **the things which they know by instinct.** They operated from intuitive musings, out of their own unholy **instinct** and lusts. They did not soundly interpret the truth of special revelation. The term translated **unreasoning** (*alogos*) literally means "without a word." That is, the apostates were like dumb animals who cannot speak reasonably because they cannot reason. No matter how highly educated apostate teachers are, how profoundly philosophical they think their teaching is, or how many mystical visions and insights they claim to have had, they still are like brute **animals.** Like the rest of reprobate humanity, "professing to be wise, they became fools" (Rom. 1:22; cf. 1 Cor. 3:18; 2 Cor. 10:5, 12; Gal. 6:3; Eph. 4:17; 2 Tim. 3:2, 4). In the end, **they are destroyed** by means of their own lying and deceiving heresies, which bring upon them the judgment of God (cf. Gen. 6:17; 19:24; 2 Kings 22:17; Jer. 30:16; Matt. 7:22–23; 13:40–42; 25:41; Heb. 10:27).

CORRELATIONS TO PAST APOSTATES

Woe to them! For they have gone the way of Cain, and for pay they have rushed headlong into the error of Balaam, and perished in the rebellion of Korah. (11)

It was George Santayana (1863–1952), American poet, philosopher, and literary critic, who said, "Those who cannot remember the past are condemned to repeat it." Such was certainly true of the false teachers in Jude's day.

Like Santayana, Jude understood the crucial importance of learning from history. He had already drawn from biblical history in sketching his portrait of the apostates in verses 5–7 (see the discussion of those verses in the previous chapter of this volume). He did so again in this section as he compared them to three influential, familiar examples from the past: Cain, Balaam, and Korah.

CAIN

Woe to them! For they have gone the way of Cain, (11*a*)

By exclaiming **Woe to them!** Jude followed the example of Christ (cf. Matt. 23:13, 14, 15, 16, 23, 25, 27, 29) and the prophets (cf. Isa. 3:9, 11; 5:8–23; 29:15; 30:1; 31:1; Jer. 13:27; 23:1; Ezek. 13:3; 16:23; 34:2; Hos. 7:13; Zech. 11:17) in pronouncing ultimate spiritual judgment on apostates. The word translated **woe** (*ouai*) is an interjection or emotional cry that is essentially like exclaiming, "Alas, how horrible it will be!"

Cain was the prototypical model of one who departed from God's truth. He was the first child of Adam and Eve, having been born after the fall. Genesis 4:1–15 contains the familiar story:

> Now the man had relations with his wife Eve, and she conceived and gave birth to Cain, and she said, "I have gotten a manchild with the help of the Lord." Again, she gave birth to his brother Abel. And Abel was a keeper of flocks, but Cain was a tiller of the ground. So it came about in the course of time that Cain brought an offering to the Lord of the fruit of the ground. Abel, on his part also brought of the firstlings of his flock and of their fat portions. And the Lord had regard for Abel and for his offering; but for Cain and for his offering He had no regard. So Cain became very angry and his countenance fell. Then the Lord said to Cain, "Why are you angry? And why has your countenance fallen? If you do well, will not your countenance be lifted up? And if you do not do well, sin is crouching at the door; and its desire is for you, but you

must master it." Cain told Abel his brother. And it came about when they were in the field, that Cain rose up against Abel his brother and killed him. Then the Lord said to Cain, "Where is Abel your brother?" And he said, "I do not know. Am I my brother's keeper?" He said, "What have you done? The voice of your brother's blood is crying to Me from the ground. Now you are cursed from the ground, which has opened its mouth to receive your brother's blood from your hand. When you cultivate the ground, it will no longer yield its strength to you; you will be a vagrant and a wanderer on the earth." Cain said to the Lord, "My punishment is too great to bear! Behold, You have driven me this day from the face of the ground; and from Your face I will be hidden, and I will be a vagrant and a wanderer on the earth, and whoever finds me will kill me." So the Lord said to him, "Therefore whoever kills Cain, vengeance will be taken on him sevenfold." And the Lord appointed a sign for Cain, so that no one finding him would slay him.

The fact that Cain's sacrifice was unacceptable demands that God had previously told him what constituted a proper sacrifice. Cain knew God required a blood sacrifice, but instead of obeying he invented his own form of worship. His inappropriate offering revealed the irreverent blasphemy of his heart, as he rejected God's revelation and operated by his own self-styled instinct and pride in what he had produced.

In light of their similarities, Jude could refer to proud, self-willed apostates as those who **have gone the way of Cain.** Cain was religious but disobedient, and when God did not accept his offering, he responded in jealous anger—even murdering his obedient brother Abel. The writer of Hebrews offered this commentary on the tragic episode: "By faith Abel offered to God a better sacrifice than Cain, through which he obtained the testimony that he was righteous, God testifying about his gifts, and through faith, though he is dead, he still speaks" (Heb. 11:4).

BALAAM

and for pay they have rushed headlong into the error of Balaam, (11b)

Here Jude unmasks the fundamental motive behind the religious interests of false teachers: They do so **for pay** (cf. Ps. 10:3; Mic. 3:11; 1 Tim. 6:10; 2 Peter 2:3). Unlike God's true shepherds (cf. 1 Tim. 3:3; Titus 1:7; 1 Peter 5:2), these ministry mercenaries follow in **the error of Balaam,** rushing **headlong into** envy and greed.

Numbers 22–24 relates the story of Balaam, with some additional references occurring in chapter 31. Balak, king of Moab, hired Balaam to curse Israel. So Balaam devised a plan by which he would lure Israel into idolatry and immorality—and ultimately God's judgment. But God used an angel along with Balaam's own donkey to prevent him from carrying out his plan. (For a fuller discussion of Balaam and his sin, see the exposition of 2 Peter 2:15–16 in chapter 7 of this volume.) As a prophet-for-hire, Balaam is a prime illustration of false teachers—those who love wealth and prestige more than faithfulness and obedience (cf. Rev. 2:14).

KORAH

and perished in the rebellion of Korah. (11c)

Numbers 16 presents the story of **Korah,** a cousin of Moses. As a Levite and a Kohathite, Korah had significant duties in the tabernacle (Num. 1:50–51; 3:6–8; 18:3; Deut. 10:8; cf. 1 Chron. 15:2). However, when he was not chosen to be a priest, he became irate. To show his contempt, Korah enlisted Dathan and Abiram (along with 250 other men) to join him in a **rebellion** against Moses' leadership.

The book of Numbers records Korah's disingenuous indictment against Moses: "You have gone far enough, for all the congregation are holy, every one of them, and the Lord is in their midst; so why do you exalt yourselves above the assembly of the Lord?" (Num. 16:3). In his pride, Korah disputed the idea that the people needed a leader and mediator, someone who could speak for God and teach them His truth (Ex. 4:10–17). He openly rebelled against the authority that God had given Moses, and he actively rallied others to support his spiritual mutiny.

God, however, responded by terminating **the rebellion of Korah** in an abrupt and decisive fashion, such that all the apostate rebels **perished.** Numbers 16:32–35 says,

> The earth opened its mouth and swallowed them up, and their households, and all the men who belonged to Korah with their possessions. So they and all that belonged to them went down alive to Sheol; and the earth closed over them, and they perished from the midst of the assembly. All Israel who were around them fled at their outcry, for they said, "The earth may swallow us up!" Fire also came forth from the Lord and consumed the two hundred and fifty men who were offering the incense.

Tragically, the consequences of the rebellion extended beyond the families of Korah, Dathan, and Abiram and the 250 men. In the aftermath of

God's judgment, many of the Israelites—having grown sympathetic to Korah's position—grumbled against Moses and Aaron. As a result, God sent a plague that killed an additional 14,700 Israelites (Num. 16:41–50). The plague's widespread devastation marked Korah's extensive influence among the people. Many of today's false teachers also have significant followings, composed of people who will share their judgment (cf. 1 Tim. 1:1–4). Yet, like Korah and his supporters, all apostate rebels will eventually experience God's wrath (cf. Mark 3:29; John 15:6; Heb. 10:26–31; Rev. 20:10–15).

COMPARISONS WITH FIVE NATURAL PHENOMENA

These are the men who are hidden reefs in your love feasts when they feast with you without fear, caring for themselves; clouds without water, carried along by winds; autumn trees without fruit, doubly dead, uprooted; wild waves of the sea, casting up their own shame like foam; wandering stars, for whom the black darkness has been reserved forever. (12–13)

In many of His parables, the Lord Jesus used natural phenomena as object lessons to illustrate spiritual truth (cf. the parable of the soils in Matt. 13:3–23; the parable of the tares and the wheat in Matt. 13:24–30, 36–43; the kingdom parables of Matt. 13:31–33, 44–50; the parables of the fig trees in Matt. 24:32–34 and Luke 13:6–9; and the parable of the lost sheep in Luke 15:3–7). The Psalms also contain many rich allusions to creation and natural phenomena (cf. Pss. 1, 8, 18, 23, 29, 33, 42, 46, 59, 68, 72, 90, 91, 97, 98, 104, 107, 114, 124, 135, 147, 148). In this passage Jude followed that well-established pattern by comparing apostates with five natural phenomena: hidden reefs, waterless clouds, fruitless autumn trees, wild sea waves, and wandering stars.

HIDDEN REEFS

These are the men who are hidden reefs in your love feasts when they feast with you without fear, caring for themselves; (12a)

Jude's description of apostates as **hidden reefs** graphically depicts the unseen danger they pose. **Reefs** are undersea coral formations usually located close to the shore. They are potentially harmful to ships because they can rip open the bottoms of their hulls, causing the vessels to sink. Like those **hidden reefs,** the apostates embedded themselves under the surface in the **love feasts** of the early church, from where they tore into unsuspecting people with their lies and wickedness. Originally, the love feast was intended to be a regular church gathering for the purpose of mutual instruction (cf. Acts 17:11), encouragement (Heb. 10:24–25), confrontation (cf. Heb. 3:13), and care (Rom. 12:10; 13:8; Gal. 5:13; Eph. 4:2, 25; 5:21; Col. 3:9; 1 Thess. 4:9; 1 Peter 4:9–10). The feast was similar to a contemporary potluck dinner held on the Lord's Day. Believers would gather to worship, hear the teaching of Scripture, celebrate Communion, and then share their common love in a meal (cf. Acts 2:42).

However, the love feast eventually became so corrupted and abused, due to the defiling influence of false teachers (cf. 1 Cor. 11:17–22), that it passed from the scene. Lacking a functioning conscience or sense of conviction, and being adept hypocrites, the apostates were able to **feast with** believers **without fear.** As Paul wrote to Timothy, such heretics are "liars seared in their own conscience as with a branding iron" (1 Tim. 4:2). The fact that their actions do terrible damage to others is of no concern to them. While the love feast was designed for believers to care for one another, the false teachers were guilty of **caring** only **for themselves.** The word rendered **caring** is from *poimainō,* "to shepherd," indicating that the apostates shepherded no one but themselves. Their only interest was self-interest and self-gratification—at the expense of anyone else.

WATERLESS CLOUDS

clouds without water, carried along by winds; (12b)

In normal weather cycles, clouds regularly produce the anticipation of rain. But **clouds without water** arrive with the mere promise of rain and then fail to deliver. Solomon said, "Like clouds and wind without rain is a man who boasts of his gifts falsely" (Prov. 25:14). Apostate teachers promise to bring the true spiritual blessing and refreshment from God, but they do not deliver on that promise. Jude likened them to clouds **carried along by** the **winds,** constantly portending rain but failing to produce it. The term translated **without water** (*anudros*) also occurs in Matthew 12:43 in reference to the wanderings of evil spirits through dry and barren places (cf. Luke 11:24–26). By describing false teachers in the same way that Luke describes demons, Jude reiterated the connection between the apostates and their satanic sources.

FRUITLESS AUTUMN TREES

autumn trees without fruit, doubly dead, uprooted; (12c)

Autumn is the season when farmers and gardeners expect to harvest the final crops of the year. If nothing comes, they must endure disappointment and hardship through the winter. The next spring they can begin again the painstaking process of fertilizing, planting, watering, and waiting for the crop to mature. With this in mind, the phrase **autumn trees without fruit** pictures the disappointing reality of a barren harvest.

Jude likened the apostates' empty profession and utter lack of spiritual life to a barren harvest. He called them **doubly dead;** first, they are fruitless because there is no life in them; second, they are **uprooted,** dead at the very core. They are like trees that have come out of the ground, disconnected from the life-giving source of water and nutrients. As Jesus said of the Pharisees, "Every plant which My heavenly Father did not plant shall be uprooted" (Matt. 15:13; cf. 3:10; 7:17–20; 13:6). Such people produce no life-changing fruit, neither in themselves nor in others.

WILD SEA WAVES

wild waves of the sea, casting up their own shame like foam; (13a)

Scripture often uses **the sea** as a symbol for those who do not know God. "The wicked are like the tossing sea," Isaiah wrote, "for it cannot be quiet, and its waters toss up refuse and mud. 'There is no peace,' says my God, 'for the wicked'" (57:20–21). In the aftermath of a storm, the seashore is littered with debris and mire, which is neither beneficial nor life-giving. That is a graphic picture of what false teachers produce. With all their empty talk and self-serving activity, they are like **wild waves.** In the end they are **casting up** only **their own shame like foam.** Their disgraceful attitudes and actions froth up to display all forms of heresy, deception, immorality, irreverence, and insubordination.

WANDERING STARS

wandering stars, for whom the black darkness has been reserved forever. (13b)

Wandering stars does not refer to heavenly bodies that continuously shine and have fixed orbits. Most likely the expression signifies a meteor or "shooting star" that flashes across the sky in an uncontrolled moment of brilliance and then disappears forever into **the black darkness** (cf. v. 6). Apostates often appear for a short time on the stage of Christianity. They promise enduring spiritual light and direction but deliver nothing but an erratic, aimless, worthless flash. The utter blackness and darkness of hell **has been reserved forever** for them (cf. 2 Peter 2:4,9,17).

Jude's striking descriptions, valid comparisons with the past, and graphic analogies to nature all paint a vivid portrait of apostates. False teachers are hypocritical deceivers, immoral sinners, materialistic hedonists, and, as a result, spiritual terrorists. They misrepresent the truth about the gospel of Christ and twist the teachings of Scripture. In contrast, true shepherds have an accurate understanding of the gospel (John 1:12–13; 3:16; Rom. 1:16–17; 1 Cor. 15:3–4) and a right view of who Jesus is (Matt. 16:16; Col. 2:9; cf. 1 Tim. 3:16). They possess a humble, submissive attitude to Christ's lordship (John 1:47–49; 20:27–28; Luke 5:8), and they understand the seriousness of the Lord's declaration, "I am the way, and the truth, and the life; no one comes to the Father but through Me" (John 14:6). False teachers, on the other hand, choose the way of Cain over the way of Christ, the error of Balaam over the truth of Christ, and the death of Korah over the life of Christ.

The Coming Judgment on Apostates (Jude 14–16)

It was also about these men that Enoch, in the seventh generation from Adam, prophesied, saying, "Behold, the Lord came with many thousands of His holy ones, to execute judgment upon all, and to convict all the ungodly of all their ungodly deeds which they have done in an ungodly way, and of all the harsh things which ungodly sinners have spoken against Him." These are grumblers, finding fault, following after their own lusts; they speak arrogantly, flattering people for the sake of gaining an advantage. (14–16)

Hell is certainly not a popular concept in Western society. In an age of tolerance and acceptance, the topic of eternal punishment is taboo; the very mention of it is considered unloving. After all, postmodern culture believes that everyone is basically good and expects that life after death (if the afterlife even exists) includes heaven for all but the most evil people.

Sadly, the political correctness and doctrinal ambiguity that characterizes the world has also permeated the church. Even among those who call themselves evangelicals, hell is regarded as a theological embarrassment. Passages that teach eternal destruction are often explained away, arbitrarily softened, or ignored altogether. As a result, society's erroneous views about God's judgment are only reinforced.

In stark contrast to the contemporary ambiguity, God's Word is unabashedly straightforward about the reality of divine judgment (cf. Gen. 6–8; Deut. 28:15–68; Isa. 1; 3; 5; 13–23; Jer. 2–9; 46–51; Ezek. 20:33–44; 25–32; Joel 3:12–16; Zech. 12:2, 9; 14:2; Mal. 3:2–6; Matt. 12:36; 25:31–46; Luke 12:48; Rom. 14:10–12; 1 Cor. 3:12–15; 5:5; 2 Cor. 5:10; Gal. 6:7; Col. 3:24–25; Rev. 6–20). Throughout its pages, themes of divine retribution, depicted in both temporal and eternal punishment, are impossible to miss. That God has judged, is judging, and will judge sinners, both with death and eternal punishment, is unmistakable. The New Testament's treatment of future judgment is especially clear and includes at least seven primary features.

First, the final aspect of God's divine wrath relates to a specific future event—namely, the second coming of Jesus Christ. At the end of the age, the Lord will return to earth to execute judgment: "He has fixed a day in which He will judge the world in righteousness through a Man whom He has appointed, having furnished proof to all men by raising Him from the dead" (Acts 17:31; cf. Matt. 24:29–30; Rom. 2:5–8, 16; 2 Peter 2:9*b;* Jude 6b; Rev. 6:16–17). No human knows the exact hour or day of the second coming—only the Father knows (Matt 24:36). But He has fixed the precise moment when His Son will return, an event which He promises will occur quickly (Rev. 22:7, 12, 20).

Second, this judgment will be general and public. For instance, at the sheep and goat judgment (which immediately precedes the millennial kingdom), Christ will call to account all the nations of the earth:

> But when the Son of Man comes in His glory, and all the angels with Him, then He will sit on His glorious throne. All the nations will be gathered before Him; and He will separate them from one another, as the shepherd separates the sheep from the goats; and He will put the sheep on His right, and the goats on the left. (Matt. 25:31–33)

No one anywhere will be able to hide his or her sins or escape responsibility for them (Matt. 10:26; Mark 4:22). The Great White Throne Judgment, at the end of earth's history, will be even more extensive—as all of God's enemies from every age are brought before Him for final sentencing (Rev. 20:7–15).

Third, God's judgment will be just and impartial (Rom. 2:11; Gal. 2:6; cf. Gen. 18:25). The apostle Paul declared that neither the openly wicked (Rom. 1:21–31) nor the self-righteous (2:1–3) will escape the judgment of God—judgment which God the Father has delegated to His Son, Jesus Christ (John 5:22, 27; cf. Matt. 16:27; Acts 10:42). Only God (in

His triune glory) is fit to judge, because only He is perfectly holy and righteous (Ex. 15:11; 1 Sam. 2:2; Ps. 47:8; Isa. 6:3; 57:15; Luke 1:35; Acts 4:27; Heb. 7:26; Rev. 3:7; 4:8).

Fourth, the promise of divine judgment is intended as a warning. The Lord designed it to produce fear of His wrath (Ex. 20:20; 2 Cor. 7:1; Heb. 10:27; 11:7; cf. John 19:8; Acts 24:25), as Jesus warned in Matthew 10:28, "Do not fear those who kill the body but are unable to kill the soul; but rather fear Him who is able to destroy both soul and body in hell." By warning men of His wrath, God graciously offers the lost an opportunity to repent (cf. 2 Peter 3:9).

Fifth, God's judgment is based on His law (Deut. 27:26; Rom. 2:12; 3:19; Gal. 3:10; James 2:10). Because their hearts are deceitful and desperately wicked (Jer. 17:9; Rom. 3:10–18; Gal. 5:19–21; Eph. 2:1–3), people are not only unable to keep God's law (Eccles. 7:20; Rom. 7:5; 8:7); they are also willfully disobedient of it (Ps. 78:10; Isa. 30:9; Jer. 9:13). Everyone has violated the law of God (Rom. 3:23; James 2:10); consequently, everyone deserves God's wrath (cf. 2 Thess. 1:6–8). But God extends forgiveness to those who genuinely believe in Jesus Christ (Rom. 10:9–10). Believers will not face God's final wrath because they have been saved through faith in the atoning work of Christ (Luke 18:13–14; Acts 3:19; Rom. 3:23–28; 4:3–5; 5:9; Eph. 1:7; Col. 2:13; 1 John 1:7), and their names are written in the Book of Life (cf. Rev. 3:5; 20:12; 21:24–27). On the other hand, those who persist in breaking God's law, showing no signs of true repentance, will be judged for their rebellious unbelief.

Sixth, God's final judgment will occur in specific phases. It will begin during the seven-year tribulation period (which immediately follows the rapture—1 Thess. 4:13–17; cf. Rev. 3:10). During the tribulation, God will unleash His wrath against the ungodly, through the seal (Rev. 6:1–8:5), trumpet (8:6–11:19), and bowl judgments (15:5–16:21). His judgment will culminate in the battle of Armageddon (19:11–21) in which He will utterly defeat His enemies. After Armageddon, the Lord will set up His earthly kingdom, during which Satan will be bound and Christ will reign in Jerusalem for one thousand years (20:1–6). Satan will then be released and lead one final rebellion, before he and his followers are cast into the lake of fire forever (20:7–15). That final sentencing (of all of God's enemies) is at the Great White Throne Judgment. So the first phase of God's judgment will be an earthly one during the tribulation period; the second and final phase will be a heavenly one at the foot of His throne.

Finally, God's retribution ultimately results in eternal damnation in hell:

> So just as the tares are gathered up and burned with fire, so shall it be at the end of the age. The Son of Man will send forth His angels, and they will gather out of His kingdom all stumbling blocks, and those

who commit lawlessness, and will throw them into the furnace of fire; in that place there will be weeping and gnashing of teeth. (Matt. 13:40–42; cf. 24:50–51; John 5:29)

During the course of His earthly ministry, the Lord had much to say about the reality of hell. In His Sermon on the Mount, Jesus warned of the danger of hell (Matt. 5:22) and spoke of the whole body entering it (5:30). This reality of a body in hell was clearly taught by the Lord in His words concerning the "resurrection of judgment" (John 5:29). In His references to hell, Jesus used the word *gehenna*. That familiar term, which identified the continuously burning city dump in the Valley of Hinnom outside Jerusalem, graphically illustrated to Jesus' listeners the fiery torment of hell (cf. Mark 9:43–48). Near the end of the Sermon, Jesus pictured false teachers as trees that do not bear good fruit and are "cut down and thrown into the fire" (Matt. 7:19).

Perhaps Jesus' most dramatic and frightening depiction of hell appears in the story of the rich man and Lazarus:

Now the poor man [Lazarus] died and was carried away by the angels to Abraham's bosom; and the rich man also died and was buried. In Hades he lifted up his eyes, being in torment, and saw Abraham far away and Lazarus in his bosom. And he cried out and said, "Father Abraham, have mercy on me, and send Lazarus so that he may dip the tip of his finger in water and cool off my tongue, for I am in agony in this flame." But Abraham said, "Child, remember that during your life you received your good things, and likewise Lazarus bad things; but now he is being comforted here, and you are in agony. And besides all this, between us and you there is a great chasm fixed, so that those who wish to come over from here to you will not be able, and that none may cross over from there to us." (Luke 16:22–26)

God reserves the severest judgment for those who hear the truth but reject it. In addressing some of the Galilean towns that refused to believe in Him, Jesus warned,

Woe to you, Chorazin! Woe to you, Bethsaida! For if the miracles had occurred in Tyre and Sidon which occurred in you, they would have repented long ago in sackcloth and ashes. Nevertheless I say to you, it will be more tolerable for Tyre and Sidon in the day of judgment than for you. And you, Capernaum, will not be exalted to heaven, will you? You will descend to Hades; for if the miracles had occurred in Sodom which occurred in you, it would have remained to this day. Nevertheless I say to you that it will be more tolerable for the land of Sodom in the day of judgment, than for you. (Matt. 11:21–24; cf. Luke 12:46–48)

Jesus also excoriated the hypocrisy and false teaching of the scribes and Pharisees. He condemned them for their sanctimonious pride, legalism, greed, and overall spiritual blindness. In response to their self-righteous duplicity, Jesus pronounced this fate on them: "You serpents, you brood of vipers, how will you escape the sentence of hell?" (Matt. 23:33; cf. the entire chapter; Matt. 16:6, 11–12; Mark 7:5–8; Luke 11:44).

Such warnings of judgment are especially applicable to apostates and false teachers. Those who claim to represent Christ yet do irreparable damage to His message (such that souls are eternally lost) will receive the severest judgment of all. The writer of Hebrews issued this stern warning to anyone who trifles with divine truth—a warning particularly ominous for false teachers:

> For if we go on sinning willfully after receiving the knowledge of the truth, there no longer remains a sacrifice for sins, but a terrifying expectation of judgment and the fury of a fire which will consume the adversaries. Anyone who has set aside the Law of Moses dies without mercy on the testimony of two or three witnesses. How much severer punishment do you think he will deserve who has trampled under foot the Son of God, and has regarded as unclean the blood of the covenant by which he was sanctified, and has insulted the Spirit of grace? For we know Him who said, "Vengeance is Mine, I will repay." And again, "The Lord will judge His people." It is a terrifying thing to fall into the hands of the living God. (Heb. 10:26–31; cf. 2 Peter 2:1–2, 20–21; 3:7; Rev. 19:20)

Jude previously pointed out that the apostates "were long beforehand marked out for this condemnation" (v. 4; cf. vv. 6, 13). Verses 14–16 reaffirm that truth and the truth of all the other New Testament judgment passages that precede it. The passage first underscores the fact of an ancient prophecy by Enoch; then it suggests three certainties regarding God's final judgment: The Lord will come, He will not come alone, and He will come to execute judgment on deserving recipients.

THE FACT OF ENOCH'S ANCIENT PROPHECY

It was also about these men that Enoch, in the seventh generation from Adam, prophesied, (14a)

These men refers to the apostates whom Jude pictured in the previous section—the false visionaries, the flouters of spiritual authority, the revilers, the brute beasts who behave by carnal instinct, the hidden reefs, the waterless clouds, the dead and uprooted trees, the wild sea waves, and the wandering stars headed for eternal blackness. Even before the Flood, **Enoch** (Gen. 5:21–24) **prophesied** that the Lord would come to judge such false teachers. By citing Enoch, Jude underscored the motivation behind God's judgment on apostasy while also reinforcing the certainty of it.

Even though this prophecy is not recorded in the Old Testament, the Holy Spirit inspired Jude (cf. 2 Tim. 3:16; 2 Peter 1:20–21) to use it because it was familiar, historically valid, and supported his overall thesis. Jude extracted the quote from the pseudepigraphal book of *1 Enoch*, with which his first-century readers were well acquainted. The book was part of the written history and tradition of the Jewish people, and rabbinical allusions to it were not uncommon.

Though he was not the author of the book, Enoch's message was passed down through oral tradition until it was finally recorded in what was called *1 Enoch*. That book, like other books such as *The Book of Jubilee, The Testament of the Twelve Patriarchs,* and *The Assumption of Moses* (from which Jude probably quoted in v. 9), was not part of the Old Testament canon; yet, since it was accurate, it was acceptable for Jude to use it to bolster his argument. None other than the apostle Paul occasionally followed the same pattern (of citing nonbiblical sources to make a legitimate spiritual point) in his teaching (cf. Acts 17:28; 1 Cor. 15:33; Titus 1:12). (For a further discussion of Jude's use of apocryphal works, see the Introduction to Jude in this volume.)

Enoch stood **in the seventh generation from Adam** (Gen. 5:4–24). He was a hero to the Jewish people because, like the prophet Elijah later (2 Kings 2:11–12), he went to heaven without dying: "Enoch walked with God; and he was not, for God took him" (Gen. 5:24; cf. Heb. 11:5). Although it was not included in the biblical record until the book of Jude, Enoch's prophecy is the earliest human prophecy found anywhere in Scripture. (The only earlier prophecy recorded in the Bible was made by God in Gen. 3:15.) In fact, Enoch's message predated the words of Moses, Samuel, and the Hebrew prophets by many centuries.

CERTAINTIES REGARDING GOD'S JUDGMENT

saying, "Behold, the Lord came with many thousands of His holy ones, to execute judgment upon all, and to convict all the ungodly of all their ungodly deeds which they have done in an ungodly way, and of all the harsh things which ungodly sinners have spoken against Him." These are grumblers, finding fault, following after their own lusts; they speak arrogantly, flattering people for the sake of gaining an advantage. (14b–16)

Enoch's prophecy and Jude's subsequent comments set forth three certainties regarding God's judgment on apostasy. The first certainty is that **the Lord** will come (cf. Dan. 7:13; Luke 12:40; Acts 1:9–11; 1 Thess. 3:13). The aorist tense of the verb translated **came** suggests Enoch's vision was so startling and convincing that he spoke as if the judgment had already occurred. The certainty of Christ's return was under attack from the false teachers, and Jude's reminder reinforced the apostle Peter's earlier teaching on this matter (cf. 2 Peter 3:1–10 and the commentary on that passage in chapter 8 of this volume).

Second, the Lord will not come alone. While He alone is the final judge, He will be accompanied by **many thousands of His holy ones. Holy ones** ("saints") could refer to believers (cf. 1 Cor. 1:2; 1 Thess. 3:13), who will return with Christ when He comes in judgment (Rev. 19:14; cf. Zech. 14:5). However, the emphasis on judgment here seems to favor viewing the **holy ones** as angels, since angels appear in other judgment contexts in the New Testament (Matt. 24:31; 25:31; Mark 8:38; 2 Thess. 1:7). The saints will have a judgment role during the millennial kingdom (Rev. 2:26–27; 3:21; cf. Dan. 7:22; 1 Cor. 6:2), but angels will serve as God's executioners when Christ returns (Matt. 13:39–41, 49–50; 24:29–31; 25:31; 2 Thess. 1:7–10).

Third, the Lord will come with a definite purpose, **to execute judgment upon** many deserving recipients. Those people are **all the ungodly** who have utterly disregarded God's law. The verb translated **to convict** (*elegchō*) means "to expose," "rebuke," or "prove guilty," which includes showing someone his error and culpability. When the Lord returns, the sins of the ungodly will be exposed and the verdict rendered accordingly. The final sentence, as noted earlier, will be eternal punishment in hell (Rev. 20:11–15; cf. Matt. 5:22; 7:19; 8:12; 10:28; 13:40–42; 25:41, 46).

All the ungodly includes the apostates (see the discussion of v. 4 in chapter 11 of this volume). As the righteous Judge, God must punish them because **of all their ungodly deeds which they have done in an ungodly way, and of all the harsh things which ungodly sinners have spoken against Him.** Enoch's fourfold use of **ungodly** (*asebēs*, "godlessness," or "impiety") to describe the apostates (cf. 2 Peter 2:5–6; 3:7) identifies their basic sinful attitude; they refused to have a proper reverence for God. All such reprobates—like the immoral, irreverent, and blasphemous false teachers—are storing up divine wrath and punishment for themselves in the day of judgment (Rom. 2:5; cf. Ps. 2:2–5; Jer. 10:10; Nah. 1:6; John 3:36; Rom. 1:18; 1 Thess. 2:16; Heb. 10:26–27). Their punishment comes because of their ungodly actions and their ungodly speech; both their works and their words betray the wickedness of their hearts.

It is certain the Lord will come to mete out judgment to the godless guilty. **These** refers once again to the apostate teachers who threatened the church (cf. vv. 4, 8, 10, 12–13). In verse 16 Jude looks particularly at the sins of their mouths. **Grumblers** occurs only here in the New Testament and is the same term the Septuagint uses to describe Israel's murmurings against God (Ex. 16:7–9; Num. 14:27, 29; cf. John 6:41; 1 Cor. 10:10). Like the ancient Israelites (Pss. 106:24–25; 107:11; Zech. 7:11), they grumbled against the truth and murmured against God's holy law. The apostates were also **finding fault** or complaining about God's holy purpose and plan. The word translated **finding fault** (*mempsimoiros*) means "to blame," and describes one who is perpetually discontent and dissatisfied. The false teachers brazenly attacked the Lord and His truth—a fact Jude illustrated earlier in his letter by comparing them with the unbelieving Israelites, the reprobates of Sodom and Gomorrah, the fallen angels, Cain, Korah, and Balaam.

In a self-centered manner, the false teachers were at odds with God because they were **following after their own lusts** (cf. vv. 4, 7; 2 Peter 2:10, 18; 3:3). This New Testament phrase commonly described the unconverted (cf. v. 18; 2 Peter 3:3). The apostates were so dominated by self that **they** spoke **arrogantly,** or as the *New King James Version* renders the expression, they used "great swelling words." They pompously puffed themselves up with an elaborate, sophisticated religious vocabulary that had an external spiritual tone and attractiveness but was void of divine truth and substance. By such speech they were also **flattering people for the sake of gaining an advantage.** The apostates were good at telling people what they wanted them to hear (cf. 2 Tim. 4:3–4), cleverly manipulating others for their own gain. They certainly did not care about proclaiming God's truth for the edification of their hearers (cf. Pss. 5:9; 12:2–3; Prov. 26:28; 29:5; Rom. 3:13; 16:18).

It was Jesus who said that "the things that proceed out of the mouth come from the heart, and those defile the man" (Matt. 15:18). In the case of false teachers, their lips reveal their discontentment, hypocrisy, lust, pride, and selfishness. Their mouths betray the wickedness of their hearts. And, as Enoch foretold, their sin will one day be exposed by the perfect Judge who will render them guilty for their spiritual crimes.

In this passage, Jude affirms the promise, the participants, and the purpose of the Lord's coming in judgment. He thus addresses the *who, what, where,* and *why* of Christ's return. The only major question that he does not answer is *when,* and the answer to that lies solely with God. As the Lord Jesus fittingly exhorted His apostles:

But of that day or hour no one knows, not even the angels in heaven, nor the Son, but the Father alone. Take heed, keep on the alert; for you do not know when the appointed time will come. It is like a man away on a journey, who upon leaving his house and putting his slaves in charge, assigning to each one his task, also commanded the door-keeper to stay on the alert. Therefore, be on the alert—for you do not know when the master of the house is coming, whether in the evening, at midnight, or when the rooster crows, or in the morning—in case he should come suddenly and find you asleep. What I say to you I say to all, "Be on the alert!" (Mark 13:32–37; cf. Luke 21:34–36)

Survival Strategy for Apostate Times (Jude 17–23)

14

But you, beloved, ought to remember the words that were spoken beforehand by the apostles of our Lord Jesus Christ, that they were saying to you, "In the last time there will be mockers, following after their own ungodly lusts." These are the ones who cause divisions, worldly-minded, devoid of the Spirit. But you, beloved, building yourselves up on your most holy faith, praying in the Holy Spirit, keep yourselves in the love of God, waiting anxiously for the mercy of our Lord Jesus Christ to eternal life. And have mercy on some, who are doubting; save others, snatching them out of the fire; and on some have mercy with fear, hating even the garment polluted by the flesh. (17–23)

As Jude's letter draws to its conclusion, one crucial question arises: How can we as believers practically contend for the truth so that we will be victorious in a day of rampant falsehood? In other words, how can we personally apply Jude's cautions regarding apostasy to our own lives and ministries? To be sure, Jude's warning is unmistakable, and it clearly demands a response. But what does that response look like? And where does it begin?

Jude, of course, recognized that his readers needed more than just a warning; they also needed a plan of attack. Instead of being merely defensive, they had to be proactive in their fight for the faith. And this meant taking action—not only in reinforcing their own spiritual armor (cf. Eph. 6:10–17), but also in coming to the aid of others in the church.

In order to do this, Jude's readers desperately needed to develop discernment. They had to be able to recognize the difference between truth and error. Otherwise, they would not know what to embrace and what to shun. They could not "contend earnestly for the faith which was once for all handed down to the saints" (v. 3) unless they were able to discern true faith from its counterfeits. Thus if they were to heed Jude's warnings, they had to begin by actively pursuing spiritual discernment.

The importance of discernment is underscored throughout the whole of Scripture (Prov. 2:3; 23:23; 1 Cor. 16:13; Phil. 1:9; Heb. 5:14; Rev. 2:2). The apostle Paul, for example, voiced his fear that the Corinthians would be led astray:

> I wish that you would bear with me in a little foolishness; but indeed you are bearing with me. For I am jealous for you with a godly jealousy; for I betrothed you to one husband, so that to Christ I might present you as a pure virgin. But I am afraid that, as the serpent deceived Eve by his craftiness, your minds will be led astray from the simplicity and purity of devotion to Christ. For if one comes and preaches another Jesus whom we have not preached, or you receive a different spirit which you have not received, or a different gospel which you have not accepted, you bear this beautifully. (2 Cor. 11:1–4)

Concerned about their lack of discernment, Paul feared that the people would be deceived by false teachers. They were far too tolerant of error, and as a result they foolishly threw open the door to apostasy.

Along those same lines, Paul admonished the Thessalonians to prize sound teaching and exercise discernment. He instructed them, "Do not despise prophetic utterances. But examine everything carefully; hold fast to that which is good; abstain from every form of evil" (1 Thess. 5:20–22; cf. 1 John 4:1–3). The believers in Thessalonica were to respond carefully to the spiritual messages they heard—examining them thoroughly to see whether or not they accorded with apostolic teaching. The messages that passed the test were to be held fast and embraced. But those that did not were to be abstained from and rejected.

Even the Jewish religious leaders and elite scholars of Jesus' day lacked spiritual perception. The Lord indicted them for being more discerning of the weather than spiritual matters:

> The Pharisees and Sadducees came up, and testing Jesus, they asked Him to show them a sign from heaven. But He replied to them, "When it is evening, you say, 'It will be fair weather, for the sky is red.' And in the morning, 'There will be a storm today, for the sky is red and threatening.' Do you know how to discern the appearance of the sky, but cannot discern the signs of the times? An evil and adulterous generation seeks after a sign; and a sign will not be given it, except the sign of Jonah." And He left them and went away. (Matt. 16:1–4)

Despite their fastidious attention to Scripture, their rigorous theological training, and their prominent status in the community, the Pharisees and Sadducees rejected the truth because they could not discern it.

Tragically, there are many in the contemporary church who also lack spiritual discernment. Such people are far better at staying in tune with cultural trends than they are at appreciating and understanding biblical doctrine. In some cases, whole churches have shifted their focus from the clear teachings of Scripture to the felt needs of sinners. They want to make the church service "comfortable" and "non confrontational." As a result, the messages they champion are theologically weak, and the people they serve are doctrinally naïve. Those churches are defenseless against error.

There are at least six reasons for the disturbing lack of discernment that characterizes much of contemporary Christianity. Obviously, the first is the recent trend among many evangelicals to minimize the importance of doctrine. Those in this camp argue that biblical clarity is both divisive and unloving—to them it puts up walls, lacks humility, and hinders unity. The reality, however, is that the church has suffered severe consequences for abandoning its commitment to sound doctrine. Such repercussions include a false sense of humility and a false faith produced by "easy believism" and watered-down gospel presentations, a false unity based on inter-religious ecumenism and theological compromise, a false commission preoccupied with political activism and legislated morality, a false worship driven by man-centered services and experience-based Christianity, and a false ministry focused solely on temporal satisfaction and external success—it all makes people feel comfortable in this life but utterly fails to prepare them for the life to come.

A second reason is that the church has become less objective in its outlook, substituting unconditional truth for moral relativism and postmodern subjectivity. Instead of seeing truth in terms of black and white, many Christians treat it as a gray area. But the Bible is clearly antithetical; it makes absolute distinctions between right and wrong, truth and error, saving faith and false professions. The Lord Jesus' teaching, for example, was black and white: He contrasted the broad way and the narrow way (Matt. 7:13–14), eternal damnation and eternal life (Matt. 24:46–51), the kingdom of Satan and the kingdom of God (Matt. 13:38), hate and love (Matt. 5:43–44), worldly wisdom and divine wisdom (cf. Matt. 11:16–19; Mark 6:2), and so forth. In contrast, the contemporary church shies away from theological absolutes, preferring instead to tolerantly embrace "every wind of doctrine" (Eph. 4:14), as if that stance were a virtue.

Third, as part of its contemporary evangelistic strategy, the church has abandoned its commitment to the power of Scripture and become preoccupied with its image. In order to reach the culture, it has become like the culture. But James wrote, "Do you not know that friendship with the world is hostility toward God? Therefore whoever wishes to be a friend of the world makes himself an enemy of God" (James 4:4; cf. 1 John 2:15–17). To be a friend of God makes us enemies of the world, and vice versa. We are kidding ourselves to think that the key to winning the lost is found in imitating them. By mimicking secular society, some believers are actually forfeiting their distinctiveness and the power of the Scripture. And if the distinct call of the gospel is lost, any hope of evangelizing the culture will also disappear (cf. Matt. 5:13).

Fourth, and in consequence of the previous point, the church's current lack of discernment stems from a failure to properly study and interpret the Scriptures. Pastoral laziness, exegetical sloppiness, and a general attitude of indifference to God's Word have plunged God's people into error. Because he understood the deadly dangers of such spiritual apathy, the apostle Paul commanded Timothy to "be diligent to present yourself approved to God as a workman who does not need to be ashamed, accurately handling the word of truth" (2 Tim. 2:15; cf. 2 Cor. 4:2). The book of Acts also commended the brethren in Berea for being "more noble-minded than those in Thessalonica, for they received the word with great eagerness, examining the Scriptures daily to see whether these things were so" (17:11; cf. 1 Thess. 2:13). As the Berean's example demonstrates, discernment cannot develop apart from a desire to know the truth and a determination to discover it. Yet this deep concern for truth is scarcely found today.

A fifth reason is the general abandonment of church discipline in evangelical circles (cf. Matt. 18:15–18). When God's people fail to confront sin and heresy, wickedness within the body goes unchecked. The congregation inevitably accumulates more and more unregenerate members—unbelievers who feel comfortable because their sin issues are never addressed. Even grievous immorality and major ethical lapses are sometimes overlooked, ignored under a false pretense of love. But a church cannot effectively promote discernment if it happily condones sin or primarily consists of unsaved sinners. After all, the congregation that thinks incorrectly about holiness shows that it also thinks incorrectly about truth.

A final reason for the church's lack of discernment is the rampant void of spiritual maturity within its ranks. Those with a superficial understanding of Scripture (cf. Mark 12:24), a weak grasp of sound doctrine, and a deficient view of God cannot be discerning. Yet those are the very people who fill most pews each Sunday. Like the unbelieving Jews of the first century, many contemporary Christians would do well to heed the admonition given by the author of Hebrews:

> For though by this time you ought to be teachers, you have need again for someone to teach you the elementary principles of the oracles of God, and you have come to need milk and not solid food. For everyone who partakes only of milk is not accustomed to the word of righteousness, for he is an infant. But solid food is for the mature, who because of practice have their senses trained to discern good and evil. (Heb. 5:12–14)

(For much more on the subject of spiritual discernment and the church's desperate need to recover this crucial ability, see John MacArthur, *Reckless Faith* [Wheaton, Ill.: Crossway, 1994], and MacArthur, gen. ed., *Fool's Gold?* [Wheaton, Ill.: Crossway, 2005], especially chaps. 1 and 12.)

If those in today's church are to honor the God of revelation and enjoy spiritual victory in their lives, despite the constant temptation to capitulate, they must begin by developing discernment. They must be able to differentiate between what is right and what is wrong, such that they will be able to pursue the one and flee the other. This calls for being serious and precise in interpreting Scripture. Otherwise, in their confusion, professing believers will fail to contend for the faith before they even enter the battle.

In this section, Jude addresses how to properly contend for the faith and prosper spiritually during increasingly more apostate times. The Lord's brother presented his readers with three crucial truths that, if faithfully applied, will grant all believers discernment: They must remember, remain, and reach out.

REMEMBER

But you, beloved, ought to remember the words that were spoken beforehand by the apostles of our Lord Jesus Christ, that they were saying to you, "In the last time there will be mockers, following after their own ungodly lusts." These are the ones who cause divisions, worldly-minded, devoid of the Spirit. (17–19)

Jude's words here echo verses 5–7 and 11–13, which reminded his readers that false teachers pose a constant threat. They were present during Old Testament times (Isa. 28:7; Jer. 23:14; Ezek. 13:4; Mic. 3:11; Zeph. 3:4), they afflicted the early church (1 John 2:18–19; 2 John 7–11; Rev. 2:2–3, 15–16; 3:9), they are active today, and they will continue to be a threat in the future (2 Thess. 2:1–4; Rev. 13; 19:19–20). Because they have always plagued God's people, their presence should not surprise believers in any era.

Like Peter (2 Peter 1:12–13), Jude exhorted his readers **to remember** the truths they had already heard—**the words that were spoken beforehand by the apostles of** the **Lord Jesus Christ** who predicted the coming of apostasy. The Lord Himself was the first one in the New Testament to warn against false teachers: "Beware of the false prophets, who come to you in sheep's clothing, but inwardly are ravenous wolves" (Matt. 7:15; cf. 24:11). As he defended his apostleship to the Corinthians, Paul echoed these same concerns:

> But what I am doing I will continue to do, so that I may cut off opportunity from those who desire an opportunity to be regarded just as we are in the matter about which they are boasting. For such men are false apostles, deceitful workers, disguising themselves as apostles of Christ. No wonder, for even Satan disguises himself as an angel of light. Therefore it is not surprising if his servants also disguise themselves as servants of righteousness, whose end will be according to their deeds. (2 Cor. 11:12–15)

The apostle gave additional warnings about false teachers in several of his other epistles (Col. 2:16–19; 1 Thess. 2:14–16; 2 Thess. 2:3–12; 1 Tim. 4:1–3; 6:20–21; 2 Tim. 2:17–19; 3:1–9; 4:1–3). Similarly, Peter warned that "there will also be false teachers . . . who will secretly introduce destructive heresies, even denying the Master who bought them, bringing swift destruction upon themselves" (2 Peter 2:1; see the commentary on 2 Peter 2 in chapters 5–7 of this volume). And the apostle John wrote, "Beloved, do not believe every spirit, but test the spirits to see whether they are from God, because many false prophets have gone out into the world" (1 John 4:1; cf. 2:18–19; 2 John 7; 3 John 9–11).

Repeatedly, Christ and the apostles **were saying** that false teachers would infiltrate the church and oppose the truth. In light of that, Jude quoted Peter's warning, **"In the last time there will be mockers, following after their own ungodly lusts"** (see 2 Peter 3:3). (That the word translated **mockers** appears in the New Testament only here and in 2 Peter 3:3 suggests that Jude quoted Peter; see the discussion of Jude's relationship to Peter in the Introduction to Jude.) The technical phrase

the last time refers to the period between Christ's first and second comings (cf. Acts 2:17; Gal. 4:4; 2 Tim. 3:1; Heb. 1:2; 1 Peter 1:5, 20; 1 John 2:18–19; James 5:3).

Peter said the mockers scoffed at the truth of Christ's return (2 Peter 3:4), and here Jude implied that they mocked the law of God (cf. the discussion of "grumblers" in chapter 13 of this volume). Both ideas, of course, are parallel since those who mock the law of God will also mock Christ's return; they do not want to be accountable to the divine Judge for their sins, either in the present or the future.

Such mockers will be **following after their own ungodly lusts,** a fact Jude already established in verses 4, 15, and 16. They will give free reign to their passions and dissipations because they have no capacity for holiness. Since their hearts are not transformed, all they can do is pursue their own ungodly desires.

Jude further described the false teachers as **the ones who cause divisions.** The word *apodiorizō* (**divisions**) refers to the motivation behind the false teachers' behavior, as well as its divisive effect. The term means "to make a distinction" and, in the case of the apostates, meant that they portrayed themselves as superior to those who taught the truth. Like the Pharisees, they were arrogant (Luke 16:15; 18:9, 11) and condescending (Matt. 23:4–5), adhering to their self-styled set of standards (cf. Mark 7:5–8)—their own elite understanding of "the truth" (cf. Matt. 16:6, 11–12). Instead of putting others before themselves (which is the key to true spiritual unity—cf. Phil. 2:1–4), they exalted themselves and their own agendas. Naturally, the end result was division and strife in the body.

Worldly-minded (*psuchikos*, lit. "soulish") is more accurately translated "sensual persons" (NKJV). With a certain deference to Greek philosophy, Jude depicted the false teachers in strictly physical terms. His materialistic description exposed them for who they really were— religious terrorists who lacked such internal qualities as a proper self-perception, the ability to reason, and a true knowledge of God. Even though the false teachers claimed a transcendental understanding of God, they did not know Him at all—they were **devoid of the Spirit** (cf. John 3:5; Rom. 8:9; 1 John 3:24; 4:13). The truth is that they were physically alive but, because they had never been regenerated by the Holy Spirit, they were spiritually dead. They were religious frauds who paid lip service to faith and spiritual life but denied such claims by their actions. As Paul told Titus, "They profess to know God, but by their deeds they deny Him, being detestable and disobedient and worthless for any good deed" (Titus 1:16).

Remain

But you, beloved, building yourselves up on your most holy faith, praying in the Holy Spirit, keep yourselves in the love of God, waiting anxiously for the mercy of our Lord Jesus Christ to eternal life. (20–21)

For those of us who are Christians to exercise discernment and protect ourselves from being led astray, we must remain on the path of sanctification. Doing so involves first **building** ourselves **up on** our **most holy faith.** We must become doctrinally strong if we would recognize error and effectively fight the battle for truth. The present, active participle translated **building yourselves up** has an imperatival sense —meaning it is not optional. Metaphorically, the idea of building up refers to personal edification and spiritual growth, and it implies the establishment of the firm foundation of sound doctrine. As in verse 3, the **most holy faith** is the objective body of biblical truth.

Practically speaking, edification centers on studying the Word of God and learning to apply it. In Acts 20:32 Paul tells the Ephesian elders, "I commend you to God and to the word of His grace, which is able to build you up and to give you the inheritance among all those who are sanctified." All the ministries of the church should result in edification (Rom. 14:19; 1 Cor. 14:12, 26; Eph. 4:16; 1 Thess. 5:11; cf. 1 Cor. 8:1). God gave the church apostles, prophets, evangelists, and pastor/teachers to proclaim His Word, which results in "the building up of the body of Christ" (Eph. 4:11–12; cf. Col. 2:6–7). Peter wrote that believers should desire the Word for spiritual growth, just as babies desire milk for their physical nourishment (1 Peter 2:2). Along those same lines, the apostle John wrote that the spiritually strong believers, those capable of successfully waging effective warfare for the truth, are those in whom the Word of God abides (1 John 2:14).

A second essential element of sanctification involves **praying in the Holy Spirit.** That expression does not refer to speaking in tongues, but to praying for that which is consistent with the Spirit's will— His desires, directives, and decrees. Although His will is revealed through the plain commands of Scripture (Deut. 17:19–20; Pss. 19:7, 11; 119:11, 105, 130; Prov. 6:23; Matt. 4:4; Luke 11:28; John 5:39; Rom. 15:4; 2 Tim. 3:16–17; James 1:25), we as believers do not always know how to practically apply it to the various issues of life. Therefore the Holy Spirit intercedes for us before the Father with genuine sympathy and inexpressible fervor (Rom. 8:26–27). Of course, the Spirit's will and the Father's will— and even praying in Jesus' name—are one and the same. When we pray **in the Holy Spirit** we submit ourselves to Him, rest on His wisdom, seek

His will, and trust in His power (cf. John 14:14–17; 1 John 5:14–15).

As we who believe pursue sanctification, we must also **keep** ourselves **in the love of God.** This is a vitally important principle, and it means to remain in the sphere of God's love, or the place of His blessing (Rom. 5:5; 8:39; 1 John 4:16). On a practical level, it means that we must stay obedient to God, since divine blessing is promised only within the sphere of obedience. As Jesus told the apostles:

> Just as the Father has loved Me, I have also loved you; abide in My love. If you keep My commandments, you will abide in My love; just as I have kept My Father's commandments and abide in His love. These things I have spoken to you so that My joy may be in you, and that your joy may be made full. (John 15:9–11; cf. 1 John 2:5)

On the other hand, if we become disobedient, we move from a position of blessing to a position of chastisement (Heb. 12:3–11).

Finally, as we pursue sanctification, we Christians must be **waiting anxiously for the mercy of** the **Lord Jesus Christ to eternal life.** The verb translated **waiting anxiously** (*prosdechomai*) means "to wait for," or "to welcome," and connotes doing so with great expectancy. Thus we are to live with eternity in view as we eagerly anticipate the Lord's return (1 Cor. 1:7; Phil. 3:20; 1 Thess. 1:10; 2 Tim. 4:8; Titus 2:12–13; cf. 1 Peter 4:7; 2 Peter 3:11–13 and the commentary on these three verses in chapter 9 of this volume). On that great future day, all of us who have trusted in Him will experience Christ's final **mercy** and enjoy the fullness of **eternal life** (cf. Rom. 2:7; 1 Tim. 6:12; 1 John 5:13) as we experience the resurrection and glorification of our bodies (John 5:24; 17:3; Rom. 5:17; 2 Tim. 1:10; 1 John 5:20; cf. Dan. 7:18).

REACH OUT

And have mercy on some, who are doubting; save others, snatching them out of the fire; and on some have mercy with fear, hating even the garment polluted by the flesh. (22–23)

Those who pose the greatest threat to the church also constitute part of its mission field. Not only are believers responsible to identify and oppose the enemy and his error; they are also commanded to reach out and evangelize the enemy with the truth. That is precisely what Jesus sought to do when He had meals with the Pharisees (Luke 7:36; 11:37–38; 14:1); while He denounced them as heretics, He also proclaimed to them the way of salvation (Luke 7:40–50; cf. 14:3–6). Nicodemus, for example, was a Pharisee who sincerely sought the truth (John 3:1–21). His honest investigation into Jesus' teachings was met with compassion and kindness from the Savior.

In these two verses Jude identifies three categories of unbelieving people who, from the church's perspective, are both a menace and a mission field. They are the confused, the convinced, and the committed.

TO THE CONFUSED

And have mercy on some, who are doubting; (22)

The heretical and deceptive statements made by false teachers, along with their licentious lifestyles, can easily confuse some people within the church. In fact, that was exactly what happened at both Corinth (2 Cor. 11:3) and Galatia (Gal. 3:1–5; cf. 1:6–9). And it still happens today. Caught in the web of deception, some find themselves thoroughly confused—unsure of what is true and what isn't. In reaching out to such people, Jude called the church to **have mercy on** them, showing kindness, compassion, and sympathy to those who **are doubting.**

Like wolves stalking sheep, false teachers prey on weak people (cf. 2 Tim. 3:6), individuals who are vacillating, unsure, and mired in doubt (James 1:6–8; cf. Pss. 73:13–16; 77:7–9). Those who are strong must show mercy to such souls as they are torn between truth and error (cf. Eph. 4:14), commitment and noncommitment (Heb. 3:7–4:13; 6:1–12). Showing mercy does not mean ignoring the seriousness of false teaching or commending the weak for their vacillation. But it does mean exhorting such people with the truth, in meekness and patience, being diligent to present the gospel to them before they are permanently caught in heresy.

TO THE CONVINCED

save others, snatching them out of the fire; (23a)

In this aspect of outreach, the challenge for believers increases. It is no longer merely a matter of showing mercy; it becomes the difficult task of rescuing those who are already convinced of false teaching. But in humility and faith we who would be faithful must be willing to be used by God to **save others.** God remains the ultimate source of salvation (Ps. 3:8; Jonah 2:9; John 1:12–13; 3:6–8; Eph. 2:8), but we are the secondary means He uses to reach sinners (cf. Acts 2:37–41; 4:1–4; 8:26–38;

13:46–48; 16:13–14). James wrote, "My brethren, if any among you strays from the truth and one turns him back, let him know that he who turns a sinner from the error of his way will save his soul from death and will cover a multitude of sins" (James 5:19–20).

Snatching translates *harpazō,* and presents the strong image of seizing something, or taking something or somebody by force. Jude undoubtedly borrowed this imagery from the prophets, specifically Amos's statement about Israel, "You were like a firebrand snatched from a blaze" (Amos 4:11; cf. Zech 3:2). Even as he penned his letter, Jude apparently knew of some who had already been drawn into the damning doctrines of the apostates. He pictured them as having been singed by the very **fire** of hell, a foreshadowing of the eternal inferno that would one day engulf them if they continued to embrace false teaching (cf. Isa. 33:14; Matt. 13:42).

The only way to rescue such people is to crush their false ideologies before it is too late. And this can be done only by the power of God's truth (2 Cor. 10:3–5). Jesus modeled this principle during His earthly ministry. To those who were confused, unsure, and filled with doubts, He patiently and gently presented the gospel (John 4:10–26; 6:26–59). But to those committed to false teaching, such as the scribes and Pharisees and their devotees, He bluntly warned of the gravity of their lost condition (Matt. 12:1–37; 15:1–14; Luke 11:37–54; John 8:12–59).

TO THE COMMITTED

and on some have mercy with fear, hating even the garment polluted by the flesh. (23*b*)

Sometimes Christians may have the opportunity to reach out to the most committed apostates. Such heretics are profoundly deceived individuals who are deeply committed to their own deceptions. In some cases, they are even the articulators of heretical doctrine and the leaders within a false system. When reaching out to such people, we who know the truth must proceed with utmost caution and clearheadedness. The admonition **on some have mercy with fear** indicates the sobering, frightening nature that outreach to such people entails. **Fear** stems from an awareness that getting too close to corrupt, apostate error could result in somehow being tainted by those lies (cf. Matt. 16:6, 12; 1 Cor. 5:6–7; 15:33; Gal. 5:7–9).

Jude used extremely graphic, coarse language to highlight the degree of danger involved in this type of outreach. **Garment** translates *chitōn* and refers to the clothing that the people of that day wore under their outer tunics—it was their underwear. The word translated **polluted** is a participial form of the verb *spiloō,* meaning "to stain," or "to spot." To be **polluted by the flesh** means "to be stained by bodily function." Just as no one wants to handle someone else's dirty underwear and be defiled physically, so we should be extremely wary of getting too close to the spiritual defilement of those corrupted by false teachers. Even in bringing the gospel to committed apostates, saints must exercise great caution and wisdom (cf. Matt. 10:16).

When the church does not deal properly with the spiritual contamination that false teachers can spread, the results can be disastrous. For example, the Lord told the church at Sardis, "I know your deeds, that you have a name that you are alive, but you are dead" (Rev. 3:1). That was because only a few in Sardis had not "soiled their garments" (v. 4). The rest had indiscriminately embraced apostasy, which damned their souls and killed the church. Sardis, along with some of the other seven churches in Revelation (especially Pergamum, Thyatira, and Laodicea), failed to heed the apostle Paul's warning:

> Now I urge you, brethren, keep your eye on those who cause dissensions and hindrances contrary to the teaching which you learned, and turn away from them. For such men are slaves, not of our Lord Christ but of their own appetites; and by their smooth and flattering speech they deceive the hearts of the unsuspecting. (Rom. 16:17–18)

The spiritual survival and prosperity of us who love Christ, especially in times of growing apostasy, requires the utmost perseverance and care. We must be defensive—remembering what Scripture teaches about the presence of false teachers. And we must also be proactive—diligently practicing the disciplines of Bible study, prayer, and obedience as we eagerly anticipate Christ's return. Finally, we must exercise bold discernment in taking the offensive and reaching out to apostates and those influenced by their heresies. The Christian life has always been a pilgrimage (Heb. 11) and a spiritual battle (Eph. 6:10–18), but its end will be triumphant (Rev. 18–22). With that truth in mind, we can take great solace and encouragement in the words of the well-known hymn "Onward, Christian Soldiers":

> Onward, Christian soldiers, marching as to war, with the cross of Jesus going on before! Christ, the royal Master, leads against the foe; forward into battle see His banners go!

> At the sign of triumph Satan's host doth flee; on, then, Christian soldiers, on to victory! Hell's foundations quiver at the shout of praise; brothers, lift your voices, loud your anthems raise!

The Saints' Guarantee (Jude 24–25)

15

Now to Him who is able to keep you from stumbling, and to make you stand in the presence of His glory blameless with great joy, to the only God our Savior, through Jesus Christ our Lord, be glory, majesty, dominion and authority, before all time and now and forever. Amen. (24–25)

All of the doctrines of salvation are absolutely essential and profoundly precious to the redeemed. But the doctrine of eternal security, more accurately known as the perseverance of the saints, stands out as the most marvelous of them all. The glory of the other aspects of salvation—such as justification, regeneration, conversion, and adoption—could not be fully appreciated if salvation were not forever. Without the assurance and confidence of eternal security, the Christian life would give way to doubt, worry, and fear as believers wondered if the other doctrines were permanent. And the thought of giving up everything to follow Christ would hardly seem worth the cost if all might be lost in the end (cf. Luke 9:23–25). Yet, because of the doctrine of eternal security, we as believers can rest assured that nothing can rob us of that saving faith that will ultimately produce an "eternal weight of glory far beyond all comparison" (2 Cor. 4:17).

If it were up to us alone to maintain our salvation, we would surely lose it. As those who still struggle with sin (1 John 1:8–10; cf. Rom. 7:15–23; 1 Cor. 1:11; 5:1; 11:18; James 1:14–15; 4:1–3), we would repeatedly forfeit our righteous standing before God. Even the apostle Paul acknowledged his continuing battle against the flesh, exclaiming, "Wretched man that I am! Who will set me free from the body of this death?" (Rom. 7:24). He recognized that he could neither gain nor maintain salvation through his own self-righteous efforts (Phil. 3:4–14).

Thankfully, true salvation is not based on our works as believers, but rather the work of Christ. It is His righteousness that covers those who trust in Him (Phil. 3:9; 2 Peter 1:1). We need not worry about keeping, or losing, our salvation because it is not based on our deeds. Instead, it is based on the unchanging person of Jesus Christ (cf. Heb. 13:8). The plan (Rom. 8:29–30), promise (Heb. 10:23), power (Rom. 1:16), and provision (2 Cor. 5:21) from God Himself guarantees our eternal destiny.

The doctrine of the perseverance of the saints (that true believers persevere in faith in the gospel to the end because the Father has granted them an unfailing faith) connects inseparably with the other doctrines of salvation. For instance, it is intimately tied to the doctrine of election (v. 1; Eph. 1:11; 1 Thess. 5:24; cf. 1 Peter 1:4–5)—God makes sure that those He chooses for eternal life will never lose it (John 10:28–29; 1 Cor. 1:8–9; Phil. 1:6). It is also eternally linked to the doctrine of justification (Rom. 5:1, 9; 8:30), by which Jesus Christ has fully paid sin's penalty for believers (1 Peter 2:24; cf. 2 Cor. 5:21) so that there is no basis on which they can be condemned (Rom. 8:1, 33–35). And it connects inseparably to the doctrines of sanctification (2 Thess. 2:13) and glorification (Heb. 2:10)—the Holy Spirit seals believers and sanctifies them (2 Cor. 1:21–22; Eph. 1:13–14), thereby certifying that all will be brought to glory (cf. Heb. 10:14–15). If we—who by faith embrace the gospel—could lose our salvation, then each of these other doctrines would be severely undermined.

As he brings his letter to a close, Jude underscores God's preserving work in salvation by means of a doxology, a word of praise to God. In so doing, Jude is in keeping with biblical precedent. Each of the five books of Psalms, for example, concludes with a doxology (41:13; 72:18–19; 89:52; 106:48; 150). The New Testament also records many other doxologies (e.g., Luke 2:13–14; 19:35–38; Rom. 11:36; 16:27; Eph. 1:3; 3:20–21; Phil. 4:20; 1 Peter 5:11; 2 Peter 3:18; Rev. 1:6), all of which focus on the glory and grace of God. They are always outbursts of praise for the greatness of salvation and the promised blessings of eternal life in heaven. For instance, Paul concluded his letter to the Romans with this doxology:

> Now to Him who is able to establish you according to my gospel and the preaching of Jesus Christ, according to the revelation of the mystery which has been kept secret for long ages past, but now is manifested, and by the Scriptures of the prophets, according to the commandment of the eternal God, has been made known to all the nations, leading to obedience of faith; to the only wise God, through Jesus Christ, be the glory forever. Amen. (16:25–27; cf. Gal. 1:3–5; 1 Tim. 1:17; 2 Tim. 4:18)

In contrast to his warnings regarding apostasy, Jude's doxology brings comfort and encouragement, reminding believers of the faithfulness and power of God. It negates fear (cf. Ps. 27:1; Prov. 1:33; John 14:27), brings joy (cf. Isa. 35:10; Matt. 5:12*a;* Rom. 15:13), and stimulates hope for the future (cf. Rom. 12:12; Eph. 4:4; Titus 1:2; 1 Peter 1:3). And it does this by emphasizing two crucial things that the Lord will do for us His saints: preserve our salvation and present us blameless before His glorious throne.

THE LORD PRESERVES THE SAINTS

Now to Him who is able to keep you from stumbling, (24*a*)

Because God is perfectly faithful, supremely powerful, and infinitely loving, He will not allow His children to fall away from saving faith or defect from the gospel so as to be lost again in their sins. Not only is He willing to preserve believers (Rom. 8:28; Eph. 1:9–11; cf. John 17:20–23), He **is** also **able** to preserve them to the end.

During His earthly ministry, Jesus taught definitively that God sovereignly secures all who believe:

> All that the Father gives Me will come to Me, and the one who comes to Me I will certainly not cast out. For I have come down from heaven, not to do My own will, but the will of Him who sent Me. This is the will of Him who sent Me, that of all that He has given Me I lose nothing, but raise it up on the last day. For this is the will of My Father, that everyone who beholds the Son and believes in Him will have eternal life, and I Myself will raise him up on the last day. . . . No one can come to Me unless the Father who sent Me draws him; and I will raise him up on the last day. (John 6:37–40, 44; cf. 10:28–29; 1 Peter 1:3–5)

Scripture is filled with many other testimonies to God's promise and power to preserve His people. In another New Testament doxology, Paul exulted to the Ephesians, "Now to Him who is able to do far more abundantly beyond all that we ask or think, according to the power that works within us, to Him be the glory in the church and in Christ Jesus to all generations forever and ever. Amen" (Eph. 3:20–21; cf. 2 Cor. 9:8). And the author of Hebrews, speaking of Jesus, echoes, "Therefore He is able also to save forever those who draw near to God through Him, since He always lives to make intercession for them" (Heb. 7:25; cf. 5:7).

Humanly speaking, the path to heaven has always been perilous (cf. Acts 14:22; 2 Cor. 6:4–10; 11:23–30; Heb. 11:32–40; Rev. 12:10–11), full of dangers from Satan and his apostate agents (Luke 22:31; Eph. 6:11–17; 1 Thess. 2:18; 3:5; 1 Peter 5:8–9; cf. Job 1:12–19; 2:6–7; Matt. 4:1–11). But, from God's perspective, the path to heaven is absolutely safe, not because believers are able to preserve themselves, but because God is able to keep them.

To keep is the translation of a military word (*phulassō*) meaning "to guard," or "to watch over." God is at His post, standing guard over believers to ensure their safety (Ps. 12:7; Prov. 3:26; 1 Cor. 1:8–9) during any assault from the enemy (cf. 1 John 5:18). He is the One who keeps them **from stumbling** into apostasy. As Jesus the Good Shepherd told His listeners:

> My sheep hear My voice, and I know them, and they follow Me; and I give eternal life to them, and they will never perish; and no one will snatch them out of My hand. My Father, who has given them to Me, is greater than all; and no one is able to snatch them out of the Father's hand. (John 10:27–29)

The Lord Jesus again entrusted His followers into the hands of His Father in His High Priestly Prayer recorded in John 17 (cf. vv. 9, 11, 15). In verses 24 and 26 (NKJV), He prayed,

> Father, I desire that they also whom You gave Me may be with Me where I am, that they may behold My glory which You have given Me; for You loved Me before the foundation of the world. . . . And I have declared to them Your name, and will declare it, that the love with which You loved Me may be in them, and I in them.

The Son's infinite love for the Father ensures that He will keep those whom the Father has given Him. And vice versa, the Father's infinite love for the Son makes certain that He will protect those whom He has given to the Son. Thus the believer is secured by both the Father and the Son.

Salvation is also guaranteed by the Holy Spirit. The apostle Paul underscored this truth while writing to the Ephesians. After emphasizing the doctrine of election, that God chose His own solely on the basis of His good pleasure (1:3–12), Paul added:

> In Him you also trusted, after you heard the word of truth, the gospel of your salvation; in whom also, having believed, you were sealed with the Holy Spirit of promise, who is the guarantee of our inheritance until the redemption of the purchased possession, to the praise of His glory. (vv. 13–14, NKJV)

In the same way that an ancient seal served as both a secure guarantee and a mark of ownership, the Holy Spirit is given to believers as divine proof of salvation. The work of the Spirit in the lives of His people confirms that they have truly been regenerated (Titus 3:3–8; cf. Gal. 5:21–22). As Paul noted elsewhere, "The Spirit Himself testifies with our spirit that we are children of God" (Rom. 8:16). Having been adopted into God's family, believers are assured by the indwelling Holy Spirit Himself that they will never be disowned.

In several places in his writings, the apostle Paul also emphasized that salvation is a gift based solely on God's grace through Christ's death. It is not based on human good works, but rather on God's working alone. In Romans 5:8–11, Paul wrote:

> But God demonstrates His own love toward us, in that while we were yet sinners, Christ died for us. Much more then, having now been justified by His blood, we shall be saved from the wrath of God through Him. For if while we were enemies we were reconciled to God through the death of His Son, much more, having been reconciled, we shall be saved by His life. And not only this, but we also exult in God through our Lord Jesus Christ, through whom we have now received the reconciliation.

Before God saved them, believers were the enemies of God (Eph. 2:1–3). There was nothing good in them that made them worthy of His love (cf. Rom. 3:10–19). Thus it was only by His infinite grace and according to His perfect plan (cf. Rom. 8:28–30) that salvation was ever even offered to them. Ephesians 2:8–9 reiterates this reality: "For by grace you have been saved through faith; and that not of yourselves, it is the gift of God; not as a result of works, so that no one may boast." Salvation is truly a free gift from God. It could not possibly be earned by human works or self-righteousness (cf. Titus 3:1–8). By the same token, it cannot be kept by human effort. The eternal security of the believer rests upon the same infinite sacrifice that brought salvation in the first place—the death of Jesus Christ (cf. Heb. 7:27). Because Christians did nothing to earn salvation, they can do nothing to lose it; they were saved by the loving power of God, and they remain saved by that same power. With this in mind, Paul joyously exclaimed,

For I am convinced that neither death, nor life, nor angels, nor principalities, nor things present, nor things to come, nor powers, nor height, nor depth, nor any other created thing, will be able to separate us from the love of God, which is in Christ Jesus our Lord. (Rom. 8:38–39)

Nothing, including personal acts of sin, can separate the true believer from his or her Savior.

Other passages in the New Testament also affirm this doctrine to be true:

You are not lacking in any gift, awaiting eagerly the revelation of our Lord Jesus Christ, who shall also confirm you in the end, blameless in the day of our Lord Jesus Christ. God is faithful, through whom you were called into fellowship with His Son, Jesus Christ our Lord. (1 Cor. 1:7–9)

Do not grieve the Holy Spirit of God, by whom you were sealed for the day of redemption. (Eph. 4:30)

For I am confident of this very thing, that He who began a good work in you will perfect it until the day of Christ Jesus. (Phil. 1:6)

May the God of peace Himself sanctify you entirely; and may your spirit and soul and body be preserved complete, without blame at the coming of our Lord Jesus Christ. Faithful is He who calls you, and He also will bring it to pass. (1 Thess. 5:23–24)

In light of the biblical evidence, one author asks,

Is it conceivable that in spite of all this, [Christians] may still fall away and be lost? Is it possible for God to predestine us to holiness, and yet we do not become holy? Can He adopt us as children and then disown us? Can He give us a guarantee of salvation and then renege on His promise? Is the human will so strong as to overcome divine power? Surely not! What more does God need to say to assure us that He will uphold us to the end? (David Clotfelter, *Sinners in the Hands of a Good God* [Chicago: Moody, 2004], 176)

Even the apostle Peter, who was continually prone to failure (such as denying Christ three times), never suggested that salvation could be lost. Instead, when he penned his first epistle, Peter recognized God's power as that which preserved salvation:

> Blessed be the God and Father of our Lord Jesus Christ, who according to His great mercy has caused us to be born again to a living hope through the resurrection of Jesus Christ from the dead, to obtain an inheritance which is imperishable and undefiled and will not fade away, reserved in heaven for you, who are protected by the power of God through faith for a salvation ready to be revealed in the last time. (1 Peter 1:3–5)

At the end of this same epistle, he returned to the theme of perseverance, writing, "After you have suffered for a little while, the God of all grace, who called you to His eternal glory in Christ, will Himself perfect, confirm, strengthen and establish you" (5:10).

The magnitude of that promise is overwhelming. God Himself perfects, confirms, strengthens, and establishes us who are His children. Though His purposes for the future involve some pain in the present, He will nevertheless give us grace to endure and persevere in faith. Even while the enemy attacks us personally, God simultaneously perfects us. He Himself is doing it. He will accomplish His purposes in us, bringing us to wholeness, setting us on solid ground, making us strong, and establishing us on a firm foundation.

To be sure, the doctrine of eternal security does not mean that people can live in patterns of unrepentant sin and still be assured of heaven. Eternal security is not a license for sin (cf. Rom. 6:1). For that matter, we who truly believe would never view it as such—since we have been given a new nature (cf. 2 Peter 1:4) that loves to obey our Master (John 14:15). Those who make a profession of faith, but then fall away into lifestyles of sin, reveal that their profession was never really genuine (cf. 1 John 2:19). But for those of us whose faith is real, the security of salvation is a joyous certainty indeed.

THE LORD PRESENTS THE SAINTS

and to make you stand in the presence of His glory blameless with great joy, to the only God our Savior, through Jesus Christ our Lord, be glory, majesty, dominion and authority, before all time and now and forever. Amen. (24b–25)

A hallmark of genuine saving faith is that it endures to the end (Matt. 24:13). **To make you stand** translates the verb *histēmi,* which more precisely in this context means "to set," "to present," "to confirm," or "to establish." At present, believers stand in grace (Rom. 5:1–4), but in the future they will also stand in glory (Col. 3:4; 1 Peter 5:10).

For fallen men to stand **in the presence of** God's **glory** should produce sheer terror. Isaiah pronounced a curse on himself (Isa. 6:5). Ezekiel fell over like a dead person (Ezek. 1:28). Peter, James, and John experienced overwhelming fear on the Mount of Transfiguration (Matt. 17:5–7; Luke 9:32–34). The apostle John fainted as one who was dead when he saw the vision of the risen and glorious Christ (Rev. 1:17). Having come face-to-face with God's glorious presence, each of these men instantly felt the full weight of his sinfulness (cf. Luke 5:8). Each fell to the ground, overwhelmed by his own sense of unworthiness.

To stand in God's glorious presence, believers must be **blameless.** Revelation 21:27 makes it clear that unrepentant sinners will not enter the glory of heaven: "Nothing unclean, and no one who practices abomination and lying, shall ever come into [the heavenly Jerusalem], but only those whose names are written in the Lamb's book of life" (cf. 22:14–15). *Amōmos* (**blameless**) means "faultless," and it is used here to describe the sinless state that believers will one day enjoy. The New Testament also uses the term to refer to the purity of sacrifices (Heb. 9:14, "without blemish"; cf. 1 Peter 1:19). Although believers, as those of us to whom God has imputed Christ's righteousness, are now positionally blameless (Rom. 4:6–8; 1 Cor. 1:30; 2 Cor. 5:21; Titus 3:7), we are still in our fleshly, sinful bodies. We are yet awaiting the resurrection, when we will receive our new glorified bodies (cf. John 5:25; 11:24–25; 1 Cor. 15:21–23, 42–44; 2 Cor. 5:1; Phil. 3:21). In heaven we will experience not only an absence of sin but also a presence of perfect holiness (1 Thess. 3:13; cf. Rev. 21:22–22:5). All our faculties will be emancipated from evil and fully devoted to the righteous worship of God forever and ever (cf. Rev. 4:6–11; 5:11–14; 19:6).

As saints in glory, we will know nothing of the fear and trauma that characterized being in God's presence on earth (see the aforementioned examples). Instead we will experience **great joy,** which will characterize every aspect of our heavenly life (cf. Rev. 7:16–17). This joy refers primarily to the divine joy (cf. Luke 15:7, 10; Zeph. 3:17) of the Father and the Son over our fellowship with other believers—a joy in which the redeemed will share for all eternity. Thus all believers will dwell with God in perfect love and holy delight forever and ever.

> There will no longer be any curse; and the throne of God and of the Lamb will be in it [the New Earth], and His bond-servants will serve Him; they will see His face, and His name will be on their foreheads. And there will no longer be any night; and they will not have need of the light of a lamp nor the light of the sun, because the Lord God will illumine them; and they will reign forever and ever. (Rev. 22:3–5)

As he ended his epistle, Jude offered praise for the present salvation and future glorification of believers: **to the only God our Savior, through Jesus Christ our Lord, be glory, majesty, dominion and authority, before all time and now and forever. Only God . . . through Jesus Christ** can accomplish the work of a **Savior.** As a result, Jude reserved the highest praise for the Son. **Glory** summarizes all the divine attributes in their powerful radiance (cf. Ex. 33:22); **majesty** signifies the absolute reign of the Father (cf. Heb. 1:3; 8:1) and the Son (cf. 2 Peter 1:16); **dominion** refers to the extent of His might and active rule over all (cf. Ps. 66:7); and **authority** denotes Christ's supreme right and privilege to do as He wills (cf. Acts 2:33–35; Phil. 2:9–11). This divine supremacy over everything in the universe encompasses all eternity (cf. Rev. 1:8): **before all time** (eternity past), **now** (the present age), and **forever** (eternity future).

Because He is all powerful, and because His glorious name is at stake, God's promise to preserve us His saints and to one day present us blameless before His throne can be trusted without reservation. To doubt the reality of that promise is to doubt God Himself. But to embrace it is to find ceaseless joy and never-ending comfort. In the words of Charles Spurgeon:

> When I heard it said that the Lord would keep His people right to the end, —that Christ had said, "My sheep hear My voice, and I know them, and they follow Me: and I give unto them eternal life; and they shall never perish, neither shall any pluck them out of My hand," I must confess that the doctrine of the final preservation of the saints was a bait that my soul could not resist. I thought it was a sort of life insurance— an insurance of my character, an insurance of my soul, an insurance of my eternal destiny. I knew that I could not keep myself, but if Christ promised to keep me, then I should be safe for ever; and I longed and prayed to find Christ, because I knew that, if I found Him, He would not give me a temporary and trumpery salvation, such as some preach, but eternal life which could never be lost, the living and incorruptible seed which liveth and abideth for ever, for no one and nothing "shall be able to separate us from the love of God, which is in Christ Jesus our Lord." (C. H. Spurgeon, from "Danger, Safety, Gratitude," sermon no. 3,074, preached January 8, 1874, *The Metropolitan Tabernacle Pulpit* [reprint, Pasadena, Tex.: Pilgrim Publications, 1978], 54:24)

Bibliography

Arndt, W. F., F. W. Gingrich and F. W. Danker. *A Greek-English Lexicon of the New Testament and Other Early Christian Literature.* Chicago: Univ. of Chicago, 1957.

Barclay, William. *The Letters of James and Peter.* Revised edition. Philadelphia: Westminster, 1976.

Bigg, Charles. *A Critical and Exegetical Commentary on the Epistles of St. Peter and St. Jude.* The International Critical Commentary. Reprint. Edinburgh: T. & T. Clark, 1975.

Bruce, F. F. *The Canon of Scripture.* Downers Grove, Ill.: InterVarsity, 1988.

Carson, D. A., Douglas J. Moo, and Leon Morris. *An Introduction to the New Testament.* Grand Rapids: Zondervan, 1992.

Green, E. M. B. (Michael). "Peter, Second Epistle of." In J. D. Douglas, ed. *The New Bible Dictionary.* Grand Rapids: Eerdmans, 1979.

_____. *The Second Epistle of Peter and the Epistle of Jude.* The Tyndale New Testament Commentaries. Grand Rapids: Eerdmans, 2002.

_____. *2 Peter Reconsidered.* London: Tyndale, 1961.

Guthrie, Donald. *New Testament Introduction.* Revised Edition. Downers Grove, Ill.: InterVarsity, 1990.

Harrison, Everett F. *Introduction to the New Testament.* Grand Rapids: Eerdmans, 1968.

Hiebert, D. Edmond. *An Introduction to the Non-Pauline Epistles.* Chicago: Moody, 1962.

_____. *Second Peter and Jude: An Expositional Commentary.* Greenville, S. C.: Unusual Publications, 1989.

Kelly, J. N. D. *A Commentary on the Epistles of Peter and Jude.* Peabody, Mass.: Hendrickson, 1988.

Kistemaker, Simon. *New Testament Commentary: Exposition of James, Epistles of John, Peter, and Jude.* Grand Rapids: Baker, 1995.

Kruger, Michael J. "The Authenticity of 2 Peter," *Journal of the Evangelical Theological Society* 42/4 (1999): 645–71.

Lenski, R. C. H. *The Interpretation of the Epistles of St. Peter, St. John, and St. Jude.* Reprint. Minneapolis: Augsburg, 1966.

MacArthur, John. *Twelve Ordinary Men.* Nashville: W Publishing, 2002.

Picirilli, Robert E. "Allusions to 2 Peter in the Apostolic Fathers," *Journal for the Study of the New Testament* 33 (1988): 57–88.

Schreiner, Thomas R. *1, 2 Peter, Jude.* The New American Commentary. Nashville: Broadman & Holman, 2003.

Vine, W. E. *An Expository Dictionary of New Testament Words.* 4 volumes. London: Oliphants, 1940. One-volume paperback edition. Chicago: Moody, 1985.

Wallace, Daniel B. "Jude: Introduction, Argument, and Outline." Biblical Studies Press. www.bible.org, 2000.

_____. "Second Peter: Introduction, Argument, and Outline," Biblical Studies Press, www.bible.org, 2000.

Warfield, Benjamin B. "The Canonicity of Second Peter." In John E. Meeter, ed. *Selected Shorter Writings of Benjamin B. Warfield*. Volume 2. Phillipsburg, N. J.: Presbyterian and Reformed, 1973.

White, William Jr. "Peter, Second Epistle of." In Merrill C. Tenney, ed. *The Zondervan Pictorial Encyclopedia of the Bible*. Volume 4. Grand Rapids: Zondervan, 1977.

Indexes

Index of Greek Words

choregōs, 39–40

dedōrēmenēs, 27
deleazō, 101
despotēs, 72, 162
diegeirō, 51
dikaios, 50
dōreomai, 30
doxa, 60, 98, 174
doulos, 19, 149–50
dusnoētos, 135

egkrateia, 41
elegchō, 189
eirēnē, 24, 132
ekpalai, 83
ekporneuō, 166
empaiktēs, 146
emporeuomai, 78
epagōnizomai, 155
epignōsis, 24, 28
epichorēgeō, 39
epiluseōs, 65
epithumia, 31
epoptai, 59
epoptes, 59
erchomai, 112
eusebeia, 28, 41–42
exodos, 52

gehenna, 85, 186
ginetai, 64–65
gnōrizō, 58
gnōsis, 24, 28
graphas, 136
graphē, 136
graphō, 136
gumanzō, 101

haireseis, 71–72
hapax, 156
harpazō, 203
histēmi, 211

huparchonta, 43
hupomonē, 41

isotimon, 20

kainos, 131
kaleō, 150
kataklusmos, 88
katastrophē, 89
katharismos, 43–44
katoikeō, 131
kerygma, 29
klētos, 150
koinōnos, 30
kurios, 162, 173
kuriotēs, 92–93, 173

lagchanō, 20
lanthanō, 118
lambanō, 43
lēhē, 43

makrothumeō, 122
maranatha, 110, 129
megaleiotēs, 60
megistos, 30
mempsimoiros, 190
miainō, 172–73
miasma, 106
miasmou, 92
muthos, 58

ouai, 176

parakaleō, 155
paraphronia, 103
paredōken, 85–86
pareisduō, 71
pareispherō, 39
parousia, 10, 59, 129
pareisduō, 158–59
patientia, 91
peirasmos, 92

Index of Scripture

2:22	26	21:1–5	62	5:10	3
3:10	181	22:13	105	5:17	26
4:12–16	62	23:13–36	69–70	6:13	19
4:18	2	24:4–5	70	6:13–16	2
4:19	3	24:11	70	6:46	28
4:25	11	24:13	27–28	7:36–40	2
5:5	49	24:24	70	9:23–25	205
5:13	196	24:29–31	111	9:27	60
5:18	49, 57	24:35	52	9:27–36	29
5:22	186	24:45–51	85	9:30–32	61
5:43–44	196	24:46	150	9:43	60
7:13–14	195	24:50–51	185–86	11:24–26	180
7:15	2, 170	25:14–30	85	11:39–52	69–70
7:15–20	147–48	25:31	111	11:44	187
7:16–20	15	25:31–33	184	12:28	25
7:17–20	181	25:41	105	12:46–48	186
7:19	186	26:6	2, 18	12:48	85
7:21–28	28	26:36–46	51	15:11–32	134
8:12	105	27:32	2, 18	15:17–24	26
10:1	19	28:7	3	16:1–8	85
10:2–4	2	28:18–19	29	16:22–26	186
10:4	2	28:19–20	19	17:28–32	89
10:14–15	89			19:12–27	85
10:16	204	**Mark**		22:27	30
10:23	111	1:21	2	22:31	3
11:16–19	196	1:29	2–3	22:31–34	50
11:21–24	186	1:32–33	2	22:42	17–18
11:23	24, 89–90	3:13	19	22:54–62	50
11:28	28	3:16–19	2	24:33–34	59
12:19–20	62	5:20	11		
12:36	184	5:30	26	**John**	
13:20–22	72	7:31	11	1:2	30
13:36–42	72	8:38	111	1:3–5	29
13:38	196	10:17–22	105	1:9	82
13:40–42	185–86	12:24	197	1:12–13	29
13:42	105	12:29–30	48	1:14	29, 82
13:47–50	72	12:32–33	48	1:16	24–25
13:55	2, 18	12:38–40	69–70	1:17	82
16–23	61	13:35–37	51	1:40–42	2
16:1–4	195	14:37	3	1:42	2, 18
16:17	2	16:20	19	1:44	2
16:28	60			3:3	31
15:13	181	**Luke**		3:3–8	29
17:1	4	2:52	30	3:15–16	27
17:1–13	61	4:14	26	3:27	28
17:24–25	3	4:16–21	62	3:33	82
19:26	26	4:38	2–3	5:23	138
20:28	30	5:1–8	2–3	5:24	27

Index of Apocryphal and Pseudepigraphal Works

Index of Subjects

Illustrations, of apostates, 169–82
Immorality, 113, 165–67, 172–73
Inability, absolute. *See* Absolute inability
Insubordination, 173–75
Internal peace, 132–35
Interpretation, 65–66
Irreverence, 173–75
Isaiah, 11, 23, 48, 57, 82, 116–17

James, 18–19, 60–62, 113, 141–49
Jeremiah, 64–65
Jerome, 9, 141
Jerusalem Council, 4, 22, 135
Jesus Christ
    atonement of, 17–18, 73–76
    church of, 1
    coming of, 57–61
    commandments of, 117
    divine nature of, 30–31
    divine power of, 26–28
    as faithful and true One, 117
    forgiveness of, 24
    as God, 23, 26–27, 29–30
    as Good Shepherd, 51, 96, 208–9
    knowledge of, 43–45
    as Lord and Master, 23–25, 72–76, 159–63
    ministry of, 207–14
    parables of, 179
    prayers of, 37–38, 152–53, 208–9
    as presenter of saints, 211–13
    relationship with Peter, 2–15
    resurrection of, 19–20, 34–35, 52–53
    righteousness of, 22–23
    as Savior, 18–31, 34–35, 38–41, 205–14
    Second Coming of, 12, 57–61, 109–46
    Sermon on the Mount, 186–87
    as Son of God, 34–35, 42, 55, 60–61
    sufferings of, 25
    teachings of, 15, 63–65, 69–79, 153–55, 186–87, 193–204
    true knowledge of, 28–30, 33–46
John the apostle, 37, 60, 62, 106–7, 110, 117, 130–31
John the Baptist, 22

Joshua, 18, 174–75
Joy, 212–13
Judas Barsabbas, 149
Judas Iscariot, 2–4, 71–72, 142, 149
Judas of Damascus, 149
Jude, teachings and writings of
    about apostates and apostate times, 157–204
    about coming judgments, 183–92
    about contention, 147–56
    introduction to, 139–46
    about saints' guarantees, 205–14
    about survival strategies, 193–204
    about warnings, 157–68
Judgments
    and the ancient world, 87–88
    on apostates, 183–92
    assurance of, 123–25
    certainties of, 188–91
    coming ones, 183–92
    day of, 120–21
    Day of Judgment, 115
    Day of the Lord vs. Day of God, 5, 120–34
    on false teachers, 81–94
    Great White Throne Judgment, 92–93, 185–86
    patterns of, 91–93
    precedent for, 84
    promise of, 83–84
Justice, divine, 34–35, 82
Justification, 25–26, 205–14
Justin Martyr, 6–7

Kant, Immanuel, 56
Kelly, J. N. D., 216
Kierkegaard, Soren, 56
Kindness, 49–50
Kingdom of God, 26, 45, 93, 112–13, 132, 158, 196
Kistemaker, Simon, 216
Knowledge, 28–30, 33–46
Korah, 145, 176, 178–79
Kruger, Michael J., 8, 11, 216

Laodicea, Council of, 9, 141. *See also* Councils
Last days, 112

Polycarp, 12
Portraits, false teachers, 67–80
Post-modern relativism, 56
Postmodernism, 183–84
Power, divine, 26–28. *See* Divine power
Practical purity, 132–33
Practice, 45
Praise, continual, 137–38
Prayer, 37–38, 152–53, 200–204, 208–9
Pre-Flood world, 119–20
Premillenialism, 10
Premiums, 102–3
Procurement, divine, 26, 28–30
Prodigal son parable, 134
Promises, divine. *See* Divine promises
Prophecies, 9, 61–66, 135–36, 171–72, 187–90
Prophecies, false, 103–4
Prophets, 116–17
Prophets, false. *See* False prophets and prohecies
Provision. *See* Divine provision
Pseudo-Christians, 72, 98
Pseudonymous works, 1–2, 12–13
Purification, 43–45
Puritanism, 96–97

Rapture, 135, 185–86
Rationalistic pantheism, 56
Rebellion
    of Korah, 178–79
    of Satan, 97–98
Redemption, 18, 205–14
Reformed theology, 17
Reformers, 56–57
Regeneration, 205–14
Rejection, 173–75
Religion, false. *See* False religion
Resurrection, 19–20, 34–35, 52–53
Revival, 204
Ridicule and mocking, 111–13
Righteousness, 22–23, 50–51, 87–88, 90–91, 107
Ritschl, Albrecht, 56
Rock (Simon Peter). *See* Peter, teachings and writings of
Rufinus, 9

Sacrilege, 72–76
Sadducees, 195
Saints' guarantees, 205–14
Salvation, 18–31, 38–41, 155–56, 205–14
Santayana, George, 176
Satan, 2, 68–82, 96–102, 108–10, 139–40, 157–65, 174–75, 185–86, 196, 204–9
Schleiermacher, Friedrich, 56
Schreiner, Thomas R., 13, 140, 216
Sea waves, wild, 180
Second Coming. *See* Jesus Christ, Second coming of; judgments
Secrecy, 71–72
Self-control, 41–42
Self-will, 95–108
Sensuality, 76–77
Sentimentalism, 155
Sermon on the Mount, 186–87
Serpent, 83–84
Silas, 11, 149
Simon
    of Cyrene, 2
    father of Judas Iscariot, 2
    half-brother of Jesus, 2
    the leper, 2
    the magician, 2
    Magnus, 140
    the Pharisee, 2
    Peter. *See* Peter, teachings and writings of
    the tanner, 2
    the Zealot, 2
Sin, 18, 33–35, 84–86, 89, 95–108, 123, 133, 152–53, 164, 210–11
Skepticism, 56
Snatching, 202–3
Sodom and Gomorrah, 81–91, 159–71
Solomon, 139
Sophocles, 39–40
Source, substance and sufficiency of believers' faith, 17–32
Spiritual progress, 136
Spurgeon, Charles, 75, 213
Stars, wandering, 180–82
Steadfastness, 136
Stigma, 77–78
Sure Word, 55–66

Titles in the
MacArthur New Testament Commentary Series

MOODY
PUBLISHERS

THE NAME YOU CAN TRUST®

1-800-678-6928 www.MoodyPublishers.org